STREET SONGS

CLARENDON LECTURES IN ENGLISH

STREET SONGS

WRITERS AND URBAN SONGS AND CRIES, 1800–1925

DANIEL KARLIN

OXFORD
UNIVERSITY PRESS

OXFORD
UNIVERSITY PRESS

Great Clarendon Street, Oxford, OX2 6DP,
United Kingdom

Oxford University Press is a department of the University of Oxford.
It furthers the University's objective of excellence in research, scholarship,
and education by publishing worldwide. Oxford is a registered trade mark of
Oxford University Press in the UK and in certain other countries

© Daniel Karlin 2018

The moral rights of the author have been asserted

First Edition published in 2018
Impression: 2

Published in the United States of America by Oxford University Press
198 Madison Avenue, New York, NY 10016, United States of America

British Library Cataloguing in Publication Data
Data available

Library of Congress Control Number: 2018947080

ISBN 978–0–19–879235–2

Printed and bound by
CPI Group (UK) Ltd, Croydon, CR0 4YY

For my brothers
Michael and David

Acknowledgements

'Cherry Ripe' by Donald Davie is reprinted from *Collected Poems* (1990) with the permission of Carcanet Press Ltd.

★

This book is based on the Clarendon Lectures for 2016. I am grateful to Oxford University's Faculty of English and Oxford University Press for inviting me to give the lectures; I would especially like to thank Robert Douglas-Fairhurst, Laura Marcus, Jacqueline Norton, and Seamus Perry for their welcome and hospitality. I am grateful, too, for the questions and comments I received from the audience on each occasion.

The Clarendon Lectures are a series of four, and have been expanded in scope and detail for this book. The section in Chapter 1 on George Gissing's *The Nether World* is based on a paper delivered at the Fifth International Gissing Conference at the University of Bristol in July 2016. Chapter 2, on Elizabeth Barrett Browning, is new. Robert Browning's 'Fra Lippo Lippi' featured in the first lecture but here has a chapter to itself (Chapter 3); James Joyce's *Ulysses* and Virginia Woolf's *Mrs. Dalloway* originally shared a lecture, but here occupy a chapter each (Chapters 4 and 5). Chapter 6, on the street cries of Paris in Proust's *La Prisonnière*, borrows from an essay I wrote on the translation of these cries: 'Traduire les cris de Paris dans La Prisonnière', published in *Son et traduction dans l'oeuvre de Proust*, ed. Emily Eells and Naomi Toth (Paris: Honoré Champion, 2018). This essay in turn developed from a paper I gave at a conference (*Traduire la sonorité dans l'œuvre proustienne/Translating Sounds in Proust*) organized under the auspices of CREA (Centre de recherches anglophones) at the Université de Paris Ouest Nanterre in June 2015; I am deeply grateful to Emily Eells for her advice and encouragement. The first idea for the Clarendon Lectures came from my love of this episode of Proust's novel.

Other material has been revised and relocated, but I would empha-size that the subject of the lectures, the appropriation of street song by poets and novelists in the nineteenth and early twentieth centuries, remains the same.

Many friends and colleagues helped me locate examples of street song in literature, all of which have enriched this book even if not all have found a place in it. Philip Kelley kindly supplied the image of Elizabeth Barrett Browning's letter to her sisters reproduced in Chapter 2, and was as always a fount of information. I am especially indebted to Anna Snaith for advice on Virginia Woolf's writings about music and song, and on the critical reception of the episode in *Mrs. Dalloway* that I discuss in Chapter 5.

Both the lectures and the book owe more than I can express to Samantha Matthews' encouragement and guidance.

Contents

List of Illustrations and Plates

Illustrations

Plates

Introduction

This book is about the appropriation of street songs and cries by poets and novelists. Appropriation is an awkward word, but 'theft' is a bit blunt; perhaps the old-fashioned offence of 'taking and driving away' might be charged on the writers I discuss. Often they drive away in unexpected directions. The following poem by Robert Herrick is a case in point:

Cherrie-ripe

Cherrie-Ripe, Ripe, Ripe, I cry,
Full and faire ones; come and buy:
If so be, you ask me where
They doe grow? I answer, There,
Where my *Julia's* lips doe smile;
There's the Land, or Cherry-Ile:
Whose Plantations fully show
All the yeere, where Cherries grow.[1]

'Cherrie-ripe' is an ancient street-vendor's cry, one of the many 'Cries of London'; Herrick's poem, published in 1648, takes this familiar cry and transposes it into a metaphor, doing something more complex, that is, than simply comparing lips to cherries.[2] The metaphor evokes a dramatic scene, in which the poet acts the part of a street-vendor.

1. Robert Herrick, 'Cherrie-ripe', *Hesperides* [1648], in *The Complete Poetry of Robert Herrick*, ed. Tom Cain and Ruth Connolly, 2 vols. (Oxford: Oxford University Press, 2013), i 20.
2. The comparison is ubiquitous, and a commonplace; Shakespeare gives it to Demetrius, spellbound by Puck and wooing the wrong lady in *A Midsummer Night's Dream*: 'O, how ripe in show / Thy lips, those kissing cherries, tempting grow!' (III ii 139–40). The street cry for cherries varies from the simple 'Cherry-ripe' to 'Ripe cherries, ripe', to more elaborate formulas specifying the variety of the fruit and its price: 'Round and sound, fivepence a pound, Duke cherries' is the title of one of Antoine Cardon's prints (after Francis Wheatley) in a series illustrating the 'Cries of London' (London, 1793–7).

Herrick was not the first poet to turn the phrase 'come and buy' to metaphorical use, and he was certainly not the last. In Byron's *English Bards and Scotch Reviewers*, a boring poet 'sends his goods to market— all alive! / Lines forty thousand, Cantos twenty-five! / Fresh fish from Helicon! who'll buy? who'll buy?'[3] 'Come buy, come buy' is the insistent, seductive call of the goblins in Christina Rossetti's *Goblin Market*, where doubts are raised both as to what is being bought and how it is to be paid for.[4] Siegfried Sassoon, in the last lines of 'The Effect', transplants the phrase to the battlefield: '*How many dead? As many as ever you wish. / Don't count 'em; they're too many. / Who'll buy my nice fresh corpses, two a penny?*'[5] A lover 'crying' the wares of his mistress has something dubious about it; I am not sure Herrick gets away with dancing on this particular edge, but I am sure he knew what he was doing, because of this song by Thomas Campion, first published in 1605 but taken here from *The third and fourth booke of ayres* of 1617:

> There is a Garden in her face,
> Where Roses and white Lillies grow;
>   A heav'nly paradice is that place,
> Wherein all pleasant fruits doe flow.
>   There Cherries grow, which none may buy
>   Till Cherry ripe themselves doe cry.
>
>   Those Cherries fayrely doe enclose
> Of Orient Pearle a double row,
>   Which when her lovely laughter showes,
> They look like Rose-buds fill'd with snow.
>   Yet them nor Peere nor Prince can buy,
>   Till Cherry ripe themselves doe cry.
>
>   Her Eyes like Angels watch them still;
> Her Browes like bended bowes doe stand,
>   Threatning with piercing frownes to kill
> All that attempt with eye or hand
>   Those sacred Cherries to come nigh,
>   Till Cherry ripe themselves doe cry.[6]

3. George Gordon, Lord Byron, *English Bards and Scotch Reviewers* (1811), ll. 389–91.
4. Christina Rossetti, 'Goblin Market' [1862], ll. 3–4 and *passim*, in *Complete Poems*, ed. R. W. Crump and Betty S. Flowers (London: Penguin Books, 2001), pp. 5–20.
5. Siegfried Sassoon, 'The Effect' [1918], ll. 16–18, in *Collected Poems 1908–1956* (London: Faber and Faber, 1961).
6. *The third and fourth booke of ayres: composed by Thomas Campian* [sic]. *So as they may be expressed by one voyce, with a violl, lute, or orpharion* (London: Printed by Thomas Snodham, 1617), in *Works: Complete Songs, Masques and Treatises*, ed. Walter R. Davis (Garden City,

Here the woman 'cries' her own wares; she possesses and will sell herself in her own good time; only when she declares herself 'ripe' may buyers approach 'with eye or hand'. Campion plays with myth: the myth of the forbidden fruit in Paradise, which lacked an angelic guard, and the classical myth of the golden apples of the Hesperides, which were guarded by a dragon, but to no avail. It is a defiant affirmation of her virtue to place it in such ill-omened company. The idea that beauty might be both self-possessed and invulnerable is denied by Herrick's poem, yet Herrick, like Campion, sees the woman's beauty as a kind of paradise, where cherries magically grow 'all the yeere', whereas the original cry of 'Cherry ripe' was a seasonal cry, linked to midsummer when cherries from Kent would be hawked around London's streets.[7]

Generations of readers seem not to have been troubled by Herrick's use of this street cry in praise of Julia's beauty; and you can add listeners to readers, given that Charles Edward Horn's setting became a concert and parlour standard in the nineteenth century, far outstripping in popularity any setting of Campion's song.[8] It was popular in part because it was felt to be so English—as one mid-Victorian encomium put it,

> Cherry ripe, cherry ripe—ripe, I cry,
> That's the ballad you should buy,
> Herrick's sparkling poetry,
> Horn's true English melody.[9]

NJ: Doubleday, 1967). The song is no. VII in the Fourth Book. Herrick's editors note that he was 'probably recalling' Campion's poem (*Complete Poetry* ii 525).

7. I differ from Tom Jones, who says of Campion's poem that 'the street cry is not incorporated into the poem, or incorporated only so as to indicate a difference between the world of the poem and the world of the street market, not their proximity. Poetic language looks down upon the language of business, the cry' (*Poetic Language: Theory and Practice from the Renaissance to the Present* [Edinburgh: Edinburgh University Press, 2012], p. 153). But it seems to me that the poetry of the cry is fully acknowledged in the structure and versification of Campion's poem.

8. Horn's setting was first performed in John Poole's comedy *Paul Pry* (1825).

9. J. R. Planché, *The Golden Branch* (1850) II ii; text from *The extravaganzas of J. R. Planché*, 5 vols. (London: Samuel French, 1879), v 210. Planché's work was founded on *Le Rameau d'Or* by Madame d'Aulnoy (Marie-Catherine Le Jumel de Barneville, Baroness d'Aulnoy (1650/1651–4 January 1705), also known as Countess d'Aulnoy: see H. Philip Bolton, *Women Writers Dramatized: A Calendar of Performances of Narrative Works Published in English to 1900* (Mansell Publishing, 1999), p. 144. The song is performed on stage by Suivanta, the waiting-woman to Princess Dumpy; 'Cherry-Ripe' is superior, Suivanta goes on, both to modern British airs, and to the blackface minstrels who were becoming fashionable in London: 'Let the belle of London balls, / Dream she "dwelt in marble halls." / Let the husband she would get, / Hope they "may be happy yet;" / But cherry ripe, cherry ripe, still I cry, / 'Twas a spell, in years gone by. / Must it yield the prize of

A less enchanted view of the Englishness of the song is given by Robert Louis Stevenson and Lloyd Osbourne in *The Wrong Box*:

England is supposed to be unmusical; but without dwelling on the patronage extended to the organ-grinder, without seeking to found any argument on the prevalence of the jew's trump, there is surely one instrument that may be said to be national in the fullest acceptance of the word. The herdboy in the broom, already musical in the days of Father Chaucer, startles (and perhaps pains) the lark with this exiguous pipe; and in the hands of the skilled bricklayer,
     'The thing becomes a trumpet, whence he blows'
(as a general rule) either 'The British Grenadiers' or 'Cherry Ripe'. The latter air is indeed the shibboleth and diploma piece of the penny whistler; I hazard a guess it was originally composed for this instrument. It is singular enough that a man should be able to gain a livelihood, or even to tide over a period of unemployment, by the display of his proficiency upon the penny whistle; still more so, that the professional should almost invariably confine himself to 'Cherry Ripe'.[10]

We shall encounter such prejudice again, often in less light-hearted form; the barrel-organ, with its banality and its wearisome, sometimes maddening repetitiveness, was a particular target in the polemic against noise pollution in the city; but there was a counterargument from those who saw it as one of the few pleasures available to the urban poor. At any rate, Stevenson and Osbourne were not mistaken in singling out 'Cherry Ripe' as a ubiquitous presence, familiar enough to serve George Eliot, for example, as a marker of Fred Vincy's idle proficiency.[11] Inevitably it migrated into visual art as well. The original 'Cries of London' had been illustrated since the late Middle Ages, and these illustrations became a recognized sub-genre in painting and print-making. In the case of cherries, as with other fruits and flowers, illustrators

song / To "Lucy Neal," or "Lucy Long?" / No—though Yankees black to view, / May be cherry colour too. / "Old Dan Tucker," with "Jim Crow," / To old Virginny back shall go— / And cherry ripe, cherry ripe, still to me, / Shall the sweetest ballad be.'

10. Robert Louis Stevenson and Lloyd Osbourne, *The Wrong Box* (1898), opening of ch. 12. The 'herdboy in the broom' is from Chaucer's *The House of Fame*, in the long section on music in the narrator's dream: 'And pipes made of grene corn, / As han these litel herde-gromes / That kepen bestis in the bromes' (iii 1224–6). 'The thing becomes a trumpet' is from Wordsworth's sonnet 'Scorn not the Sonnet' (1827), referring to Milton: 'The Thing became a trumpet; whence he blew / Soul-animating strains— alas, too few!' (*Poems* 635)—or in the case of 'Cherry Ripe', 'alas, too many'.

11. George Eliot, *Middlemarch* (1872), bk. ii, ch. 16; Rosamond Vincy is flirting with Lydgate: ' "Ah, there is Fred beginning to strum! I must go and hinder him from jarring all your nerves," said Rosamond, moving to the other side of the room, where Fred having opened the piano, at his father's desire, that Rosamond might give them some music, was parenthetically performing "Cherry Ripe!" with one hand.'

who aimed at something more than a plain documentary record might choose to represent the scene as one of childhood innocence or erotic suggestion, and the best-known image of 'Cherry Ripe' combines the two. It is John Everett Millais' painting of 1879 (Plate 1), whose subject's pose may derive from a painting by Joshua Reynolds but whose title is traceable, ultimately, to Herrick and Horn.

Cherry-Ripe, which Millais sold to the *Graphic* magazine and which was reproduced in chromolithography by the hundreds of thousands, became one of the great visual clichés of the period. An 'expensive print' of it hangs on the wall of Rosalind Connage's bedroom in Scott Fitzgerald's *This Side of Paradise*, and this would seem a fitting end, if anything ever did have an end.[12] But it doesn't, of course. In 1915 the Spanish artist Juan Gris painted *Les Cerises* (Plate 2) and when the picture caught the eye of that quintessentially English poet and critic Donald Davie, it took him back to Herrick:

Cherry Ripe
On a Painting by Juan Gris

No ripening curve can be allowed to sag
On cubist's canvas or in sculptor's stone:
Informal fruit, that burgeons from the swag,
Would spoil the ripening that is art's alone.

This can be done with cherries. Other fruit
Have too much bloom of import, like the grape,
Whose opulence comes welling from a root
Struck far too deep to yield so pure a shape.

And Cherry ripe, indeed ripe, ripe, I cry.
Let orchards flourish in the poet's soul
And bear their feelings that are mastered by
Maturing rhythms, to compose a whole.

But how the shameful grapes and olives swell,
Excrescent from no cornucopia, tart,
Too near to oozing to be handled well:
Ripe, ripe, they cry, and perish in my heart.[13]

---

12. F. Scott Fitzgerald, *This Side of Paradise* (1920), bk. 2, ch. 1: 'A girl's room: pink walls and curtains and a pink bedspread on a cream-colored bed. Pink and cream are the motifs of the room, but the only article of furniture in full view is a luxurious dressing-table with a glass top and a three-sided mirror. On the walls there is an expensive print of "Cherry Ripe," a few polite dogs by Landseer, and the "King of the Black Isles," by Maxfield Parrish.'
13. Davie's poem was first published in *A Winter Talent and Other Poems* (London: Routledge and Kegan Paul, 1957). Gris's painting is in the Solomon R. Guggenheim Museum, New York (bequest of Richard S. Zeisler, 2007).

In this strange, exacting poem, cherries are an emblem of 'feelings that are mastered by / Maturing rhythms', and that 'flourish in the poet's soul', whereas the 'shameful grapes and olives' represent feelings that cannot be disciplined: 'Too near to oozing to be handled well', they 'perish in [his] heart', incapable, that is, of utterance, of being born into language.

Juan Gris's painting suggests this thought; its formal severity contains the cherries in a pattern of inorganic materials, while these materials themselves (especially the blue and pink dots) have something fruit-like about them; but Davie could have drawn the contrast between 'informal fruit' and 'the ripening that is art's alone' without bringing in the cry of 'Cherry ripe'. He does so, I think, because its occurrence in Herrick's poem (and perhaps in Campion's, too; he will have known them both) has just this quality of chastened, deliberate art, by which a London street cry does not irrupt into the poem but is invited, so to speak, to take its place in the metrical dance. And yet, when you have made these concessions to the poem's idea, it is disturbing that the cry itself should return at the end, attributed now to the 'shameful' fruits, which seem to be 'crying' themselves: 'Ripe, ripe, *they* cry'; it is as though the summative energy of the poem channels itself in excess, in overripeness, and in death. The grand poise of the penultimate stanza, with its imperative 'Let orchards flourish', its mastery and composure, risks seeming a rhetorical flourish; the third line, in particular, ending as no other line in the poem on a prepositional enjambment ('mastered by / Maturing rhythms'), now seems more precarious than composed. The poem is more self-doubting than it proclaims itself to be, and that, too, may reflect back on Herrick's poem, so confident that it has just enough 'bloom of import', and not 'too much'.

'Cherrie-ripe' traces an arc from the sixteenth century to the twentieth, and encompasses literature, art, music, social history... but some boundaries, however artificial, need to be drawn. This book, to repeat, is about what street songs are doing in works of literature, not about the songs themselves. Street song has a rich and varied history, of which the 'cries' of London and Paris are only a fraction, and this history has been, and continues to be, intensively studied by literary critics as well as musicologists and social historians. The street ballad alone has accumulated an immense library, musical archive, and gallery of images, and the ballad, though we think of it as the predominant form of urban song, was only one of many kinds that circulated in city streets. Every social and political cause, from temperance to women's rights, every movement from trades-unionism to Fascism, every religious denomination, has at one time or another been sung in the streets. Besides these collective forms of song, individuals have sung on street corners, or at the doors of their houses, or on their way home from theatres and pubs, since cities began; and all have been the subject of dispute, whether with other citizens or the authorities. Questions about who is allowed to sing in the streets of a city, what they sing and how it is valued socially, economically, and politically, the place of song in defining, or transgressing, the boundaries of public urban spaces—these questions have not just a history but a currency; they are living questions subject to complex and sometimes acrimonious contemporary debate. But I am not a musicologist or a historian or a social geographer; street song has found its way into works of literature, and those works are my concern. And as the example of 'Cherry-Ripe' indicates, what interests me is something that goes beyond mere reference, or that adds local colour to a realist fiction: something that plays a specific part in an artistic design.

I begin with one of the primal myths of music and song, transposed to the city and treated with reverence, with irony, and with bitter disillusion. William Wordsworth's 'Power of Music' represents street music as an unqualified blessing, yet the blind fiddler, as the title of the poem suggests, is not subject to his audience, not dependent on their charity, but dominant over them, a figure for the poet's own assertion of power over the immense indifferent urban scene. In proclaiming his musician 'An Orpheus!', Wordsworth was summoning the miraculous and sacred power of music and song, but any allusion to Orpheus is shadowed by his tragic fate, and Wordsworth's poem recalls, by inversion, William Hogarth's *The Enrag'd Musician* (1741), one of the most famous and influential images of urban noise in our culture. In Hogarth's print, a mob of exuberant urban noise-makers (including rival and degraded forms of street music and song) advance on the figure of the 'classical' violinist, himself a bathetic version of divine harmony. The closest verbal equivalent to Hogarth's urban 'soundscape' comes in James Clarence Mangan's poem 'Khidder' (1845), but Mangan does not try to emulate Hogarth's brilliant synoptic composition; his vision is disintegrative, which is another way of bringing the fate of Orpheus, rather than his power, into focus. The violence with which street singers are faced is evident in George Gissing's *The Nether World* (1889), whose title indicates that Orpheus will descend into the hell of the city in vain.

Chapter 2 returns—at least to begin with—to street song as a source of pleasure, and, in the optimistic opening of Part One of Elizabeth Barrett Browning's *Casa Guidi Windows* (1851), a sign of political regeneration. Hearing a little child singing 'O bella libertà' in a street in Florence in 1847, Barrett Browning projects a future for Italy in which the poetry of loss and lament, the false consolation for subjection to foreign tyranny, will be replaced by a modern song of enlightenment and freedom. The hopes she and others had for the longed-for triumph of the 'Risorgimento', the movement for Italian unity and independence, were raised by the revolutions of 1848 and crushed in the defeats that followed, and the second part of *Casa Guidi Windows* reflects with mordant irony on her own false consciousness and on the blustering cowardice of the people in whom she had placed her faith. The figure of the child in the street is replaced by that of her own child, born in 1849; yet Barrett Browning returns, in a number of later poems, to the child singing of liberty, especially in poems written in the last year of her life, when the prospects for a united Italy were again resurgent. These poems do not form a coherent group, but show the poet returning to the imagery she had deployed in *Casa Guidi Windows* in a ferment of mixed feelings. I end this chapter by suggesting that a disturbing shadow lies over the image of the original figure of the child singing of liberty, a shadow cast by a poem set in another country and dealing, apparently, with a quite different 'scene' of dispossession.

Barrett Browning's child singer was in part a homage to her husband's treatment of this figure in *Sordello* and, especially, *Pippa Passes*; and Robert Browning, who loved and admired his wife's poetry and set it above his own, responded by taking up the themes of *Casa Guidi Windows* in a number of poems published in his 1855 collection, *Men and Women*. I concentrate on the street songs that infiltrate the monologue of the painter-monk, Fra Lippo Lippi, caught playing truant in the red-light district of Renaissance Florence. Lippi, a child of the streets who has attracted the patronage of the Catholic Church and, more important, of the ruler of Florence, Cosimo de' Medici, plays throughout his monologue with songs derived from a Tuscan folk-song known as the *stornello*. It was hearing these 'whiffs of song' sung by carnival-goers in the street, Lippi claims, that tempted him to break bounds in the first place. As he tells the story of his life to the officer of the watch who has arrested him (but who will let him go, of course—dropping the Medici name makes sure of that), he quotes, or makes up, half a dozen of his own *stornelli*. He appropriates the form, you might say, for his own purpose—but as is the way with dramatic monologue, the *stornelli* say more about him than he intends. Browning's appropriation of the *stornello* overrides Lippi's; it becomes one of the indices of Lippi's failure as an artist, a failure he attributes to his enforced dependency on the Church and the ruling class, but whose roots go deeper than he is willing to acknowledge. Here Browning picks up the politics of *Casa Guidi Windows*, as he does explicitly in 'Old Pictures in Florence', a poem which functions as the 'antitype' to 'Fra Lippo Lippi' and which declares that 'Pure Art's birth [is] still the Republic's'. Renaissance Florence demands, from the artist, a continual negotiation with Church and state, a continual surrender of autonomy. It is not as far from the Florence of the nineteenth-century 'Risorgimento' as it might appear.

The *stornelli* Lippi sings, though he turns and twists them to his own ends, keep their integrity in Browning's poem; only one is left incomplete, and there is no implication that street song in itself is a degraded or denatured form. On the streets of Dublin, by contrast, a crippled sailor growls out fragments of an English ballad about a crippled sailor, 'The Death of Nelson'; this popular song, almost as widely disseminated as 'Cherry-Ripe', functions, in James Joyce's *Ulysses*, as a mocking reminder of British rule—a mockery that cuts both ways. At the same time, the dubious celebration of the 'one-handled adulterer', as Stephen Dedalus calls Nelson, fits the plot of sexual conquest and betrayal played out between Leopold Bloom, his wife Molly, and her lover Hugh 'Blazes' Boylan. (Other English songs, notably 'My Girl's a Yorkshire Girl', repeat this double theme of political and sexual potency; and this song, too, is heard only in broken shards.) Yet the wandering sailor's associations reach to the deepest sources of the book: to Ulysses, to Sinbad, to Homer. Joyce's observation of an ill-featured, ill-natured urban 'type' is exact, credible, 'realistic' (and has a surprising 'real-life' origin in a one-legged Irish sailor who caused a disturbance in the royal box at Ascot in 1832); yet his figure, and the song he sings, correspond to other 'types' in the novel, intricately doubled and bonded: for Ulysses is both adulterer and cuckold, and Homer both beggar and bard. In the final section of the novel devoted to Bloom, and in Molly's concluding monologue, these threads of association are woven together, as Bloom falls asleep to the rhythms of a prose poem or language game that begins with Sinbad, and Molly, recalling the moment she said yes to Bloom's proposal of marriage, remembers also her first lover—an English sailor.

Urban realism is also the foundation of the episode at the heart of Virginia Woolf's *Mrs. Dalloway* in which an old woman is heard singing outside Regent's Park underground station. Several years before she wrote the novel, Woolf recorded in her diary 'An old beggar woman, blind, sat against a stone wall in Kingsway', whom she saw on a 'drive to Waterloo on top of a bus', and she included a vignette of this familiar urban type in *Jacob's Room*. In both the diary entry and the earlier novel, however, there is an insistence that the 'beggar woman' is not, in fact, begging—not 'singing for coppers', but 'for her own amusement', 'from the depths of her gay wild heart'. But in *Mrs. Dalloway* the old woman's hand is definitely 'exposed for coppers'; it seems as though Woolf wanted to ground the image in a more familiar form of urban transaction (Peter Walsh, crossing Marylebone Road, puts a shilling in her hand), even though what she actually does with this street song is, in one sense, the most complex and problematic of all the instances in this book. For the song itself cannot be fixed: it is given to us, first, as a string of meaningless syllables, which are then 'translated' by the narrator of the book into an ancient, primordial song of sexual love, and then heard in the form of a modern German *lied*—a melancholy *fin-de-siècle* art-song which you might expect to hear not far away in the concert rooms of Wigmore Hall, but which is inconceivable as a song sung by a beggar on a London street in 1925. The solid foundation of realism dissolves in Woolf's playful handling, but she has good reasons for refusing to pin the song down to a single determinate form. The characters who see and hear the old woman—Peter Walsh, Rezia, and Septimus Smith—do not really 'see' her for what she is, and cannot therefore 'hear' what she is singing. To them she is stationary in more than the physical sense—fixed in her ignoble urban category. They do not understand that she is not begging, but offering; and they pass her by.

The old woman 'singing of love…love which prevails' incarnates one of the most enduring aspects of street song; and Eros features not only in ballads and ditties (where 'true crime', patriotic exploits, and comedy rival it in popularity) but, as we have seen with 'Cherrie-ripe', in the cries of street traders. In an episode of *La Prisonnière*, the sixth volume of Marcel Proust's *À la recherche du temps perdu*, the narrator listens from his bedroom to the *cris de Paris*, which like the 'Cries of London' had long been enshrined in music and visual art. The pleasure the narrator takes in associating the cries he hears with Gregorian plainchant, or the music of Debussy and Mussorgsky, suggests that his interest is purely aesthetic, and at times the intricacy and refinement of his thoughts make the episode seem like a parody or auto-pastiche of 'Proustian' style. But this aesthetic surface is a mask; in the street-vendors' cries the narrator hears a different song, the song of the Sirens, tempting his lover Albertine into the streets, 'translating' foodstuffs and trades into offers of sexual pleasure, and in particular promising to satisfy her desire for other women. Albertine's lesbianism is the secret each withholds from the other—she refusing to admit what he refuses to tell her he already knows—and this secret is cried in the street. The narrator's treatment of the *cris de Paris* is the most extreme instance of the appropriation of street song I have come across, the most selfish, the most mercilessly exposed; yet it is also the most eloquent, the most attuned to the beauty of form and language. The last work I consider in this book may match it—but only by taking street song out of the domain of sound.

This work is Walt Whitman's short poem 'Sparkles from the Wheel', which also describes an encounter with a street trader, but not one who is crying his wares. 'A knife-grinder works at his wheel sharpening a great knife': this is what the narrator sees, and the 'sparkles from the wheel' form the knife-grinder's song. Although we think of Whitman as a quintessential city poet, the kind of specific, individual urban anec-dote recorded in this poem is actually quite rare in his work. 'Sparkles from the Wheel', with its narrator observing a group who are watching the knife-grinder's magical performance, circles back to Wordsworth's 'Power of Music', with which I began. But the way the narrator places himself in the scene, the description of the old man at work, the implied politics of the urban landscape, are all radically different. Whitman seems at first glance more unassuming than Wordsworth, less willing to offer an explicit judgement of the meaning of what he observes ('An Orpheus! An Orpheus!'), less polemical in his presentation of a pleasure which is accessible to the urban poor and denied to the indifferent rich. Needless to say, it is not that simple. The knife-grinder practises one of the most ancient of all trades, but also one of the 'lowest' in terms of social status (and the one whose noise was held to be even more grating than a barrel-organ). He has a long literary and visual history, but there are very few images that ennoble his 'art', and some that carry the darkest intimations of violence. For a poet to identify with a knife-grinder is not the same as identifying with a fiddler, or a singer—who may per-form execrably as individuals, but whose art is touched with the sacred.

Whitman deliberately refrains from investing the knife-grinder, this 'sad sharp-chinn'd old man with worn clothes and broad shoulder-band of leather', with attributes 'above his station'. Realism dictates his portrait as much as it does that of Joyce's 'onelegged sailor' or Woolf's 'old beggar woman'. What is transcendent is not the knife-grinder himself, but his utterance—or rather the poet's apprehension of that utterance. The sparkles from the wheel are magical, volatile, gone. The group of attentive children whom the narrator joined is also gone, and so is the narrator himself, if any of them were ever real. What remains is the subject of this book.

I

Orpheus in the city

An Orpheus! an Orpheus! yes, Faith may grow bold,
And take to herself all the wonders of old;—
Near the stately Pantheon you'll meet with the same
In the street that from Oxford hath borrowed its name.

His station is there; and he works on the crowd,
He sways them with harmony merry and loud;
He fills with his power all their hearts to the brim—
Was aught ever heard like his fiddle and him?

What an eager assembly! what an empire is this!
The weary have life, and the hungry have bliss;
The mourner is cheered, and the anxious have rest;
And the guilt-burthened soul is no longer opprest.

As the Moon brightens round her the clouds of the night,
So He, where he stands, is a centre of light;
It gleams on the face, there, of dusky-browed Jack,
And the pale-visaged Baker's, with basket on back.

That errand-bound 'Prentice was passing in haste—
What matter! he's caught—and his time runs to waste;
The Newsman is stopped, though he stops on the fret;
And the half-breathless Lamplighter—he's in the net!

The Porter sits down on the weight which he bore;
The Lass with her barrow wheels hither her store;—
If a thief could be here he might pilfer at ease;
She sees the Musician, 'tis all that she sees!

He stands, backed by the wall;—he abates not his din;
His hat gives him vigour, with boons dropping in,
From the old and the young, from the poorest; and there!
The one-pennied Boy has his penny to spare.

O blest are the hearers, and proud be the hand
Of the pleasure it spreads through so thankful a band;
I am glad for him, blind as he is!—all the while
If they speak 'tis to praise, and they praise with a smile.

That tall Man, a giant in bulk and in height,
Not an inch of his body is free from delight;
Can he keep himself still, if he would? oh, not he!
The music stirs in him like wind through a tree.

Mark that Cripple who leans on his crutch; like a tower
That long has leaned forward, leans hour after hour!—
That Mother, whose spirit in fetters is bound,
While she dandles the Babe in her arms to the sound.

Now, coaches and chariots! roar on like a stream;
Here are twenty souls happy as souls in a dream:
They are deaf to your murmurs—they care not for you,
Nor what ye are flying, nor what ye pursue![1]

W ordsworth's 'Power of Music' is an exemplary instance of the way
poetry both celebrates, and appropriates for its own use, the art
with which it is twinned. 'Power of Music', first published in 1807, was,
according to Wordsworth, 'taken from life' during his residence in
London in the preceding year.[2] The narrator who describes the musician's power, his 'empire' over his audience, is not himself subject to
that power; it works on the labouring urban poor (chimney sweep,
baker, 'prentice, 'Newsman', lamplighter, porter, costermonger—down
to the 'one-pennied Boy', perhaps a crossing sweeper) and on figures
of destitution and lack, a cripple with his crutch, a mother and her
(probably illegitimate) child. The narrator is an educated man, as his
opening exclamation, 'An Orpheus! an Orpheus!' suggests, and he
rejoices in the power of music to alleviate the sufferings of the poor,
not his own. And yet he identifies with the musician who, though blind,
stands 'like a centre of light' in the dark city. The opening allusion to
Orpheus is not, after all, frivolous or complacent; despite the poem's
tripping anapaests, its disguise as 'light verse', the myth in its primal
form makes itself felt: here is the godlike musician, the blind bard

1. William Wordsworth, 'Power of Music', in *The Poems*, 2 vols., ed. John O. Hayden
   (Harmondsworth: Penguin Books, 1977), i 691–3.
2. Note dictated by Wordsworth to Isabella Fenwick in 1843; the 'Fenwick Notes' were
   first published in Christopher Wordsworth's *Memoirs of William Wordsworth* (1851) and
   as headnotes to the poems in the *Poetical Works* of 1857.

who both takes his listeners captive and sets them free. 'He works on the crowd', 'He sways them', 'He fills with his power all their hearts to the brim'; the 'prentice is *caught*, the newsman is *stopped*, the lamplighter is *in the net*, the mother's spirit *in fetters is bound*; yet the musician also performs miracles of healing and redemption for the weary, the hungry, the mourner, the sinner. One image captures this doubleness, that of the tall man, the 'giant in bulk': 'Not an inch of his body is free from delight'. Pleasure, which Wordsworth elsewhere defines as the only true purpose of poetry, is given here on condition that the recipient *not be free* from it; the hearers are possessed by the music, in the same way that the musician or poet is traditionally said to be possessed by the god.[3]

Everything that is said of music here applies to song, as the opening reference to Orpheus suggests. Almost any reference to Orpheus has a dark aspect, given his eventual fate; but what Wordsworth does with the myth of Orpheus' silencing and dismemberment is at the heart of the poem's own double nature.

To understand why, you need to appreciate the isolation of the musician and the crowd from the general noise of the city. Cities are noisy places, and the street musician or singer is in perpetual competition with ambient noise, as Wordsworth knew well. In book 7 of *The Prelude*, in which he describes his residence in London in the early 1790s, he evokes the 'Babel din' of the city, in which street song, whether performed by a 'minstrel band / Of Savoyards' or an 'English ballad-singer', is on a level with 'a company of dancing dogs', or 'some female vendor's scream, belike / The very shrillest of all London cries'.[4]

3. On the 'necessity of producing immediate pleasure' as a condition of 'the Poet's art', see the Preface to *Lyrical Ballads* (in the expanded text of 1802): 'it is a homage paid to the native and naked dignity of man, to the grand elementary principle of pleasure, by which he knows, and feels, and lives, and moves. We have no sympathy but what is propagated by pleasure' (*Lyrical Ballads*, ed. Michael Mason [Harlow: Longman, 1992], pp. 73–5). Wordsworth's tribute to the skill of the musician runs counter to the taxonomy proposed by Henry Mayhew in *London Labour and the London Poor* (1852); in the section on 'Street Musicians and Street Vocalists', he states: 'The Street Musicians are of two kinds—the skilful and the blind. The former obtain their money by the agreeableness of their performance, and the latter in pity for their application rather than of their harmony. The blind Street Musicians, it must be confessed, belong generally to the rudest class of performers'.

4. William Wordsworth, *The Prelude* (1850) vii 176–83. I cite the 1850 text, the first published edition, because it is the one that other authors mentioned in this book (e.g. Gissing and Whitman) would have known; the 1805 manuscript was not published until 1926. In the case of this particular passage, there is in fact no difference between the two versions. Subsequent line references are given in the text.

The sounds of the city culminate in Bartholomew Fair, where voices compete with one another in 'anarchy and din, / Barbarian and infernal': hucksters who 'stretch the neck and strain the eyes, / And crack the voice in rivalship', 'buffoons against buffoons / Grimacing, writhing, screaming'; and the musicians are like factory workers: 'him who grinds / The hurdy-gurdy, at the fiddle weaves, / Rattles the salt-box, thumps the kettle-drum, / And him who at the trumpet puffs his cheeks' (ll. 686–7, 695–702).

Phrases like 'Babel din', and adjectives like 'Barbarian and infernal', are clichés of writing about London, and about cities in general, and continued to circulate a century and more after the poem appeared. And what applies to writing applies to visual imagery as well. Indeed, the musician in 'Power of Music' consciously or unconsciously recalls a famous and influential image of urban noise, Hogarth's print of 'The Enrag'd Musician' (Figure 1.1).

Figure 1.1. William Hogarth (1697–1764), *The Enrag'd Musician* (engraving, 1741)

Here the 'power of music' is exhaustively, comically, cruelly eviscerated, as a riot of street noise overwhelms the indignant violinist at the window. It is a controlled riot, composed by a maestro, who has 'orchestrated' every instrument in the picture, from the bawling ballad singer to the boy with his drum, from the cats on the roof to the parrot on the lamp post—perched just below a poster advertising *The Beggar's Opera*, whose heroine, of course, is named Polly. The carnival of uproar is presided over by a great goddess, the glorious milkmaid with her improbable bucket. Wordsworth is very likely to have known this image; in effect his poem turns Hogarth's scene inside out, putting the violinist on the street, denuding that street of any other sound than that of the traffic over which he triumphs, disarming the London crowd of the threat it poses and transforming it into an enchanted audience for the performance of a god.

Hogarth's treatment of the violinist has been read as a satire on this stuck-up foreigner's pretensions, yet he, too, is Orpheus—a snooty Orpheus, perhaps, but the crowd of unbridled noise-makers who surge towards him are not as genial as they look. When you consider that they include a knife-grinder and a sow-gelder, the violinist might have cause to worry. After all, the episode of the death of Orpheus is marked in book 11 of Ovid's *Metamorphoses* not just by violence but by noise:

> But rash
> And heady riot out of frame all reason now did dash,
> And frantic outrage reigned. Yet had the sweetness of his song
> Appeased all weapons, saving that the noise now growing strong
> With blowing shawms, and beating drums, and bedlam howling out,
> And clapping hands on every side by Bacchus' drunken rout,
> Did drown the sound of Orpheus' harp. Then first of all stones were
> Made ruddy with the prophet's blood, and could not give him ear.[5]

This is the passage that so haunted Milton, who takes it up in the invocation to book 7 of *Paradise Lost*:

> But drive far off the barbarous dissonance
> Of Bacchus and his revellers, the race
> Of that wild rout that tore the Thracian bard
> In Rhodopè, where woods and rocks had ears

5. Arthur Golding (trans.), *The Fifteen Books of P. Ovidius Naso, entitled Metamorphosis, translated out of Latin into English meter* (1567) xi 13–20. I have modernized the spellings.

> To rapture, till the savage clamour drowned
> Both harp and voice; nor could the Muse defend
> Her son.[6]

It is this 'savage clamour' that is transposed into Hogarth's picture; but Wordsworth's poem deliberately lowers its volume. The noise of the urban crowd should be overwhelming the musician's performance, especially considering where that performance is taking place. His musician's 'station' is said to be near the 'stately Pantheon' in Oxford Street, but 'stately' is probably ironic, since Wordsworth is alluding not to the elegant high-society assembly rooms designed by James Wyatt in 1772, and described by Horace Walpole as 'the most beautiful edifice in England', which had burned down twenty years later, but its more showy replacement, a venue for concerts and masquerades.[7] Nor would the musician's audience be patrons of this establishment. They are standing on the street, while the 'coaches and chariots' of the rich go past. Far from being deafened *by* the noise of traffic, they are deaf *to* it—the roar has sunk to a murmur. And Wordsworth celebrates this 'dream', this suspension of the usual conditions of urban life, by directly addressing the rich: in the line 'Now, coaches and chariots! roar on like a stream', 'roar' is an imperative verb, as the comma makes clear; Wordsworth is not saying that the coaches and chariots are roaring on like a stream, but defying them to do their worst.

What power enables Orpheus to triumph over his adversaries? The poem's title tells us that it is the power of music; but there is another power at work in the poem, and another Orpheus at play. Think again about the space of performance. For though this space is specifically named, though you can point to it on a modern map and indeed visit the Oxford Street Marks & Spencer which stands on the site where the Pantheon stood and bears its ghostly name, and though buskers are playing on Oxford Street now as they have been since that day in 1806,

6. John Milton, *Paradise Lost*, ed. Alastair Fowler, 2nd ed. (Harlow: Pearson Education, 1998 [Longman Annotated English Poets]), vii 32–8. As has often been remarked, Milton makes Bacchus complicit in Orpheus' death, whereas in Ovid we are reminded that Orpheus himself was 'the chaplain of his [Bacchus'] orgies' (xi 76) and that the god took vengeance on the Thracian women by metamorphosing them into trees.

7. This is probably what Thomas De Quincey had in mind when he quoted the phrase in *Confessions of an English Opium-Eater* in 1821, observing that it was 'near "the *stately* Pantheon" (as Mr Wordsworth has obligingly called it)' that he found the druggist who sold him his first dose of opium (Thomas De Quincey, *Confessions of an English Opium-Eater* [1821], ed. Alethea Hayter [London: Penguin Books, 1986], p. 70).

the real space of the poem is just that, the page where Wordsworth works *his* crowd, his readers, and where the blind musician is transformed, metamorphosed into the figure of the poet's imagination. Street song, as I will argue over the course of this book, is always, in the grasp of a great writer, subject to the power of words.

Cities were from the beginning vocal places, in which songs performed in public spaces carried news, spread ideas, challenged or reinforced prevailing attitudes, and helped make the political weather. Songs were also the cheapest and most readily accessible form of entertainment for the urban poor, something that George Gissing, as we shall see, took seriously both for good and ill. Yet the status of street song has always been questionable, in a way that rural folk-song, for example, has not. The traditional folk-song or ballad has the prestige of authenticity, whereas urban song is compromised by association with mass culture, and with commercial modes of production and distribution. It also carries the stigma of urban noise. Street songs might be treated as one of a number of obtrusive elements of the urban soundscape, which destroyed not just peace and quiet generally, but specifically the peace and quiet of intellectual labour.[8] Keats, writing to his sister Fanny in July 1820, complained of its effect on his precarious regime of recovery from the haemorrhage he had suffered in February: 'I read the greatest part of the day, and generally take two half hour walks a day up and down the terrace which is very much pester'd with cries, ballad singers, and street music'.[9] As a component of urban noise, street music was also represented as the enemy of music itself. Hogarth's 'Enrag'd Musician', attempting to practise his civilized art in competition with the racket in the street, is only one of a huge number of polemical images and texts, in which the street singer is no better than the bawling beggar, the milkmaid crying her wares, or the knife-grinder. As cities became larger and noisier, street singers had to be loud, and their appeal was no longer to a community, socially homogeneous and sympathetically attuned, but to the alienated, unstable, fluctuating urban crowd.

8. On this subject, see John M. Picker, *Victorian Soundscapes* (Oxford: Oxford University Press, 2003), esp. ch. 2, 'The Soundproof Study: Victorian Professional Identity and Urban Noise' (pp. 41–81). Picker notes that the mathematician Charles Babbage, who waged a vigorous campaign against all forms of street music in the 1860s, included '*The human voice in its various forms*' in his pamphlet *A Chapter on Street Nuisances* (1864).

9. Letter of 22 July 1820, in *Letters of John Keats*, ed. Hyder E. Rollins, 2 vols. (Cambridge: Cambridge University Press, 2012), ii 309. Edition originally published by Harvard University Press in 1958.

The most graphic account of this environment in nineteenth-century verse comes in a passage from James Clarence Mangan's remarkable 'Khidder', a (very) free translation of a work by the German poet and Orientalist Friedrich Rückert. 'Khidder' tells the story of a time traveller who visits, at intervals of a thousand years, the same location— successively an ancient classical city, a pastoral wilderness, a lake, a wood, and, finally, a modern city. In each location he encounters a native of the place, who assures him that the particular landscape he sees has always been there. All the descriptions occupy around twenty to thirty lines, in irregular couplets, except the last, which is much longer and more detailed. And in contrast to the preceding landscapes, which are predominantly represented in visual terms, the city is evoked almost entirely through sound:

> How rose the strife
> Of sounds! the ceaseless beat
> Of feet!
> The noise of carts, of whips—the roll
> Of chariots, coaches, cabs, gigs—(all
> Who keep the last-named vehicle we call
> Respectable)—horse-tramplings, and the toll
> Of bells; the whirl, the clash, the hubbub-mingling
> Of voices, deep and shrill; the clattering, jingling,
> The indescribable, indefinable roar;
> The grating, creaking, booming, clanking, thumping,
> And bumping,
> And stumping
> Of folks with wooden legs; the gabbling,
> And babbling,
> And many more
> Quite nameless helpings
> To the general effect; dog-yelpings,
> Laughter, and shout, and cry; all sounds of gladness,
> Of sadness,
> And madness,—
> For there were people marrying,
> And others carrying
> The dead they would have died for to the grave—
> (Sadly the church bell tolled
> When the young men were burying the old—
> More sadly spake that bodeful tongue
> When the old were burying the young)—
> Thus did the tumult rave

Through that fair city—nor were wanting there
Of dancing dogs or bear,
Or needy knife-
Grinder, or man with dismal wife,
That sang deplorably of *"purling groves*
And verdant streams, all where young Damon roves
With tender Phillida, the nymph he loves,
And softly breathe
The balmy moonbeam's wreathe,
And amorous turtle-doves"—
Or other doleful men, that blew
The melancholiest tunes—the which they only knew—
On flutes and other instruments of wind;
Or small dark imps, with hurdy-
Gurdy,
And marmoset, that grinned
For nuts, and might have been his brother,
They were so like each other;
Or man
That danced like the god Pan,
Twitching
A spasmy face
From side to side with a grace
Bewitching,
The while he whistled
In sorted pipes, all at his chin that bristled;
Or fiddler, fiddling much
For little profit, and a many such
Street musics most forlorn
In that too pitiless rout quite overborne.[10]

Mangan does something extraordinary with cliché here: almost every element in his soundscape is taken from a familiar catalogue of urban sounds—human, animal, man-made—yet the effect is fresh, sharp, funny, poignant; you can't tell, as you jump or are flung from one image to the next, whether you are going to land on satire, or pathos; in its wilful inconsistencies of tone and acrobatic form, the poem itself is like the 'man / That danced like the god Pan, / Twitching / A spasmy face / From

---

10. James Clarence Mangan, 'Khidder', ll. 126–84, in *Poems, Many Hitherto Uncollected* (Dublin: O'Donoghue and Co., 1903), pp. 167–8. The poem first appeared anonymously in the *Dublin University Magazine* in 1845; Mangan had published an earlier version of Rückert's poem in 1840. See Matthew Campbell, *Irish Poetry under the Union, 1801–1924* (Cambridge: Cambridge University Press, 2013), p. 105.

side to side with a grace / Bewitching'. Mangan touches on most of
the kinds of street song I discuss in this book, but I want to concentrate
on two aspects which he emphasizes at the start of the passage and at
its end: the *strife of sounds* and the *pitiless rout*. These bear directly on
'Power of Music', which is echoed in the 'chariots [and] coaches' of l. 130
and in the 'fiddler, fiddling much / For little profit' of ll. 181–2. Mangan,
like Hogarth, represents a cacophony of sounds in competition with
each other, but unlike Hogarth, his art does not seek to comprehend
these sounds in a single masterful 'scene'. Instead, the verse enacts what
it describes, in an unpatterned sequence of long and short lines, some
end-stopped, others not, some simply recorded, others accompanied
by an authorial comment—and these comments themselves are not all
of a kind, as though the poem were at odds with itself. When it comes
to music and song, however, Mangan's attitude is clear. Like Woody
Allen's joke at the start of *Annie Hall* (1977) about the hotel food being
'terrible—and such small portions', Mangan's view of street music is
that it's terrible—and so inaudible. From the pastoral ballad performed by
the 'man with dismal wife, / That sang deplorably of "purling groves /
And verdant streams"' to the hurdy-gurdy operated by 'small dark imps'
(compared to monkeys, in a common racial slur), street music and
street song are as far from Wordsworth's idealized image of the urban
Orpheus as it is possible to get. And yet these degraded performers are
still subject to Orpheus' fate. Wordsworth, as we have seen, had emphasized the volume of sound produced by his street musician: he is 'merry
and *loud*' (l. 6), and 'abates not his *din*' (l. 25). But in Mangan's poem an
avalanche of noise—'grating, creaking, booming, clanking, thumping'—
falls onto the hapless singers and musicians. They are 'In that too pitiless rout quite overborne'; the 'pitiless rout' takes us back to Ovid, and
to Milton, as, in the modern city, even a degraded Orpheus stands no
chance against the city's 'indescribable, indefinable roar'.

Mangan's animus against street song isn't, of course, the whole story.
Robert Browning's merry monk, Fra Lippo Lippi, sings Tuscan folk-
songs when he is arrested in the red-light district of Florence. Proust's
narrator hears, from his bedroom window, the *cris de Paris*, the cries of
the itinerant street-sellers, as a form of secular liturgy. The street singer
can be a romantic figure, or a figure of modernity, and sometimes both at
once. George Gissing was certainly not immune to the romantic aspect
of street music and street song. On his visit to Italy in the autumn of
1888, he recorded in his diary his first impressions of Naples, among

them 'the soft note of the street-organs' and 'the long musical cry of
sellers going about the streets at night'.[11] Other diary entries mention
'a male soprano singing to a guitar' in the Piazza del Duomo in
Florence, the all-night 'singing and shouting in the streets' in Bologna,
which suggested that the people 'seem to live a merry life', and especially
the singing on the 'streets'—that is, the canals—of Venice (*Diary* 114, 126).
Of one such singer—'a woman's voice, exquisitely rich & true'—Gissing
wrote: 'This is "street" music, but such a voice I have never heard anywhere but in great concert halls, never'.[12]

These mentions of street music and street songs—and there are
many more of them from Gissing's Italian journeys—are almost always
benign. He noted that outside Naples the street-organ seemed to have
disappeared from Italian cities, and remarked: 'I regret this bitterly. My
whole life is brightened by a little music, however poor'.[13] Gissing's
enjoyment of the street-organ puts him at odds with most 'respectable'
opinion in the nineteenth century, according to which the street-organ
was a blight on the urban scene. Allan W. Atlas suggests that Gissing
might have come across a work by the Reverend Hugh Reginald Haweis,
Music and Morals, published in 1871, in which the 'organ-man' is described
as 'a very Orpheus in hell!'

I bless his music. I stand in that foul street where the blessed sun shines, and
where the music is playing; I give the man a penny to prolong the happiness of
those poor people, of those hungry, pale, and ragged children, and, as I retire,
I am saluted as a public benefactor; and was ever pleasure bought so cheap and
so pure?[14]

Atlas sees this sentiment as analogous to that which the narrator of
Gissing's novel *Thyrza*, published in 1887, expresses as an aside, when the
novel's hero, Gilbert Grail, hears a street-organ outside a pub in Lambeth:

---

11. *London and the Life of Literature in Late Victorian England: The Diary of George Gissing,
    Novelist*, ed. Pierre Coustillas (Hassocks: Harvester Press, 1978), p. 61. Hereafter *Diary*.
    I am indebted to two articles by Allan W. Atlas: 'George Gissing's Concertina', *Journal
    of Musicology* 17.2 (Spring 1999), pp. 304–18, and 'George Gissing on Music: Italian
    Impressions', *The Musical Times* 142 (Summer 2001), pp. 27–37.
12. *The Collected Letters of George Gissing*, ed. Paul F. Mattheisen, Arthur C. Young, and
    Pierre Coustillas, 9 vols. (Athens, OH: Ohio University Press, 1990–7), iv 34–5; cited
    in Atlas, 'Gissing on Music', p. 29.
13. *Letters* iv 21, cited in Atlas, 'Gissing on Music', p. 28.
14. Cited in Atlas, 'Gissing's Concertina', p. 309. Atlas adds: 'Gissing had probably read
    Music and Morals, and certainly knew Haweis at least by reputation. We know from an
    entry in his diary on 9 March 1892 (*Diary* 272) that Gissing had just read another of
    Haweis's books, *My Musical Life* (London, 1884).'

Grail drew near; there were children forming a dance, and he stood to watch them.

Do you know that music of the obscure ways, to which children dance? Not if you have only heard it ground to your ears' affliction beneath your windows in the square. To hear it aright you must stand in the darkness of such a by-street as this, and for the moment be at one with those who dwell around, in the blear-eyed houses, in the dim burrows of poverty, in the unmapped haunts of the semi-human. Then you will know the significance of that vulgar clanging of melody [...][15]

And yet Gissing is not really echoing Haweis's praise of music as a redeeming power. If anything, it's the contrary: the music of the barrel-organ, the children's dancing, are like a coded language in which the misery and suffering of the poor are articulated, if you know how to listen and look. The music of the people gives you an insight into 'the dim burrows of poverty' in the same way that the American slave Frederick Douglass claimed that the supposedly happy singing of his fellow slaves on the plantation where he was born 'would do more to impress some minds with the horrible character of slavery, than the reading of whole volumes of philosophy on the subject could do'.[16]

It is also clear that street music in London is not the same as in Italy. In part, this difference belongs to a conventional opposition between the image of poverty and the common people in Britain and Italy (or southern France, or Spain). Mediterranean poverty seemed to many British visitors less sordid, less degraded than the home-grown kind, and Mediterranean cities less hopelessly immiserated. The image of the cheerful foreigner is itself a stereotype of British fiction, epitomized by the irrepressible (and musical) John Baptist Cavaletto in Dickens's *Little Dorrit*.[17] But in Gissing's case there is a more specific reason. In a novel such as *The Nether World* which so severely limits the scope for redemption, and which treats conventional idealism with such scepticism, music could no more function as a means of salvation than religion, or

---

15. George Gissing, *Thyrza: A Tale* [1887], ed. Jacob Korg (Brighton: Harvester Press, 1984), ch. 9, p. 111.

16. Frederick Douglass, *Narrative of the Life of Frederick Douglass, an American Slave* [1845], ed. William L. Andrews and William S. McFeely (New York: W. W. Norton, 1997), ch. 2, p. 19.

17. 'He's a merry fellow', remarks Mr Pancks to Mrs Plornish in Bleeding Heart Yard; and Mrs Plornish confirms it: 'he plays with the children, and he sits in the sun—he'll sit down anywhere, as if it was an arm-chair—and he'll sing, and he'll laugh!' (Charles Dickens, *Little Dorrit* [1857], ed. Helen Small and Stephen Wall [London: Penguin Books, 2003], ch. 25, p. 324).

romantic love, or intellectual superiority. Instead, music and street song are appropriated as elements in the novel's symbolic design, in which the London slum is equated to hell, from which escape is not just impossible but, to its inmates, virtually inconceivable.

The street singer who articulates this symbolic design first appears in chapter 5 of *The Nether World*, which is set mainly in the slum district of Clerkenwell in central London in the late 1870s. The 'procession' referred to in the opening sentence is the funeral of an old woman, Mrs Peckover's mother-in-law, conducted with gin-soaked solemnity and vulgar pomp, and offering the neighbourhood the required display of respectability, as well as a free show:

> The procession moved slowly away, and the crowd, unwilling to disperse immediately, looked about for some new source of entertainment. They were fortunate, for at this moment came round the corner an individual notorious throughout Clerkenwell as 'Mad Jack.' Mad he presumably was—at all events, an idiot. A lanky, raw-boned, red-headed man, perhaps forty years old; not clad, but hung over with the filthiest rags; hatless, shoeless. He supported himself by singing in the streets, generally psalms, and with eccentric modulations of the voice which always occasioned mirth in hearers. [...] At present, having watched the funeral coaches pass away, he lifted up his voice in a terrific blare, singing, 'All ye works of the Lord, bless ye the Lord, praise Him and magnify Him for ever.' Instantly he was assailed by the juvenile portion of the throng, was pelted with anything that came to hand, mocked mercilessly, buffeted from behind. For a while he persisted in his psalmody, but at length, without warning, he rushed upon his tormentors, and with angry shrieks endeavoured to take revenge. The uproar continued till a policeman came and cleared the way. Then Jack went off again, singing, 'All ye works of the Lord.' With his voice blended that of the costermonger, 'Penny a bundill!'[18]

The Nether World has been held to represent, with unflinching truthfulness, the actual conditions of life in the district of London it describes. But I am not concerned here with the general picture of poverty and degradation that Gissing paints, nor with the political, moral, and aesthetic judgements he delivers. I want to ask some more specific questions. What kind of figure is 'Mad Jack'? Is he a 'type', and, if so, is he accurately drawn? What is he singing, and why?

There were street singers in Victorian London, but Mad Jack doesn't resemble any of the ones who figure in contemporary social history. He is a composite figure, made up of different elements and deployed

18. George Gissing, *The Nether World* [1889], ed. Stephen Gill (Oxford: Oxford University Press, 1992), pp. 42–3.

for a specific purpose which relates not to social history, but to the novel in which he is placed. The phrase he sings—'All ye works of the Lord, bless ye the Lord, praise Him and magnify Him for ever'—recurs in the novel not because it is plausible that we should always hear him singing the same thing, but because it is marked by dramatic irony. The funeral scene takes place in chapter 5; Mad Jack next appears in chapter 8, as one of the main characters of the novel, Pennyloaf Candy, makes her way home through Shooter's Gardens:

> As Pennyloaf drew near to the house, a wild, discordant voice suddenly broke forth somewhere in the darkness, singing in a high key, 'All ye works of the Lord, bless ye the Lord, praise Him and magnify Him for ever!' It was Mad Jack, who had his dwelling in the Court, and at all hours was wont to practise the psalmody which made him notorious throughout Clerkenwell. A burst of laughter followed from a group of men and boys gathered near the archway. (p. 75)

Pennyloaf pays no heed to Mad Jack; she is not, of course, privy to Gissing's design, in which, at the other end of the novel, she will cradle her dead husband in her arms in a miserable lodging in the same building, with a crowd of people on the staircase outside, 'talking, shouting, whistling'; and as the corpse is taken away on a stretcher, in a savage reductive parallel to the showy funeral in the earlier episode, Mad Jack appears again: 'Above the noise of the crowd rose a shrill, wild voice, chanting: "All ye works of the Lord, bless ye the Lord; praise Him and magnify Him for ever!"' (ch. 37, p. 347). The pattern in which this phrase is used tells us that Gissing is aiming at something more, or other than, a 'realistic' effect.

The statement that Mad Jack 'supported himself by singing in the streets, generally psalms' does not ring true if what is meant is that he is a professional street singer, representative or typical of a larger class. In *London Labour and the London Poor*, for example, Henry Mayhew gives a detailed survey of street singers and musicians, and none of those he mentions has a religious repertoire.[19] Collections of Victorian

---

19. Henry Mayhew, *London Labour and the London Poor; a Cyclopædia of the Condition and Earnings of Those That Will Work, Those That Cannot Work, and Those That Will Not Work*, 4 vols. (London: Griffin, Bohn, 1861). Hereafter 'Mayhew', followed by volume and page number. Vol. 3 is subtitled 'The London Street-Folk'; the section on 'Street Musicians' is on pp. 158–90, and the section on 'Street Vocalists' is on pp. 190–204. This edition is accessible online at https://babel.hathitrust.org. Mayhew's book began as a series of articles in the *Morning Chronicle* in 1849–50, published in three volumes in 1851; a fourth volume was added in 1861. The 'vocalists' include 'Street Negro Serenaders', 'Street Glee-Singers', and 'Street Ballad-Singers, or Chaunters'.

street ballads contain religious songs, of course; some are sectarian, others devoted to particular causes such as temperance or the evils of gambling; but the singing of psalms is something that took place in church, and it would have been considered unseemly to try to make money from it. Most ballad singers performed, and sold, ballads on traditional subjects such as crime and sexual misadventure, and street singers relied on popular songs of the day, refreshing their stock as taste and fashions changed. One of Mayhew's informants told him that he began as a 'glee-singer', and that he and his companions 'rarely went out till the evening' and chose their pitches 'in quiet streets or squares, where we saw, by the light at the windows, that some party was going on' (iii 195). Ballad singers, the same informant said, 'looked at the bill of fare for the different concert-rooms, and then went round the neighbourhood where these songs were being sung, because the airs being well known, you see it eased the way for us' (iii 196). Although Mayhew's survey relates to the late 1840s, and traditional ballads were in decline by the end of the century, it is doubtful that a popular taste for psalm-singing on the streets existed in Gissing's day.

The idea that Mad Jack is a professional street singer is in any case contradicted by his name, and what it connotes. 'Mad he presumably was—at all events, an idiot'—that's definite enough. According to this view, he is a different 'type', the neighbourhood lunatic, an urban variant of the village idiot, but without the pastoral gloss bestowed on such figures by (for example) Wordsworth. His singing is compulsive, and forms part of his craziness; he is exhibiting his condition, and pre-sumably attracts some charity, though who from is a puzzle. The phrase 'supported himself by singing in the streets' doesn't quite fit this view, but then Gissing's representation can't be made coherent; no single 'reading' of Mad Jack makes sense of him. He is not a street singer, not even one of those described by Mayhew as 'of the worst description of singers', who 'have money given to them neither for their singing nor songs, but in pity for their age and infirmities' (iii 196). The fact that his madness takes a religious bent allows Gissing to exploit him as a disfig-ured or denatured prophet, a holy fool who comments on the action without being conscious of his role.[20]

20. The outlandishness of a street singer performing a religious song, and its association with madness, occur in the final scene of Rudyard Kipling's 'The Man Who Would Be King' (1888). 'Peachey' Carnehan has returned, crippled and crazed, from his adventure

Gissing states that Mad Jack supported himself by singing psalms, and refers to him practising his 'psalmody'. But what Mad Jack sings is not a psalm. 'All ye works of the Lord, bless ye the Lord, praise Him and magnify Him for ever' is the opening of the *Benedicite*, a canticle in the old Roman Catholic Latin liturgy which was adopted by the Church of England and is found in the Book of Common Prayer.[21] The exact designation of Mad Jack's chant may seem a bit pedantic, but it does matter here. Gissing jotted down the following entry in his scrapbook: ' "Mad Jack" who sings psalms. His dream in which he is told that slums are Hell, & the people in them were once wicked rich in a former life'.[22] This dream does not feature in the episode from chapter 5, but in chapter 37, entitled 'Mad Jack's Dream'. In this chapter, Mad Jack appears three times. He is first encountered by Bob Hewett, on the run from the police and taking refuge in Shooter's Gardens:

At the bottom of the steps, where he was in all but utter darkness, his foot slipped on garbage of some kind, and with a groan he fell on his side.
'Let him that thinketh he standeth take heed lest he fall,' cried a high-pitched voice from close by.
Bob knew that the speaker was the man notorious in this locality as Mad Jack. Raising himself with difficulty, he looked round and saw a shape crouching in the corner.
'What is the principal thing?' continued the crazy voice. 'Wisdom is the principal thing.'   (p. 337)

Neither of these biblical quotations comes from a psalm. The first, 'Let him that thinketh he standeth take heed lest he fall', is from 1 Corinthians 10:12, and has an obvious application to Bob's fate: not only has he just slipped and fallen, but he is dying from the internal injuries he received when he was struck by a cab in the street; his physical fall is itself an image of his fall from grace; he is 'in all but utter

---

with Daniel Dravot in 'Kafiristan', and the narrator sees him 'crawling along the white dust of the roadside, his hat in his hand, quavering dolorously after the fashion of street-singers at Home. There was not a soul in sight, and he was out of all possible ear-shot of the houses. And he sang through his nose, turning his head from right to left:— "The Son of Man goes forth to war, / A golden crown to gain; / His blood-red banner streams afar— / Who follows in his train?" ' (in *Rudyard Kipling* [Oxford Authors], ed. Daniel Karlin [Oxford: Oxford University Press, 1999], p. 86). The song is an adaptation of a hymn by Bishop Reginald Heber (1783–1826).

21. *Oxford Dictionary of the Christian Church*, 2nd ed. [rev.], ed. F. L. Cross and E. A. Livingstone (Oxford: Oxford University Press, 1983), p. 153.
22. *George Gissing's Scrapbook*, ed. Bouwe Postmus (Amsterdam: Twizle, 2007), p. 396.

darkness', on his way to hell.[23] The second quotation, 'Wisdom is the principal thing', is from Proverbs 4:7; not just this verse but the whole chapter bears on Bob's deeply unwise career.[24]

For Mad Jack's second appearance in the chapter, the perspective shifts to Pennyloaf Candy, who has become Bob Hewett's wife. Pennyloaf has been searching for her husband, and returns to her old lodgings in Shooter's Gardens without realizing that Bob has taken refuge there. On her way, she passes through 'The Court', a blind alley lined with 'baked-potato ovens' which have just been lit:

Now the lighting of fires entails the creation of smoke, and whilst these ten or twelve ovens were getting ready to bake potatoes the Court was in a condition not easily described. A single lamp existed for the purpose of giving light to the alley, and at no time did this serve much more than to make darkness visible; at present the blind man would have fared as well in that retreat as he who had eyes, and the marvel was how those who lived there escaped suffocation. (p. 344)

As with 'utter darkness', the quotation from *Paradise Lost* indicates where we are: 'A dungeon horrible, on all sides round / As one great furnace flamed, yet from those flames / No light, but rather darkness visible' (i 62–4).[25] In Gissing's grimly bathetic version, the fire and smoke of the baked-potato ovens are the backdrop against which Mad Jack rants to the crowd about his dream, in which an angel appeared to him in the midst of 'a light such as none of you ever saw', and revealed that the slum dwellers were rich, hard-hearted people and are now being punished in the afterlife: ' "This life you are now leading is that of the damned; this place to which you are confined is Hell! [...] This is Hell—Hell—Hell!" ' (p. 345). This time Pennyloaf does listen: 'the last cry was so terrifying that [she] fled to be out of hearing'. But there is no escape from Mad Jack; his final appearance is the one already quoted, when he is heard singing his refrain as Bob Hewett's body is carried away.

23. 'Utter' in this usage is akin to 'outer' (*OED* I.1), as in the 'outer darkness' where there is 'weeping and gnashing of teeth' (Matthew 8:12).
24. Another image of falling occurs in v. 11–12, in which the putative author of Proverbs, Solomon, addresses his son: 'I have taught thee in the way of wisdom; I have led thee in the right paths. When thou goest, thy steps shall not be straitened; and when thou runnest, thou shalt not stumble'.
25. A few lines further on, Milton also refers to hell as the rebel angels' 'prison ordained / In utter darkness' (ll. 71–2).

What connects Mad Jack's repeated phrase, 'All ye works of the Lord, bless ye the Lord, praise Him and magnify Him for ever', with his dream of the angel revealing that the slum is hell? The origin of the *Benedicite* is an apocryphal addition to the Book of Daniel: it is sung by Shadrach, Meshach, and Abednego in the 'fiery furnace' into which they have been thrown because they defied King Nebuchadnezzar's order to worship his golden image. The 'fiery furnace', in English translations of the Bible, is associated with hell; typologically the miraculous preservation of the three men, who are joined in the furnace by God's angel, figures Christ's ability to save the faithful Christian from the fires of hell. The sordid potato ovens of Shooter's Gardens are doubly infernal: they allude to Milton's hell, but also to Daniel's fiery furnace; the angel in Mad Jack's vision may be clothed in an unearthly light, but it is not the light of redemption; he is not a messenger of salvation but of despair. The *Benedicite* forms part of this pattern of savage inversion: Mad Jack's refrain reminds us not of God's power to save, but of the absence of any such power in the nether world.

Mad Jack may not be a realistic figure, but some of the elements that make him up are drawn from Gissing's own observation and can be documented in the social history of the period. Take, for example, the cruelty with which he is treated by the crowd assembled to watch the funeral procession. Gissing could have read Mayhew's harrowing account of the 'Poor Harp Player', 'A poor, feeble, half-witted looking man [. . .] wretchedly clad, his clothes being old, patched, and greasy. He is well-known in London, being frequently seen with a crowd of boys at his heels, who amuse themselves in playing all kinds of tricks upon him' (*Mayhew* iii 174). As the harp player laments:

Mine's not a bad trade now, but it's bad in the streets. I've been torn to pieces; I'm torn to pieces every day I go out in the streets, and I would be glad to get rid of the streets for 5s. a-week. The streets are full of ruffians. The boys are ruffians. The men in the streets too are ruffians, and encourage the boys. The police protect me as much as they can. I should be killed every week but for them; they're very good people. I've known poor women of the town drive the boys away from me, or try to drive them. It's terrible persecution I suffer—terrible persecution. The boys push me down and hurt me badly, and my harp too. They yell and make noises so that I can't be heard, nor my harp. The boys have cut off my harp-strings, three of them, the other day, which cost me 6½d. or 7d. I tell them it's a shame, but I might as well speak to the stones.

How close the *harp-strings* are to *heartstrings!*—and how sharp the
reminder of the margins by which life on the streets is measured: '6½*d*.
or 7*d*'. The harp player is a pathetically reduced version of Orpheus; his
instrument, the phrase 'torn to pieces', his voice and music shouted
down, the complaint 'I might as well speak to the stones' recall Milton's
allusion to the 'wild rout' whose 'savage clamour drowned / Both harp
and voice'; unlike Wordsworth's musician, this one has no power to
compel attention, and cannot move the stony-hearted to pity. In the
myth, it was the Mænads who made up the 'wild rout' that tore
Orpheus to pieces; here they are boys, street-children; Gissing, as we
shall see, returns them to their original gender in a later passage of the
novel. Yet the poor harp player's account has a chink of light: the 'poor
women of the town' (prostitutes) are not Mænads, but try to help him;
the police are 'very good people' (Figure 1.2).

Gissing is bleaker: no one, male or female, shows Mad Jack any mercy;
in the scene in chapter 5 where we first meet him, 'he was assailed by
the juvenile portion of the throng, was pelted with anything that came to

Figure 1.2. Death of Orpheus, from *Les métamorphoses d'Ovide en latin et françois*,
trans. Pierre du Ryer (Amsterdam, 1702)

hand, mocked mercilessly, buffeted from behind', and when a policeman
does appear, he is only interested in 'clear[ing] the way'. And Gissing
lays more emphasis than Mayhew on the stigma of mental illness. In
this community the strong bully the weak, and take pleasure in doing
so, whether as individuals or collectively; in the novel's cityscape the
crowd is at best repulsive, at worst malignant; an indifferent mass or a
threatening mob.

I have suggested that religious song was not a prominent feature of
the London streets in the period of the novel, and I think this is true
of those who, like Mad Jack, are represented as solitary figures; but
an exception may be made for a different kind of religious activity, in
which music was coming to play an increasingly important part. This is
the Salvation Army, whose evangelical campaigns had been supported
by bands since the mid-1880s, and whose parades and street-corner
meetings were a familiar spectacle by the time the novel was published.
Gissing took a dim view of the Salvation Army's appeal. He recorded
watching its Christmas Day procession in 1886:

Many bands, marching and playing at intervals; girls with tambourines. The only
healthy faces were those of a few girls evidently making sport of the outing.
No pretty faces. The men poor cripples, epileptic and cretinous. Grotesque
religious inscript[ion]s. round their hats. Sudden outbursts of hymns, and gesticulation. The pathos of it all.   (*Gissing's Scrapbook* 420)

Mad Jack is, so to speak, multiplied here; or to put it the other way, he
is himself a one-man Salvation Army, an epitome of its ugliness and
futility, with his 'sudden outbursts' and 'gesticulation'. It is a paradox
Gissing does not attempt to resolve that he is both a true prophet—
and we know that true prophets are mocked and persecuted—and
an absurd caricature; that he piercingly anatomizes the social conditions that make the slums a living hell, without bringing any enlightenment or relief. How could he? The mockery that greets his
singing, like that of the girls 'making sport' of the Salvation Army
outing, conveys the message the novelist wants to enforce: that conventional religion is simply not up to the task, has no purchase on
the 'nether world', and indeed reflects its physical debility and mental derangement.

There is another kind of street song in *The Nether World*; it offers a
secular alternative to Mad Jack's 'psalmody', but it is no more appealing.

This is the raucous communal singing that marks the excursion to the Crystal Palace in chapter 12:

> At Holborn Viaduct there was a perpetual rush of people for the trains to the 'Paliss.' As soon as a train was full, off it went, and another long string of empty carriages drew up in its place. No distinction between 'classes' to-day; get in where you like, where you can. Positively, Pennyloaf found herself seated in a first-class carriage; she would have been awe-struck, but that Bob flung himself back on the cushions with such an easy air, and nodded laughingly at her. Among their companions was a youth with a concertina; as soon as the train moved he burst into melody. It was the natural invitation to song, and all joined in the latest ditties learnt at the music-hall. [...] Towards the end of the journey the young man with the concertina passed round his hat.
>
> (pp. 105–6)[26]

Gissing despised the music-hall, which he associated with the vices of poverty, prostitution, alcoholism, and obscenity: 'the latest ditties learnt at the music-hall' are likely to be bawdy songs whose appeal lay in their mastery of obscene innuendo. Nothing redeems this kind of singing; it forms part of a cacophony comparable to the 'indescribable, indefinable roar' in Mangan's 'Khidder', but more invidious, because it is shot through with class hatred; it is the sound of 'the people' at play:

> Vigorous and varied is the jollity that occupies the external galleries, filling now in expectation of the fireworks; indescribable the mingled tumult that roars heavenwards. Girls linked by the half-dozen arm-in-arm leap along with shrieks like grotesque mænads; a rougher horseplay finds favour among the youths, occasionally leading to fisticuffs. Thick voices bellow in fragmentary chorus; from every side comes the yell, the cat-call, the ear-rending whistle; and as the bass, the never-ceasing accompaniment, sounds myriad-footed tramp, tramp along the wooden flooring. [...] Up shoot the rockets, and all the reeking multitude utters a huge 'Oh' of idiot admiration. (p. 111)

The 'grotesque mænads' are not there by accident; these shrieking girls are brought on stage because of an extraordinary interlude in the Crystal Palace episode, one that concerns not song, and certainly not street song, but orchestral music, performed in what Gissing calls the 'vast amphitheatre' at the centre of the Palace, the Concert Room which had been completed in 1868. Bob Hewett and Pennyloaf Candy

---

26. Among the 'Street Musicians', Mayhew records a 'Concertina Player on the Steamboats' who comments that in summer 'The passengers come to go to the Crystal Palace in the morning part. Those that are going out for pleasure are my best customers' (iii 183).

make their way to this space, 'filled with thousands of faces', and are momentarily spellbound:

Here at length was quietness, intermission of folly and brutality. Bob became another man as he stood and listened. He looked with kindness into Pennyloaf's pale, weary face, and his arm stole about her waist to support her. Ha! Pennyloaf was happy! The last trace of tears vanished. She too was sensible of the influences of music; her heart throbbed as she let herself lean against her husband.   (p. 109)

This music is not from the music-hall; it is the music of Beethoven, of Mendelssohn, of Brahms; and Gissing allows himself an outburst of his own about the civilizing power of music in a regenerated social world:

Well, as every one must needs have his panacea for the ills of society, let me inform you of mine. To humanise the multitude two things are necessary— two things of the simplest kind conceivable. In the first place, you must effect an entire change of economic conditions: a preliminary step of which every tyro will recognise the easiness; then you must bring to bear on the new order of things the constant influence of music. Does not the prescription recommend itself? It is jesting in earnest. For, work as you will, there is no chance of a new and better world until the old be utterly destroyed. Destroy, sweep away, prepare the ground; then shall music the holy, music the civiliser, breathe over the renewed earth, and with Orphean magic raise in perfected beauty the towers of the City of Man.   (ibid.)

Here, at last, is Orpheus in the Nether World, not just an image or accompaniment of divine creativity but the creative force itself. Of course Gissing suspects his own enthusiasm; he ushers it in with defensive sarcasm, and the exaltation—or gush—of the last sentence is at odds with almost everything else in the book.[27] The praise of 'music the civiliser' is isolated and singular; Gissing acknowledges no kinship between the harmony that converts Bob and Pennyloaf, for a brief moment, into Adam and Eve, and the 'barbarous dissonance' of the Bank Holiday crowds. The music of the streets is simply a variety of urban noise, as it is in this passage from the opening of chapter 4, which describes the 'junction of highways' at the Angel, Islington:

Here was the wonted crowd of loiterers and the press of people waiting for tram-car or omnibus—east, west, south, or north; newsboys, eager to get rid of their last batch, were crying as usual, 'Ech-ow! Exteree speciul! Ech-ow! Steendard!'

27. On 13 June 1888, Gissing noted in his diary how 'terribly wearisome' he found writing this chapter: 'it is poor stuff, all this idealism; I'll never go in for it again' (*Diary* 32).

and a brass band was blaring out its saddest strain of merry dance-music. The lights gleamed dismally in rain-puddles and on the wet pavement. With the wind came whiffs of tobacco and odours of the drinking-bar.   (p. 30)

The oxymoron—'its saddest strain of merry dance-music'—echoes the 'doleful men, that blew / The melancholiest tunes' in Mangan's 'Khidder', and suggests that the pleasure being offered here is illusory, a mask that conceals a reality as grating as the cries of the newsboys, as depressing as that of the 'rain-puddles', as sordid as 'the odours of the drinking-bar'. The five senses are equally assaulted on London's streets, but the sense of hearing is especially battered and brutalized. Music in this environment brings neither healing nor consolation, but is one of the voices of misery itself.

2

The child in the street

I heard last night a little child go singing
   'Neath Casa Guidi windows, by the church,
O bella libertà, O bella! stringing
The same words still on notes he went in search
So high for, you concluded the upspringing
   Of such a nimble bird to sky from perch
Must leave the whole bush in a tremble green,
   And that the heart of Italy must beat,
While such a voice had leave to rise serene
   'Twixt church and palace of a Florence street!
A little child, too, who not long had been
   By mother's finger steadied on his feet,
And still *O bella libertà* he sang.

These are the opening lines of *Casa Guidi Windows*, the first major poem published by Elizabeth Barrett Browning following her marriage to Robert Browning in September 1846.[1] They are at the centre of a network of children and song in EBB's work, but this is the only occasion on which the poet/narrator hears, or imagines, a song sung in a city street. Within *Casa Guidi Windows* itself, the child who sings at the opening of the poem is displaced, and silenced, by another child; and in the last poem of the series, 'Nature's Remorses', the same child again withholds his voice. In both cases this other child is EBB's own son.

Before I begin discussing the lines from *Casa Guidi Windows*, I need to set the scene for readers who may not be familiar with the context

---

1. All quotations from Elizabeth Barrett Browning's work are taken from *The Works of Elizabeth Barrett Browning*, ed. Sandra Donaldson et al., 5 vols. (London: Pickering & Chatto, 2010), hereafter *Works*. *Casa Guidi Windows* is in vol. 2, pp. 481–566. From this point I refer to Elizabeth Barrett Browning as 'EBB'.

they take for granted. The poem's general historical setting is that of the Risorgimento, the movement for Italian unity and independence that followed the Congress of Vienna in 1815. This post-Napoleonic settlement confirmed the division of Italy into seven states and spheres of influence: Piedmont-Sardinia, Lombardy-Venetia, Parma, Modena, Tuscany, the Papal States, and Naples-Sicily. Austria was the major foreign power: it directly governed Lombardy-Venetia, and its influence extended through much of the peninsula. The partition of Italy was intended to reverse the liberal and republican gains that had been made, however unevenly, during the revolutionary years that followed Napoleon's invasion of Italy in 1800. The Risorgimento was not really a national movement until its very last phase, in the late 1850s; it is best understood as a collective term for the opposition to foreign rule and autocracy, which mainly took the form of political and cultural agitation, and intermittently of armed insurrection. There were many local variations. Tuscany, where Robert and Elizabeth Barrett Browning settled after their marriage and flight from England in 1846, was governed by an unremarkable Grand Duke of Austrian descent who seems mainly to have wanted a quiet life. More dramatic events were taking place elsewhere, especially in Rome, where a new Pope, Pius IX, elected in June 1846, was making liberal noises and raising hopes that the Catholic Church would actually sponsor political reform.

The Brownings made their first home in Pisa, but during the winter of 1846–7 they decided to move to the larger (and cheaper) city of Florence—despite their reluctance to become part of what they believed to be its vulgar, frivolous, gossipy community of fellow expatriates.[2] They took rooms in Via delle Belle Donne, on the north bank of the Arno and not far from the Cathedral, until July, when they moved to Casa Guidi, in Piazza San Felice, on the south bank and close to the Pitti Palace and the Boboli Gardens (Figure 2.1).[3]

Their first wedding anniversary, 12 September 1847, coincided with the celebrations in Florence to mark the Grand Duke, Leopold II,

2. Robert Browning had inoculated EBB with his horror of 'the English' in Florence during their courtship: 'As for the travelling English, they are horrible and, at Florence, unbearable...their voices in your ear at every turn...and such voices!' (10 July 1846, *The Brownings' Correspondence*, vol. xiii, ed. Philip Kelley and Scott Lewis [Winfield, KS: Wedgestone Press, 1995], p. 147; hereafter *Correspondence*).
3. Strictly speaking, 'Casa Guidi' was 'Palazzo Guidi', and the Brownings so referred to it until after the birth of their son in 1849, when they began calling it 'Casa Guidi' (*Correspondence* xiv [1998] 262 n. 14).

Figure 2.1. Frontage of Casa Guidi, Florence

granting a Civic Guard. Leopold's concession was taken as a sign of his willingness, despite his own Austrian ancestry, to distance himself from the autocratic and repressive policies of Austrian rule in Italy; if he could not be expected to embrace the cause of Italian unity and independence, he was at least prepared, it seemed, to accommodate popular feeling. EBB described the scene in a letter to her sisters Arabella and Henrietta: from the front windows on the first floor of Casa Guidi she and Browning witnessed an 'infinite procession' of 'deputations and companies of various kinds', 'the magistracy', 'the priesthood', 'troops of peasants & nobles, and of soldiers fraternizing with the people', all on their way to the Piazza Pitti, 'where the Duke & his family stood in tears at the window to receive the thanks of his people' (Figure 2.2).[4]

4. *Correspondence* xiv 300. These windows are not the ones referred to in the opening lines, which belonged to the Brownings' own apartment. As EBB explained, 'We went to a window in our palazzo which had a full view, and I had a throne of cushions piled up on a chair' (p. 301).

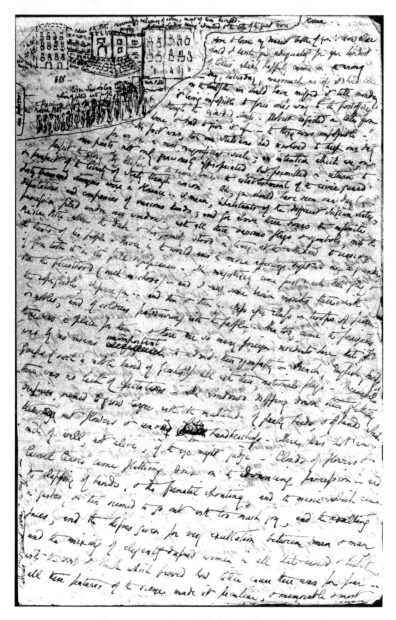

Figure 2.2. Elizabeth Barrett Browning, first page of letter to her sisters Arabella and Henrietta Moulton-Barrett, Florence, 13 September 1847. The locations in the sketch, in EBB's tiny cramped writing, have been deciphered by the editors of *The Brownings' Correspondence* (vol. 14, p. 307). In the centre, above the crowd: 'Piazza San Felice alive & filled with people'; to the right: 'viva P. IX'; to the left: 'The procession ending up at Piazza Pitti'; vertical in left margin: 'our palazzo' [i.e. Casa Guidi]; above in left margin: 'via maggio'; top margin: 'Palace of the Pitti—surrounded by balconies of stone, most of them thronged'; below (starting at 'balconies'): 'Foreign ladies being admitted to the top of the great tower'.

The procession is recorded in the first part of *Casa Guidi Windows*
and is accompanied by EBB's cautious, though on the whole optimistic, assessment of the likelihood of genuine political progress, not just
in Tuscany but in Italy as a whole, where the actions of Pope Pius IX,
'Pio Nono', loomed larger than those of the Grand Duke. But as we
have seen, this is not where the poem actually begins. The 'little child'
singing 'O bella libertà' does not belong to the procession, but is an
isolated, singular figure.

Casa Guidi Windows is not the first poem in which EBB associated
song with the figure of the child and with liberal politics, but there is
a measurable distance between poems written before her marriage and
move to Italy and those that followed. In 'A Reed', one of the poems
that appeared in *Blackwood's Magazine* in 1846, but which had been
written some years earlier, the poet refuses to serve the ruling order,
but does not dedicate her art to its overthrow:

> I
>
> I am no trumpet, but a reed:
> No flattering breath shall from me lead
>   A silver sound, a hollow sound.
> I will not ring, for priest or king,
> One blast that in re-echoing
>   Would leave a bondsman faster bound.
>
> II
>
> I am no trumpet, but a reed,—
> A broken reed, the wind indeed
>   Left flat upon a dismal shore;
> Yet if a little maid, or child,
> Should sigh within it, earnest-mild,
>   This reed will answer evermore.   (ll. 1–12)[5]

The collocation of 'priest or king' is a commonplace inherited from
the French Revolution, which circulated in the mid-nineteenth century in writings about France, Spain, and Italy. The fact that Britain
was ruled by a queen, not a king, and that 'priest' connotes Roman
Catholicism, not the Church of England, protects EBB's flank here; so
does the syntax of lines 5–6, which singles out for reprobation poems
that would 'leave a bondsman faster bound', and allows at least the
possibility of poems addressed to 'priest or king' that don't have this

5. A draft of the poem appears in a notebook of 1842; a second draft, closer to the text
   published in *Blackwood's*, appears in a notebook of 1844–6 (*Works* ii 367).

noxious effect. After all, EBB had contributed her 'flattering breath' to the 'blast' of sentiment that greeted the accession of Queen Victoria in 1837, in 'Victoria's Tears' and 'The Young Queen'; these poems can claim at least not to support tyranny and slavery. On the other hand, the positive link between the figure of the child and political liberty is missing; instead, the 'little maid or child' who are imagined as the poet's readers are separated from the political realm, and indeed seem outside of history: they will find in the poems a timeless, 'earnest-mild' response to their 'sigh'.

According to Marjorie Stone and Beverly Taylor, 'The multiple signed copies of "A Reed," combined with its first-person declarations, suggest that it can be read as a kind of signature poem for EBB, testifying obliquely to her values, modes of self-representation, and sense of identity'.[6] But the evidence may be read another way: the verses that poets choose to inscribe in albums, or as keepsakes, often correspond to what the recipient wants to believe about them, not what the authors believe about themselves. EBB was to take up the image of the poet as 'reed' with less plangency in the late poem 'A Musical Instrument', in which the making of a poet out of a reed by the 'Great God Pan' is brutally denaturing.[7] Nor do the modesty and limited ambition of 'A Reed' match the self-image of the poet of *Casa Guidi Windows*, who proposes a closer union between herself and the child, by making the child not a reader of poetry but himself a singer.

Although *Casa Guidi Windows* marked a departure for EBB in that it was the first separate, large-scale work she had published on a political theme, she was already known as a poet who was interested in social causes, and whose politics were liberal, if not radical. What was perhaps more surprising was the change in tone. Her best-known poem on a social issue, 'The Cry of the Children', had given 'voice' to children working in mines and factories, but this voice did not purport to be colloquial:

> 'For, all day, the wheels are droning, turning,—
>   Their wind comes in our faces—
> Till our hearts turn—our heads with pulses burning,
>   And the walls turn in their places.

---

6. *Elizabeth Barrett Browning: Selected Poems*, ed. Marjorie Stone and Beverly Taylor (Peterborough, ON: Broadview, 2009), p. 203.
7. 'A Musical Instrument' was published in *Cornhill Magazine* in July 1860, and reprinted in *Last Poems* (1862); *Works* v 57.

> Turns the sky in the high window blank and reeling,
>   Turns the long light that drops adown the wall,
> Turn the black flies that crawl along the ceiling,
>   All are turning, all the day, and we with all. [. . .]'
>   (ll. 77–84. I retain 'heads' in l. 79,
>   the first edition reading.)

The poet here imagines, and versifies, the children's anguish; without elaborate diction (the only poeticism is 'adown' in l. 82), and with a minimum of syntactical inversion, she yet plays on a highly wrought rhetorical instrument. The word 'turn' is itself turned into different grammatical forms, corresponding to the children's literal, bodily, mental experience; the last line masterfully sums up the paradox of their entrapment.[8] The question of realism is moot; no reader would take these lines to be 'spoken', let alone accuse their author of bad faith. The 'cry' is not directly heard by the poet, but abstracted from a text.[9] The case of *Casa Guidi Windows* is different.

'I heard last night a little child go singing. . .' The opening line seems artless, unpremeditated, anecdotal. Whatever else may follow, readers are invited to think of the event—the hearing, or overhearing, of a song in the street—as having 'really happened'. The title of the poem contributes to this effect, and even more the preface to the volume:

This poem contains the impressions of the writer upon events in Tuscany of which she was a witness. 'From a window,' the critic may demur. She bows to the objection in the very title of her work. No continuous narrative nor exposition of political philosophy is attempted by her. It is a simple story of personal impressions, whose only value is in the intensity with which they were received, as proving her warm affection for a beautiful and unfortunate country, and the sincerity with which they are related, as indicating her own good faith and freedom from partisanship.

8. The rhetorical artifice is deepened by literary allusion: the poem's buried 'intertext' is Tennyson's 'Mariana', originally published in 1832, recently revised and reprinted in the two-volume *Poems* of 1842. 'The Cry of the Children' was first published in *Blackwood's Magazine* in August 1843, and included in *Poems* of 1844 (*Works* i 431). EBB's rhyme 'dreary/weary' (ll. 29–31) echoes Tennyson's refrain ('dreary/aweary'); 'the long light that drops adown the wall' and 'the black flies that crawl along the ceiling' would not be out of place in the earlier poem. The children, like Mariana, are trapped in a condition of despair and stasis linked to diurnal and seasonal cycles, marked by weeping, by images of exhaustion, and by longing for death.
9. The source of many of the details is the report of the Royal Commission for the Employment of Children in Mines and Factories (1841), one of whose authors was EBB's epistolary friend and fellow poet R. H. Horne; she acknowledges his work for the Commission in a note to ll. 113–16.

The claim being put forward here is powerful, once you strip away its covering of self-deprecation. It is also a problematic claim. To be a 'witness' implies that your testimony will be the truth, the whole truth, and nothing but the truth, that you will not bear *false witness* (the ninth commandment); yet a witness may be both '[free] from partisanship' and unreliable. (And does not 'warm affection for a beautiful and unfortunate country' count as 'partisanship'?) A 'simple story of personal impressions' implicitly declares its superiority to 'continuous narrative' or the 'exposition of political philosophy', on the grounds of 'intensity' and 'sincerity'—both qualities we have to take on trust. 'Sincerity', in particular, by attaching itself to the way in which the impressions are 'related', lends some of its prestige to the impressions themselves, stands as a guarantor of their truth. And if we believe in the writer's sincerity, then the 'intensity' with which she conveys the 'impression' of hearing the child singing in the street beneath the windows of Casa Guidi will reinforce the 'reality-effect' of that impression—will help to persuade us that it was one of the 'events in Tuscany of which she was a witness'.

Yet several things about this opening gambit are suspect. The notation of time—'last night'—is, on the one hand, deliberately vague, with the unreality of a ballad opening ('As I walked out this morning...'); on the other hand, it might make you wonder what so very young a child is doing unaccompanied on the street. Other problems present themselves. When EBB began writing the poem, she was not living in Casa Guidi, and the first drafts of the poem do not in fact mention that location. The poem began life as 'A Meditation in Tuscany'; another manuscript has 'A Hope in Italy'; the first line originally read 'Under our windows by Felice church'; the little child was singing 'Evviva libertà, evviva'.[10] No source for the exact phrase 'O bella libertà' has been found in any Italian song or poem of the period. It is plausible without being documented.[11] In this opening sequence, at least, EBB

10. As noted above, the Brownings were living in Casa Guidi in the summer of 1847, when the Grand Duke granted a Civic Guard. But they moved out on 19 October, and from 29 October were living at an address in the Piazza Pitti; it was there that EBB began writing 'A Meditation in Tuscany'. They did not return to Casa Guidi until 9 May 1848. For a full textual history of *Casa Guidi Windows*, see the edition by Julia Markus (New York: The Browning Institute, 1977), pp. 115–30; the textual variants for the title and opening lines are recorded on p. 120.
11. 'Viva la libertà' occurs in, e.g., 'L'Addio del Volontario Toscano' [The Farewell of the Tuscan Volunteer]; 'O Giovani Ardenti' [O ardent youths] has the refrain 'Viva

is not bearing witness to her 'impressions', but setting the scene for her 'meditation'. The child in the street loses a little of his anecdotal veri-similitude and seems more like a figure of speech—the poet's speech, which is also song. In this guise he joins a literary family, or tribe—Romanticism's children, we might call them—in whose performances questions of agency or responsibility are deemed not to arise. 'Realism', that discordant voice, tells us that small children sing by imitation, by instruction, by coercion, in any case unthinkingly. If there was a little child—*so* little a child—singing 'O bella libertà' in the street, Realism would unkindly point out that he could know nothing of the meaning of the word, or of its symbolic import. Whatever purpose the 'real' child may have had is effaced, covered over by the role into which he has been co-opted. 'Meaning' does not belong to him, but is projected onto him; he is a form of the pathetic fallacy.

In letters written around the date at which the poem was conceived, EBB never singles out an individual Italian person, whether child or adult, as 'voicing' the aspiration for liberty in the way that the child does in her poem. On the contrary, her attention is caught by communal events, and her 'impressions' are almost always of crowds, not individuals:

At night there was an illumination, & we walked just to the Arno to have a sight of it,.. and *then*, the streets were as crowded as a full route in London might be, only with less pushing probably [...] And even *then*, the people were *embracing* for joy. It was a state of phrenzy or rapture, extending to the children of two years old, several of whom I heard lisping .. "*Vivas*," with their little fat arms clasping their mothers['] necks.[12]

These plural 'children of two years old'—'lisping' rather than singing—are the closest we get in EBB's letters to the solitary 'little child' who 'not

l'Italia indipendente, / Viva l'unione, la libertà!' The evidence suggests that variants of 'Viva' and 'Evviva' are the standard exclamations. 'Bella' occurs in the chorus of Hebrew Slaves in Verdi's opera *Nabucco* (1842), which became one of the anthems of the Risorgimento: 'O mia Patria sì bella e perduta' [O my country, so beautiful and lost]. 'Bella' and 'libertà' are in close proximity, but not joined, in Francesco dall'Ongaro's 'La Bandiera Tricolore': 'E la bandiera di tre colori / sempre è stata la più bella: / noi vogliamo sempre quella, / noi vogliam la libertà!' [And the flag of three colours has ever been the most beautiful: we ever wish for that [flag], we wish for liberty!]. For the Brownings' friendship with Dall'Ongaro, see Chapter 3, p. 68 n. 10. See among other collections Palermo Giangiacomi's *Inni e canzoni del Risorgimento*, ed. Ivana Pellegrini (Ancona: Italic, 2011). For other occurrences of 'viva', 'bello', and 'libertà' in opera, see below, p. 50.

12. Letter of 13 September 1847 (see Figure 2.2); *Correspondence* xiv 301.

long had been / By mother's finger steadied on his feet', and who, as we have seen, was at first heard singing 'Evviva'.[13]

I do not mean to suggest that a child on its own could not be heard singing in the streets of Florence. But the evidence we have is at a tangent to the specific scene that EBB describes. 'In the fall of 1847 children all over Italy were singing songs of liberty', Julia Markus declares; that is too vague to be of much use, and the detail Markus goes on to add is discouraging. She cites the *Tuscan Athenaeum*, an English-language weekly newspaper edited by Thomas Adolphus Trollope, which ran for thirteen issues between 30 October 1847 and 22 January 1848. In its issue of 18 December, the newspaper

reported that hymns to Pio Nono, the songs of liberty of the day, were 'gradually sinking into nursery songs for youths under 10 years of age.' On 22 January 1848, it quipped:

Given: All Florence.
To Find: A boy of 6 years old who does not sing *Pio Nono*.[14]

If this commonplace rote-learned song is what EBB heard, it is not what the speaker of *Casa Guidi Windows* conveys; on the contrary, the image of the child is presented in a syntax that runs over the line-endings, following his breathless improvisations—'stringing / The same words still on notes he went in search / So high for, you concluded the upspringing / Of such a nimble bird to sky from perch / Must leave the whole bush in a tremble green'. The child has not long learned to walk without being 'steadied on his feet'; his singing has a toddler's precarious independence, like that of the nation, Italy, whose emblem he is; at the same time, he has the natural 'upspringing' of a 'nimble bird'. His song is not mimicry, but with all its musical daring it has the child's, and bird's, quality of repetition, of insistence: 'stringing / The same words still [...] And still *O bella libertà* he sang'.

The soaring notes carry a physical, even an erotic charge: 'the upspringing / Of such a nimble bird to sky from perch / Must leave

13. EBB repeated this detail in a letter to Mary Russell Mitford: 'Grave men kissed one another, & graceful young women lifted up their children to the level of their own smiles, and the children themselves mixed their shrill little "*vivas*" with the shouts of the people' (*Correspondence* xiv 312).
14. Markus, p. 72.

the whole bush in a tremble green'.[15] They are evidence of life: the body trembles, the heart beats: indeed, 'the heart of Italy *must* beat', repeating the coercion of '*Must* leave'; the child's insistence is matched by that of the speaker (who claims merely to be bearing witness, who abjures 'partisanship'). The bird's 'upspringing... Must *leave* the whole bush in a tremble green', but reciprocally the 'voice *had leave* to rise serene / 'Twixt church and palace of a Florence street'. Who grants this 'leave'? The topography of the street, "'Twixt church and palace', is that of Blake's 'London':

> How the Chimney-sweeper's cry
> Every blackning Church appals,
> And the hapless Soldier's sigh
> Runs in blood down Palace walls.[16]

These sounds from the street make their mark on the 'built environment' of state religion and state power, but in EBB's handling the child's song has breathing space *between* 'church and palace', his song has 'leave to rise'—in part because the censorship of Church and state has been relaxed.[17] In Florence, at least in the hopeful autumn of 1847, 'church and palace' seem less forbidding, less obvious emblems of tyranny, just as the 'Florence street' itself is less threatening than a street in London. 'You never see drunkenness nor brutality in any form in the gladness of these Tuscans', she assured her sisters. 'You never see fighting with fists, nor hear blasphemous language. It is the sort of gladness in which women may mingle and be glad too'.[18]

The fusion of pastoral and urban motifs suggests that the child singer is a made-up figure; he is there not by accident, 'overheard' as he passes beneath the speaker's window, but by design. The whole scene is

---

15. Aurora, walking with Romney: 'But then the thrushes sang, / And shook my pulses and the elms' new leaves' (*Aurora Leigh* i 1110–11).

16. William Blake, 'London' [*Songs of Innocence and of Experience*, 1794], in *Blake's Poetry and Designs*, ed. Mary Lynn Johnson and John E. Grant (New York: W. W. Norton, 1979), p. 53. Both of the Brownings knew Blake's work by this period. In a letter to Mary Russell Mitford of 6 April 1842, EBB states: 'M^r. Kenyon had just lent me those curious "Songs of innocence" [sic] &c with their wild glances of the poetical faculty thro' the chasms of the singer's shattered intellect' (*Correspondence* v 308). She wrote to the same correspondent on 22 February 1848: 'M^r. Tulk often comes in to us to talk to Robert about Blake's poems & drawings' (*Correspondence* xv [2005] 26).

17. Press censorship in Tuscany was relaxed in the autumn of 1847; that was why the *Tuscan Athenaeum* 'had leave' to publish.

18. Letter of 13 September 1847; *Correspondence* xiv 301.

improbable, yet the mask or illusion of probability is necessary to the design itself. It is necessary that the song of Italian freedom should come from a child, and from the street: these two features form a powerful alliance against the self-indulgent, lettered tradition of melancholy, of lamentation over Italy's fallen greatness, that the poet goes on to satirize. Like Browning's Fra Lippo Lippi, who traces his vocation as a painter to the quick wits of a street urchin, EBB's singer has the freedom of the city before he begins singing of 'libertà'. Anonymous, 'popular', lively, he is a renovator, with whom the poet wishes to identify herself, in opposition to 'rhymers sonneteering in their sleep':

> Through all that drowsy hum of voices smooth,
> The hopeful bird mounts carolling from brake,
> The hopeful child, with leaps to catch his growth,
> Sings open-eyed for liberty's sweet sake!
> And I, a singer also, from my youth,
> Prefer to sing with these who are awake,
> With birds, with babes, with men who will not fear
> The baptism of the holy morning dew
>
> [...]
>
> Than join those old thin voices with my new,
> And sigh for Italy with some safe sigh
> Cooped up in music 'twixt an oh and ah,—
> Nay, hand in hand with that young child, will I
> Go singing rather, '*Bella libertà,*'
> Than, with those poets, croon the dead or cry
> '*Se tu men bella fossi, Italia!*' (ll. 151–68)

The Italian quotation is from the sonnet 'Italia, Italia, o tu cui feo la Sorte', by Vincenzo da Filicaja (1642–1707), already cited by EBB in ll. 20–6:

> I thought how Filicaja led on others,
> Bewailers for their Italy enchained,
> And how they called her childless among mothers,
> Widow of empires, ay, and scarce refrained
> Cursing her beauty to her face, as brothers
> Might a shamed sister's,—'Had she been less fair
> She were less wretched,'—[19]

19. Filicaja's sonnet was first published in *Poesie toscane* (1707); the octave reads: 'Italia, Italia, o tu cui feo la Sorte / Dono infelice di bellezza, onde hai / Funesta dote

The most famous of the 'others' whom Filicaja 'led on' is Byron,
who incorporates a translation of the sonnet in Canto IV of *Childe
Harold's Pilgrimage*:

> Italia! oh Italia! thou who hast
> The fatal gift of beauty, which became
> A funeral dower of present woes and past,
> On thy sweet brow is sorrow plough'd by shame,
> And annals graved in characters of flame.
> Oh God! that thou wert in thy nakedness
> Less lovely or more powerful...[20]

Byron is less accurate than EBB in one respect—there is no 'nakedness'
in Filicaja's poem—but more accurate in another, since he gives both
parts of the line 'Deh fossi tu men bella, o almen più forte'. EBB cheats
a little by excluding the second alternative, so that the poet seems
only to be wishing that Italy were 'Less lovely' and not that she were
'more powerful'. This partial reading helps to explain the substitution
of 'O bella libertà' for 'Evviva libertà' in the child's song, since *bella* is
precisely the term that EBB objects to in the 'Bewailers for their Italy
enchained'. Now it is liberty that is beautiful, and the poet determines,
like the child, to sing 'for liberty's sweet sake'—the object of desire has
shifted from *Italia* to *libertà*. As though to complete this symbolic trans-
fer, the time frame of the scene dissolves: 'I heard *last night* a little child
go singing... The baptism of the holy *morning* dew'. The child and bird
'upspringing' return to their 'natural' time, and EBB alludes to scenes
in two poems by her husband that she loved and admired: the dewy
morning in which the 'child barefoot and rosy' ascends the hill at the end
of *Sordello*, and the 'dew-pearled' morning of Pippa's first song in *Pippa
Passes*.[21] In both of these poems the bird ascending is the lark, as it should

d'infiniti guai / Che in fronte scritti per gran doglia porte; / Deh fossi tu men bella,
o almen più forte, / Onde assai più ti paventasse, o assai / T'amasse men chi del tuo
bello ai rai / Par che si strugga, e pur ti sfida a morte!'

20. George Gordon, Lord Byron, *Childe Harold's Pilgrimage* iv 370–6 (st. 42), in *The Major
Works*, ed. Jerome J. McGann (Oxford: Oxford University Press, 2000 [Oxford World's
Classics]), p. 160.

21. Robert Browning, *Sordello* (1840) vi 849–62: 'Lo, on a heathy brown and nameless
hill / By sparkling Asolo, in mist and chill, / A child barefoot and rosy [...] that boy
has crost / The whole hill-side of dew and powder-frost [...] Up and up goes he, singing all the while / Some unintelligible words to beat / The lark, God's poet, swooning
at his feet' (*The Poems of Browning*, vol. 1, ed. John Woolford and Daniel Karlin [Harlow:
Longman, 1991], p. 768); *Pippa Passes* (1841) i 215–19: 'The year's at the spring, / And day's

be; in *Casa Guidi Windows* the poet claims the power of earliness, of newness, which belongs to the bird and the child; figuratively she will leave the house in which she is 'Cooped up' and descend into the street, to go with the child 'hand in hand'. For 'O bella libertà' is her own freedom, too.

In 1848, the 'Year of Revolutions' across Europe, there were popular uprisings in Palermo and Naples, and in Rome the founding of a Republic; Pope Pius IX, no longer the darling of the liberal cause, fled the city, and it would take a French army to restore him.[22] In Tuscany, Leopold II initially accepted the demands for a constitution and sent troops to fight alongside the army of the Kingdom of Sardinia against the Austrians; but by the autumn of 1848 he was having second thoughts, and after fleeing from Florence, he began negotiating with the Austrians and with the exiled Pope. In Florence a republic was declared in February 1849, but the following month the decisive victory of the Austrians at Novara effectively put a stop to this phase of the Risorgimento. The Tuscans themselves were divided and irresolute; in the end, one of the rival factions took control of what government there was, and invited the Grand Duke to return, which he did in July 1849—preceded by a 10,000-strong Austrian army of occupation. From the balcony of their apartment in Casa Guidi, the Brownings saw the Austrian troops march past to take possession of the city.

In Part Two of *Casa Guidi Windows*, EBB reflects on these events with rueful indignation, both at the behaviour of the Florentines and at her own naïveté in mistaking patriotic bombast and flag-waving for the real thing. The opening lines return to the child singing in the street, but he is now a compromised figure:

> I wrote a meditation and a dream,
>   Hearing a little child sing in the street.
> I leant upon his music as a theme,
>   Till it gave way beneath my heart's full beat,
> Which tried at an exultant prophecy
>   But dropped before the measure was complete—

at the morn: / Morning's at seven; / The hill-side's dew-pearled: / The lark's on the wing, / The snail's on the thorn; / God's in his heaven— / All's right with the world!' (ibid., vol. 2, pp. 39–40).

22. The siege of Rome and the fall of the Roman Republic are the backdrop to the other major English Risorgimento poem of the period, Arthur Hugh Clough's *Amours de Voyage* (wr. 1849, first publ. 1858 in the *Atlantic Monthly*).

Alas, for songs and hearts! O Tuscany,
    O Dante's Florence, is the type too plain?
Didst thou, too, only sing of liberty,
    As little children take up a high strain
With unintentioned voices, and break off
    To sleep upon their mothers' knees again?   (ll. 1–12)

EBB does not quite admit that the 'little child' in Part One was fictive, but she does acknowledge that, if he really existed, he belonged to the category of 'little children [who] take up a high strain / With unintentioned voices'.[23] This 'natural' childishness is a demeaning metaphor, or 'type', of the behaviour of 'Dante's Florence'—behaviour which the great scorner of his native place and fellow citizens would recognize.[24] The crowds whose fervour had made such an impression on her had 'chalked the walls with bloody caveats / Against all tyrants' and 'fired muskets up the air / To show that victory was ours of right' (ll. 153–6), but were not, in the end, actually prepared to risk their lives for the cause of liberty. Indeed, the word itself is caught up in this bathetic story: EBB recoils from 'the trilling on an opera stage, / Of "libertà" to bravos—(a fair word, / Yet too allied to inarticulate rage / And breathless sobs, for singing, though the chord / Were deeper than they struck it!)' (ll. 226–30). When the little child sang the word in the street, it did not seem to have this weight of 'inarticulate rage / And breathless sobs', but now that it has retreated indoors, so to speak, it has shrunk to a mere performance. Opera had long been a vehicle for coded political sentiment, transposed from other countries or historical periods—EBB might be thinking of the famous duet *Suoni la tromba* at the end of Act 2 of *I puritani*: 'Suoni la tromba, e intrepido / Io pugnerò da forte; / Bello è affrontar la morte / Gridando: libertà!'[25] The syntax of 'trilling… "libertà" to bravos' allows for the word to be sung 'to the

23. *OED* cites only this occurrence of 'unintentioned'; the positive form, 'intentioned', is defined as 'Having intentions (of a specific kind)'. The sense is that small children 'take up' a song without having a serious purpose, but note the transferred epithet which attributes this lack of purpose to the 'voices' and not the children themselves.
24. The childishness of the Florentines is alluded to again later in Part Two: 'Ye played like children,—die like innocents. / Ye mimicked lightnings with a torch,—the crack / Of the actual bolt, your pastime circumvents.'
25. 'Sound the trumpet, and fearless I will fight with all my strength: it is beautiful to face death crying "Liberty!"' ' *I Puritani* (1835), music by Vincenzo Bellini, libretto by Count Carlo Pepoli (a political exile); the opera is set during the English Civil War. On the political dimension of opera in the period, see Anthony Arblaster, *Viva la Libertà: Politics in Opera* (London: Verso, 1997).

cheers (bravos) of the audience', and for it to be sung 'to an audience
made up of bravos'—an ironic tribute to Florentine gumption.[26] Not
just talk, but song is cheap.

EBB is careful not to endorse the stereotype that the Italians,
like other peoples of southern Europe, lack the earnestness and resolve
of the northern nations. 'Let none dare to say, "Here virtue never
can be national["]', she declares (ll. 215–16). Nor is Tuscany the
whole of Italy: 'Life throbs in noble Piedmont', while the Papacy,
'Rome's clay image', will, the poet predicts, be 'shovelled off like
other mud / To leave the passage free in church and street' (ll. 731–5).
Her analysis of why the revolution failed, and what needs to happen
for it to succeed, may be questionable, but it is concrete and specific.
Yet the poem does not end there. It moves to more visionary ground:
and here, though EBB's hope is again invested in a child, this child
is not Italian:

> And I, who first took hope up in this song,
> Because a child was singing one... behold,
>   The hope and omen were not, haply, wrong!
> Poets are soothsayers still, like those of old
>   Who studied flights of doves,—and creatures young
> And tender, mighty meanings, may unfold.
>
>   The sun strikes, through the windows, up the floor;
> Stand out in it, my own young Florentine,
>   Not two years old, and let me see thee more!
> It grows along thy amber curls, to shine
>   Brighter than elsewhere. Now, look straight before,
> And fix thy brave blue English eyes on mine,
>   And from thy soul, which fronts the future so,
>   With unabashed and unabated gaze,
>   Teach me to hope for, what the angels know
> When they smile clear as thou dost.   (ll. 740–51)[27]

The child in the street at the beginning of Part One of the poem is
recalled only to be effaced. Not only is his nationality usurped by a
'young Florentine' who is actually English (his 'amber' hair and blue
eyes are pointedly mentioned) but his song is usurped by the new child's

26. OED defines *bravo* as 'a daring villain... a reckless desperado'; alternatively, EBB may
    intend it to carry the sense of a cowardly boaster, like Parolles in *All's Well That Ends Well*.
27. The Brownings' son, Robert Wiedemann Barrett Browning, who became known as
    'Penini' and then 'Pen', was born in Casa Guidi on 9 March 1849. In *Works* 1. 748 has
    'my soul', the reading of EBB's 1856 *Poetical Works*; I retain the first edition reading.

silence. EBB's son utters his meaning, his soul, through his 'brave blue English eyes', and the communion between mother and child is enacted through the reciprocity of their gaze. The gap between lines 741 and 742 marks the shift to an aesthetic of sight, dominated by the sun that strikes '*through* the windows', a phrase repeated further on in the passage:

> Stand out, my blue-eyed prophet!—thou, to whom
>   The earliest world-day light that ever flowed
> Through Casa Guidi windows, chanced to come!   (ll. 757–9)

The poet is no longer looking from her window, no longer listening to a sound from the street.[28] She is refiguring the Annunciation; she is already in the presence of her promised redeemer, but she also has power over him—power to exhort, power to 'place' him where she can get most from him, like a painter placing a model in a carefully planned composition. The child smiles up at her, and his smile, perforce a silent gesture, is what finally enables her to 'trust God' (l. 776) and affirm her belief in divine providence: 'This world has no perdition, if some loss' (l. 780). The poem's last lines take a decisive turn away from the human scale:

> Such cheer I gather from thy smiling, Sweet!
>   The self-same cherub-faces which emboss
> The Vail, lean inward to the Mercy-seat.   (ll. 781–3)

The allusion conflates two passages from Exodus which describe the construction, housing, and ornamentation of the Ark of the Covenant. The first, referring to the 'Vail', is from 36:35: 'And he made a vail of blue, and purple, and scarlet, and fine twined linen: with cherubims made he it of cunning work'. These cherubims on the woven hangings around the Ark, EBB suggests, are of the same kind as the golden figures on its cover, described in the next chapter:

And he made two cherubims of gold, beaten out of one piece made he them, on the two ends of the mercy seat;
    One cherub on the end on this side, and another cherub on the other end on that side: out of the mercy seat made he the cherubims on the two ends thereof.

---

28. The change had been anticipated earlier in the poem, though in a sadder and more embittered tone: 'But wherefore should we look out any more / From Casa Guidi windows? Shut them straight, / And let us sit down by the folded door, / And veil our saddened faces and, so, wait / What next the judgment-heavens make ready for. / I have grown too weary of these windows' (ll. 425–30).

And the cherubims spread out their wings on high, and covered with their wings over the mercy seat, with their faces one to another; even to the mercy seatward were the faces of the cherubims. (37:7–9)

EBB chose this image with great care. It refers not to the temple in Jerusalem, but the 'tabernacle' in the wilderness; however glorious the vail and golden cherubim may be, they still belong to a sojourning-place, not a permanent home. Italy is not yet free; the child's 'smiling' brings 'cheer' for the future, but is not a celebration of something accomplished. The 'mercy seat' is the cover or lid of the Ark; the English term derives from Luther's *Gnadenstuhl*, an interpretative translation of the Hebrew *kappōret*, a word associated with atonement or propitiation. Luther envisaged God 'enthroned over [the Ark] in mercy, invisibly present where the wingtips of two cherubim met above it, guarding the divine presence'.[29] But what EBB noticed, I think, was the extra-ordinary precision of the sculpted gesture: the cherubims 'with their faces one to another' repeat the rapt, reciprocal, exclusive gaze between her and her son. The phrase 'lean inward to the Mercy-seat' sharpens and clarifies the slightly clumsy and archaic phrasing of the biblical text; it emphasizes the distance that separates the guileless (and childless) spectator who looked out from her window at the beginning of the poem from the wiser, more knowing, more conscious artist who sets her seal on it at the end.

A decade was to pass before Italy became a unified and independent nation. When it did so, there was no longer any realistic chance of its being a republic; the only feasible outcome was the formation of an Italian monarchy, headed by Victor Emanuel II, King of Sardinia-Piedmont, with the support of France under the Emperor Napoleon III. EBB followed the events of 1859–61 with passionate attention; the loyalty of those who, like her, would have preferred an Italian republic was tested almost to destruction. The settlement of 1861 allowed Austria to retain control of the Veneto region, and while some of the Papal States were annexed by the new kingdom, Rome itself remained under papal rule (and French protection). EBB did not live to see the cession of the Veneto to Italy in 1866 and the final annexation of Rome itself in 1870.

29. *Oxford Companion to the Bible*, ed. Bruce M. Metzger and Michael D. Coogan (Oxford: Oxford University Press, 1993), p. 56.

Old revolutionary partisans, among them Garibaldi, had to come to terms with the new order; Garibaldi's support was crucial in bringing Victor Emanuel to power. In 'The King's Gift', based on an anecdote about King Victor Emanuel sending a necklace to Garibaldi's sixteen-year-old daughter, the child who sings a song of liberty is the medium of reconciliation between revolutionary republicanism and monarchical power:

I

Teresa, ah, Teresita!
Now what has the messenger brought her,
Our Garibaldi's young daughter,
    To make her stop short in her singing?
Will she not once more repeat a
Verse from that hymn of our hero's,
    Setting the souls of us ringing?
Break off the song where the tear rose?
    Ah, Teresita!

II

A young thing, mark, is Teresa:
Her eyes have caught fire, to be sure, in
That necklace of jewels from Turin,
    Till blind their regard to us men is.
But still she remembers to raise a
Sly look to her father, and note—
    'Could she sing on as well about Venice,
Yet wear such a flame at her throat?
    Decide for Teresa.'

III

Teresa! ah, Teresita!
His right hand has paused on her head—
'Accept it, my daughter,' he said;
    'Ay, wear it, true child of thy mother!
Then sing, till all start to their feet, a
New verse ever bolder and freer!
    King Victor's no king like another,
But verily noble as *we* are,
    Child, Teresita!'[30]

30. 'The King's Gift' appeared in the *Independent* on 18 July 1861, three weeks after EBB's death, and then in *Last Poems* (1862) (*Works* v 94–5); I have retained 'Sly' in l. 15, following the text of *Last Poems*, where the editors of *Works* emend to 'Shy'. Teresa Garibaldi (1845–1903) was the Garibaldis' third child.

The song Teresa is singing—'that hymn of our hero's, / Setting the souls of us ringing'—is almost certainly Luigi Mercantini's 'Canzone Italiana', commissioned by Garibaldi in 1858 and known as 'L'Inno di Garibaldi' [Garibaldi's Hymn]. The lyrics marry high-flown rhetoric with geographical precision: 'Si scopron le tombe, si levano i morti, / i martiri nostri son tutti resorti!...Son l'Alpi e tre mari d'Italia i confini, / col carro di fuoco rompiam gli Appennini', and it has a blunt refrain: 'Va fuori d'Italia, va fuori che è l'ora, / Va fuori d'Italia, va fuori o stranier'.[31] And geography matters: the necklace comes from Turin because, although Rome had been formally declared the capital of the new nation, the *de facto* seat of government was in Turin, and would remain there until the Pope was dislodged. Teresa's 'sly' question, ' "Could she sing on as well about Venice, / Yet wear such a flame at her throat?["]', puts her father on the spot, since under the terms of the Treaty of Villafranca between France and Austria in July 1859, Austria had retained control of the Veneto region—a compromise which Garibaldi had denounced. But Teresa does not really mean, or is not really allowed, to rebuke her heroic father. EBB's playful rhymes ('Teresita'/'repeat a', 'to be sure in'/'Turin') reassure the reader that the great man is not being cut down to size. The child submits herself—is made, by the poet, to submit—to the father's word, which will 'decide for [her]' whether she may accept the king's gift. And Garibaldi, with a gesture at once kindly and commanding ('His right hand has paused on her head'), puts the child in her place. 'King Victor's no king like another', he assures her—is made, by the poet, to assure her—and she may therefore accept the gift and sing a 'New verse ever bolder and freer!' Yet it is hard to see how this new song could be 'freer' when the singer wears a royal chain around her neck. 'O bella libertà' is vague in one respect, but perfectly plain in another—as plain as 'l'Inno di Garibaldi', for that matter.

'The King's Gift' is one of a group of poems about Italy in *Last Poems* which record EBB's fluctuating feelings about the awkwardness, the shabbiness, occasionally the anguish of 'victory'. 'The King's Gift' may be thought to cover over some of the pangs of success, but the

---

31. 'The tombs burst open, the dead rise up, our martyrs have all come forth! [...] The Alps and three seas are the borders of Italy, with a chariot of fire we shall burst through the Apennines'; 'Get out of Italy, get out for now is the time, / Get out of Italy, get out, O foreigner' (my translation).

same cannot be said of 'Mother and Poet'. In this poem EBB confronts the consequences of revolutionary struggle for children who sing songs of freedom, and for poets who compose them.

Let us assume that the 'little child' singing 'O bella libertà' in the street in 1847 was three years old. In 1861 he would be seventeen—old enough to think for himself, to enlist, to fight for the cause he sang about in his borrowed enthusiasm. Old enough to die for it, and for his mother, a famous poet, to imagine what it might be like to have encouraged him:

> Dead! One of them shot by the sea in the east,
>   And one of them shot in the west by the sea.
> Dead! both my boys! When you sit at the feast
>   And are wanting a great song for Italy free,
>   Let none look at *me*!

These are the opening—and closing—lines of 'Mother and Poet'. A note at the end (probably supplied by Robert Browning) informs the reader: 'This was Laura Savio, of Turin, a poetess and patriot, whose sons were killed at Ancona and Gaeta'.[32] 'O bella libertà' now takes on a darker, a more savage tone; it is not song but *prating*, 'pompous or overbearing talk, "preaching" ':

> *I* made them indeed
> Speak plain the word *country*. *I* taught them, no doubt,
> That a country's a thing men should die for at need.
>   *I* prated of liberty, rights, and about
>   The tyrant cast out.
> And when their eyes flashed . . O my beautiful eyes! . .
>   *I* exulted; nay, let them go forth at the wheels
> Of the guns, and denied not. But then the surprise
>   When one sits quite alone! Then one weeps, then one kneels!
>   God, how the house feels!   (ll. 21–30)

The poet *in* the poem, Laura Savio, may recoil from her art, but the poem's author, EBB, has not forgotten hers. The singular 'I', four times emphatically stressed, is set in opposition to 'their eyes . . . my beautiful

---

32. 'Mother and Poet' appeared in the *Independent* on 2 May 1861, and then in *Last Poems* (1862) (*Works* v 103). A draft of the poem has the title 'The Childless Poetess' crossed out. EBB apparently believed that the two sons who died, Alfredo and Emilio, were Savio's only children, though in fact the youngest, Federico, remained at home with her (*Works* v 108 n. 3).

eyes', where the plural form signifies her possessive love, the maternal extension of her selfhood. 'My beautiful eyes' are not *her* beautiful eyes, but the beautiful eyes of the children who are so completely, so unthinkingly *hers*, who at her behest will 'indeed / Speak plain', turn her words into deeds. The singular 'i' sounds also in 'die', in 'denied', and before 'eyes' leaps out of ambush in the word 'surprise': 'But then the surprise / When one sits quite alone! Then one weeps, then one kneels!' Now 'I' is extinguished in 'quite alone', becomes *one, one, one,* incurably solitary and bereft. With some hesitation at bringing biography so plainly into play, I would suggest that Savio's anguish was sharpened for EBB by the thought that, after all, her own child had not been sacrificed, that Pen Browning, with his 'brave blue English eyes', was free to absorb and echo his mother's passion for the cause of Italian freedom.[33] But in another of the *Last Poems*, which follows 'Mother and Poet' and concludes the sequence about Italy, she gave him a profoundly significant non-speaking part.

'Nature's Remorses', subtitled 'Rome, 1861', tells the story of Maria Sophia, the last Queen of Naples, who with her husband King Francis II had taken refuge in Rome after the fall of Gaeta to the forces of Victor Emanuel. During the siege of Gaeta the young Queen—she was only nineteen—behaved with flamboyant courage, rallying the defenders and defying the besiegers.[34] In 'Mother and Poet' she appears as the 'fair wicked queen' who sat 'at her sport / Of the fire-balls of death crashing souls out of men' (ll. 77–8); but this bitter view belongs

33. 'Little Pen is very fierce upon politics. He said to me yesterday, "I hope Austria wont sell Venetia, mama." "And why not pray," I asked—"Because then people will say, the Italians fight with *money*—Now I want real fighting—with *guns*—" There's a Pen for you! Does'nt he do me credit, Arabel?' (25–6 December 1859, *The Letters of Elizabeth Barrett Browning to Her Sister Arabella*, ed. Scott Lewis, 2 vols. [Winfield, KS: Wedgestone Press, 2002], ii 439).

34. Her fame, burnished by friends and political opponents alike, lasted throughout her long life (1841–1925), and reached its literary apotheosis in Proust's depiction of her in *À la recherche du temps perdu*. When M. de Charlus is publicly humiliated by the vulgar, bourgeois Verdurins, the Queen of Naples, seemingly the mildest and most affable of *grandes dames*, shows her true mettle: outraged at the slight to one of her own rank, she conducts M. de Charlus from the *salon* with an implacable expression of disdain for her upstart hosts. He may lean on her arm, she tells him; it is strong enough for that. 'Vous savez qu'autrefois à Gaète il a déjà tenu en respect la canaille' [You know that long ago, at Gaeta, it already held the rabble at bay] (Marcel Proust, *La Prisonnière* [The Captive], in *À la recherche du temps perdu* [In Search of Lost Time], Paris: Gallimard, 1988 [Bibliothèque de la Pléiade], iii 825; my translation). Note that the Queen was still living when *La Prisonnière* was published—posthumously—in 1923. She outlived Proust, too.

to Laura Savio, and in 'Nature's Remorses' EBB tells a different story. She represents Maria Sophia as born and brought up in the stifling artificial atmosphere of dynastic privilege, 'swaddled away in violet silk' and 'royally blind' to the goings-on of the real world (ll. 6–7). She floats on a breeze of fantasy to marriage and Italy, 'To live more smoothly than mortals can, / To love and to reign as queen and wife' (ll. 20–1), only to discover that 'The lion-people ha[d] left its lair' (l. 27) and that 'a fire-stone ran in the form of a man, / Burningly, boundingly, fatal and fell, / Bowling the kingdom down!' (ll. 31–3; the 'fire-stone' is Garibaldi). She finds in herself the courage her feeble Bourbon husband lacks: 'Her high heart overtopped / The royal part she had come to play' (ll. 40–1), and 'She braved the shock and the counter-shock / Of hero and traitor, bullet and knife' (ll. 45–6). Now she is in exile in Rome, and the poet does her a kind of poetic justice, turning the impulse of pity another way, imagining a brave young woman moved, consoled, restored—not to her throne, but to her natural womanhood:

> Ah poor queen! so young and serene!
>   What shall we do for her, now hope's done,
>   Standing at Rome in these ruins old,
>   She too a ruin and no more a queen?
>   Leave her that diadem made by the sun
>   Turning her hair to an innocent gold.
>
> Ay! bring close to her, as 'twere a rose, to her,
>   Yon free child from an Apennine city
>   Singing for Italy,—dumb in the place!
>   Something like solace, let us suppose, to her
>   Given, in that homage of wonder and pity,
>   By his pure eyes to her beautiful face.
>
> (sts. xi–xii, ll. 61–72)

The child who sang 'O bella libertà' in the street here undergoes his last metamorphosis, into 'yon free child from an Apennine city / Singing for Italy'. But this metamorphosis is also a rebirth, for here, again, is EBB's own son, Pen, who had played his part at the end of *Casa Guidi Windows*. In April 1861, in Rome, Pen caught a glimpse of Maria Sophia, and, as EBB wrote to Isa Blagden, brought home to his mother a tender and winning report of her: 'Oh mama, she IS so very pretty! [...] So fair! such golden hair! & looking so melancholy'.[35] But

---

35. Letter of 13 April 1861, in *Florentine Friends: The Letters of Elizabeth Barrett Browning and Robert Browning to Isa Blagden 1850–1861*, ed. Philip Kelley and Sandra Donaldson

of course he doesn't 'sing for Italy' in the presence of the royal person-
age whose path he crosses; he is 'dumb in the place', and his 'pure eyes'
pay 'homage' to her 'beautiful face'. Her political power has lapsed, but
her female power remains; the child's 'homage' is 'pure' because it is not
a man's expression of sexual appetite (Pen was twelve years old), just as
her 'diadem' is made of the 'innocent gold' of sunlight in her blonde
hair. The final stanza sums up the poem's trajectory, in which Maria
Sophia's unnatural devotion to 'queendom and dogmas of state' comes
close to destroying her 'womanhood':

> Nature, excluded, savagely brooded,
>   Ruined all queendom and dogmas of state,—
>   Then in reaction remorseful and mild,
> Rescues the womanhood, nearly eluded,
>   Shows her what's sweetest in womanly fate—
>   Sunshine from Heaven, and the eyes of a child.
>   (st. xiii, ll. 73–8)

At this point a disturbing connection between Maria Sophia and EBB
suggests itself. If 'what's sweetest in womanly fate' is summed up in the
formula 'Sunshine from Heaven, and the eyes of a child', then what of
the poet whose 'queendom' is the domain of art, and who had, in
recent years, 'braved the shock and the counter-shock' of political con-
flict, whose verse—as some of her critics complained—was steeped in
'dogmas of state'?[36] 'Standing at Rome in these ruins old, / She too a
ruin': this was how EBB thought of herself in these last months of life,
at least in her dark moments, when 'hope' seemed 'done'. Had Nature,
then, punished her for misdirecting her creative energies? Yet the child
remains, the child who is hers; Maria Sophia was childless.[37]

(Winfield, KS and Waco, TX: Wedgestone Press and Armstrong Browning Library of
Baylor University, 2009), p. 445. The Brownings were spending the winter in Rome;
they returned to Florence in June, and EBB died there a month later.

36. When she first discovers her vocation, Aurora Leigh declares: 'The name [poet] / Is
royal, and to sign it like a queen / Is what I dare not,—though some royal blood /
Would seem to tingle in me now and then' (i 934–7). Later, when he recants his scepticism as to her genius, Romney Leigh calls her 'a woman and a queen' (viii 331).
Criticism of EBB both for her political views and for making those views the subject
of her poems was especially vocal after the publication of *Poems Before Congress* (1860).

37. Her husband suffered from phimosis (inability to retract the foreskin) and the marriage was unconsummated. It is doubtful whether EBB knew about this, or that
Maria Sophia was conducting a love affair while in Rome and became pregnant,
giving birth to an illegitimate daughter in November 1862. These are ironies beyond
the poem's conscious scope, though they circulate in its orbit.

Behind the short, compressed first lines of *Casa Guidi Windows* lies a
hinterland whose recessive planes thicken and darken. In the farthest
background, a world and a shift of mind away, lies a dead child singing
to its mother. The poem is 'The Runaway Slave at Pilgrim's Point', in
which the slave kills the child she has borne to her master.[38]

> My own, own child! I could not bear
>   To look in his face, it was so white.
> I covered him up with a kerchief there;
>   I covered his face in close and tight:
> And he moaned and struggled, as well might be,
> For the white child wanted his liberty—
>   Ha, ha! he wanted the master-right.
>
> He moaned and beat with his head and feet,
>   His little feet that never grew—
> He struck them out, as it was meet,
>   Against my heart to break it through.
> I might have sung and made him mild,—
> But I dared not sing to the white-faced child
>   The only song I knew.   (ll. 120–33)

The 'white child [who] wanted his liberty' anticipates the 'little child'
who sings 'O bella libertà' in the street below Casa Guidi; Italy, his
mother, is also a slave cursed by her beauty, whose song of innocence
has been defiled. The poet's claim, in 'A Reed', to abjure verse that
might 'leave a bondsman faster bound', in favour of 'earnest-mild'
responses to a 'little maid, or child', is cruelly exposed here, as though
to enforce the lesson that the 'master-right' will always catch up with
the fugitive lyric. Yet this is not the whole story. When the mother
buries her child, 'scoop[ing] a hole beneath the moon', the song returns
with uncanny power:

> [...] when it was all done aright,..
>   Earth, 'twixt me and my baby, strewed,..
> All, changed to black earth,.. nothing white,..
>   A dark child in the dark!—ensued
> Some comfort, and my heart grew young.
> I sate down smiling there and sung
>   The song I learnt in my maidenhood.

38. 'The Runaway Slave at Pilgrim's Point' was first published in the anti-slavery annual
    The Liberty Bell in December 1847 (dated 1848), and then in EBB's collected *Poems*
    (1850) (*Works* i 409).

And thus we two were reconciled,
  The white child and black mother, thus;
For, as I sang it soft and wild,
  The same song, more melodious,
Rose from the grave whereon I sate.
It was the dead child singing that,
  To join the souls of both of us.   (sts. 26–8, ll. 176–96)

The mother's singing is toned down, corrected by the child's 'more melodious' performance. It is 'more melodious' because it is, simultaneously, of the earth, earthy—'changed to black earth'—and spiritual, transcendent, able 'To join the souls of both of us'. The syllable *us* quietly foreshadows this outcome: mother and child are 'reconciled' in an inconspicuous rhyming sequence: 'And thus…thus…melodious…us'. The unemphatic presence of the word 'us' in the polysyllabic 'melodious' is a shock felt at a great depth, and an emblem of reunion. The child sings of his release, and of his mother's freedom from the 'master-right' he had unwittingly claimed. And yet, though the song that effects their reunion '[rises] from the grave', it portends no resurrection. When EBB heard the child's song in the street outside her window, in the happy, hopeful autumn of 1847, perhaps it seemed possible that Italy might no longer play the role of slave-mother, and that the song of freedom might not be death-devoted.

3

Lippi sings the blues

In fifteenth-century Florence, a monk, Filippo Lippi, is arrested by the night watch after an evening on the town. Lippi also happens to be a famous painter, and a protégé of the ruler of Florence, Cosimo de' Medici, and he gets out of trouble by dropping the name of his powerful patron (Plates 3 and 4).

But just wriggling out of a tight spot isn't enough for Lippi. He catches the officer of the watch shaking his head, with a kind of indulgent censoriousness—yes, 'brother Lippo's doings, up and down' are well known in Florence, but after all a monk shouldn't be breaking bounds and chasing after girls, should he? (l. 40).[1] Lippi determines to set the officer straight, to justify his conduct by telling the story of his life—how he became a monk, and then a painter, and how his fleshly appetites have been thwarted and denied in both of these careers. This is the premise of Robert Browning's poem 'Fra Lippo Lippi', published in *Men and Women* in 1855. As we have seen, Browning had been living in Italy since the autumn of 1846, and in Florence since 1847, in Casa Guidi on the south bank of the Arno, not far from the Pitti Palace. He and his wife, Elizabeth Barrett Browning, considered themselves honorary citizens, and Browning boasted of his intimate knowledge of the city's history and architecture, its churches, palaces, paintings, and sculpture, and also of its popular culture, its markets and festivals, its street life, and—in this poem—its street songs.[2]

1. All quotations from Browning's poems are from the texts of the first editions, in *The Poems of Robert Browning*, ed. John Woolford, Daniel Karlin, and Joseph Phelan (Longman Annotated English Poets): vols. i and ii, Harlow: Longman, 1991; vol. iii, Harlow: Pearson Education, 2007; vol. iv, Harlow: Pearson Education, 2012; hereafter *Poems of RB*. 'Fra Lippo Lippi' is in iii 522–51.
2. Three other major poems of *Men and Women* are set in Florence. Two of them, like 'Fra Lippo Lippi', are based on historical figures: 'Andrea del Sarto' (*Poems of RB* iii 292–310) and

Lippi explains to the officer of the watch how he came to be out after midnight:

> Here's spring come, and the nights one makes up bands
> To roam the town and sing out carnival,
> And I've been three weeks shut within my mew,
> A-painting for the great man, saints and saints
> And saints again. I could not paint all night—
> Ouf! I leaned out of window for fresh air.
> There came a hurry of feet and little feet,
> A sweep of lute-strings, laughs, and whiffs of song,—
> *Flower o' the broom,*
> *Take away love, and our earth is a tomb!*
> *Flower o' the quince,*
> *I let Lisa go, and what good's in life since?*
> *Flower o' the thyme*—and so on. Round they went.
> Scarce had they turned the corner when a titter,
> Like the skipping of rabbits by moonlight,— three slim shapes—
> And a face that looked up . . . zooks, sir, flesh and blood,
> That's all I'm made of! Into shreds it went,
> Curtain and counterpane and coverlet,
> All the bed furniture—a dozen knots,
> There was a ladder! down I let myself,
> Hands and feet, scrambling somehow, and so dropped,
> And after them. I came up with the fun
> Hard by St. Laurence, hail fellow, well met,—
> *Flower o' the rose,*
> *If I've been merry, what matter who knows?*
> And so as I was stealing back again
> To get to bed and have a bit of sleep
> Ere I rise up to-morrow and go work
> On Jerome knocking at his poor old breast
> With his great round stone to subdue the flesh,
> You snap me of the sudden.   (ll. 45–75)[3]

The 'whiffs of song' that Lippi hears in the street are called in Italian *stornelli*. The *stornello* was a popular verse form which originated in Tuscany in the fifteenth century and spread across central and southern Italy. Its metrical pattern has some historical and regional variations;

'The Statue and the Bust' (pp. 342–59). The third, 'Old Pictures in Florence' (pp. 311–41), is set in contemporary Florence; I discuss this poem in more detail below (p. 70).

3. Lippi's action—first leaning out of the window, then hearing a song in the street— recalls, but inverts, the action of the speaker in the opening lines of *Casa Guidi Windows*.

the one Browning seems to have drawn on is a three-line poem, in which the first line, of five syllables, invokes the name of a flower or plant, and is followed by two hendecasyllables, the first of which is unrhymed, and the second of which rhymes with the first line. Here are a couple of examples, from a volume of Tuscan popular songs published in Florence in 1856, the year after *Men and Women*. There are hundreds like them.

Fior di piselli.	Flower of the pea.
Vanne dall'amor mio, e digli, digli…	Go to my love, and tell her, tell her…
Che son nel letto, e conto i travicelli.	That I am in bed, and counting the rafters.
Fior d'amaranti.	Flower of the amaranth.
Voi siete ventarola a tutti venti:	You are a weather-vane [turning] in every wind:
Avete un core, e lo donate a tanti.	You have [only] one heart, and give it to many.

Browning has compressed this form into a couplet, eliminating the middle line, so that the short opening phrase naming the flower is followed by a single longer line, of ten or eleven syllables, rhyming with the flower's name. The *stornello* was originally a form of poetic contest, in which one verse would be 'capped' by another; but there is in fact no indication in Lippi's recital that the *stornelli* were being sung responsively. On the contrary, they become more and more personal to him as the poem proceeds.

Where did Browning get his knowledge of this Italian folk-song? The volume from which I have quoted, edited by Giuseppe Tigri, a priest and man of letters from Pistoia, is evidence of the growing interest in the nineteenth century, not just in Italy but across Europe, in folk art and culture, one of the legacies of Romanticism and specifically Romantic nationalism. Tigri himself pays tribute to earlier collections of songs, notably by the poet, scholar, and linguist Niccolò Tommaseo (who was later to compose the inscription in memory of Elizabeth Barrett Browning on the wall of Casa Guidi). In 1841 Tommaseo published *Canti popolari toscani*[,] *corsi*[,] *illirici*[,] *greci*—itself a testimony to his own multicultural background, as an ethnic Italian born in Croatia who had lived as a political exile in Corsica. Besides being a collector and editor, Tommaseo composed *stornelli* of his own, some of them with a political edge, and these circulated as popular songs during the period of the Risorgimento. Browning may well have known Tommaseo's work, but his immediate knowledge of the *stornello* probably came from within the Anglo-Florentine expatriate community in Florence to which, with whatever ambivalence and standoffishness, the Brownings belonged.[4] Thomas Adolphus Trollope, in his memoir *What I Remember*, recalls his first wife Theodosia Garrow Trollope translating 'the curiously characteristic *stornelli* of Tuscany, and especially of the Pistoja mountains'. The Brownings knew the Trollopes, and it is more than likely that Browning knew of Theodosia's efforts; all those years later her husband recalled 'the especial difficulty of translating them', and boasted that 'there were not—are not—many persons who could cope with the especial difficulties of the attempt as successfully as she did'.[5] This was in 1887—still in Browning's lifetime. Notice, however, that Trollope tags the *stornello* as a rural form. It belongs to 'the Pistoja mountains', not to urban Florence. Folk-songs tend to originate in the country, not the town, and the *stornello* is no exception. Thomas identifies it with the 'contadini', the peasants; besides praising Theodosia's translations, he also mentions 'a number of pen-and-ink drawings illustrating these *stornelli*', whose 'spirited, graphic, and accurately truthful characterisation of the figures could only have been achieved by an artist very intimately acquainted [...] with the subjects of her pencil'.[6] These 'figures' are all depicted in rural settings; no one, in Lippi's phrase, is 'roaming the town'. In Browning's poem, on the other hand, the *stornello*, like so many peasants in the period in which the poem was composed, has migrated to the city, abandoning the harvest festival, so to speak, for the carnival. Now the song is on the street, in the mouths of loose women and lecherous monks. A memory of *Pippa Passes* lurks in the shadows here—the scene in Part IV in which it is proposed that Pippa, the innocent child singer, should be seduced and trafficked into prostitution in Rome, where 'the courtesans perish off every three years'. It is through her singing that Pippa

---

4. On Browning's characterization of 'the English' in Florence, see Chapter 2, n. 2.
5. Thomas Adolphus Trollope, *What I Remember*, 2 vols. (London: Richard Bentley, 1887), p. 361. I am indebted for this reference to Alison Chapman's *Networking the Nation: British and American Women's Poetry and Italy, 1840–1870* (Oxford: Oxford University Press, 2015), pp. 61–2.
6. *What I Remember*, pp. 361–2. In an earlier chapter (in which his conservative politics come to the fore) Trollope associates the *stornello* with the supposed political apathy of the Tuscan peasantry in the early years of the *Risorgimento*: 'They ate their bread [...] or even their chestnuts in the more remote and primitive mountain districts, drank their sound Tuscan wine from the generous big-bellied Tuscan flasks holding three good bottles, and sang their *stornelli* in cheerfulness of heart, and had no craving whatsoever for those few special liberties which were denied them' (pp. 192–3). On the political turn given to the *stornello* by Francesco dall'Ongaro, see p. 68 below.

is to be entrapped.[7] And there are broader reasons for remembering
Pippa Passes—a work in which Browning recorded some of his earliest
and strongest impressions of Italy following his first trip in 1838. One
of the episodes in this drama concerns the mission of a young Italian
revolutionary, Luigi, to assassinate the Austrian Emperor. Browning did
not wait until he began living in Florence to support the cause of
Italian independence.

Although 'Fra Lippo Lippi' is set in Renaissance Italy, it is not insulated
from contemporary political conditions and does not occupy an idealized
aesthetic space. On the contrary, as with many of Browning's historical
fictions, the present is overlaid on the past. Florence under the Medici
in the fifteenth century is also, in some of its aspects, Florence under
Austrian occupation in the aftermath of the failed revolution of 1848–9.
There was an Austrian garrison in the city until 1855, and you were just
as likely as in Lippi's day to be stopped in the street after midnight by
a military or police patrol and asked to explain your business. There
was censorship, and the Church, for the most part, worked hand in
glove with the secular authorities. The 'Italian person of quality' who
speaks another of the *Men and Women* poems, 'Up at a Villa—Down in
the City', passes this kind of repression off lightly—it is, for him, one
of the invigorating aspects of city life—but the form of the dramatic
monologue allows a less agreeable reality to show through:

> At the post-office such a scene-picture—the new play, piping hot!
> And a notice how, only this morning, three liberal thieves were shot.
> Above it, behold the archbishop's most fatherly of rebukes,
> And beneath, with his crown and his lion, some little new law of the
>   Duke's!   (ll. 43–6)[8]

To the speaker, the execution of three nationalists ('liberal thieves' is
clearly a euphemism) is on a par with 'the new play'; the city is a place
of spectacle, to be relished as long as you hold no dissenting political
views, are not the target of one of those sinister-sounding 'fatherly
rebukes', and are not likely to fall foul of 'some little new law of the

---

7. Robert Browning, *Pippa Passes* iv 172 (*Poems of Browning* ii 98). The proposition is made
   to the Bishop by the corrupt steward of his older brother's estate, to which Pippa is
   (unknowingly) the rightful heir; the Bishop is tempted, and says 'Why, if she sings,
   one might …' (l. 186); just at this moment Pippa's voice is heard outside, singing her
   fourth song ('Over-head the tree-tops meet'), and the Bishop is saved from temptation.
8. 'Up at a Villa—Down in the City', subtitled 'As Distinguished by an Italian Person of
   Quality', *Poems of Browning* iii 147. The 'scene-picture' is a poster advertising the 'new play'.

Duke's' which will further restrict the political freedom you care nothing about. Browning's own opinion of Leopold II is concisely expressed in an epigram which again links Church and state, as the Grand Duke takes part in another public spectacle, the 'pedilavium' or ceremonial washing of the feet of the poor on Maundy Thursday:

> The G.^d Duke wash'd and kiss'd ten poor men's feet.
> You'll say His Grace is gracious to inferiors:
> But even Tuscan toes must now taste sweet
> To one who kisses Austria's p——!⁹

A regime whose brutality is masked by euphemism and hypocrisy, and in which power demands its tribute of flattery: this is the context in which the Florence of the Medici, however glamorous its 'Renaissance' aura, is connected to the Florence of the 1850s. Lippi, the would-be revolutionary in painting, has come to terms with the repressive, but also munificent, regime of his patrons, the secular rulers of Florence and the Catholic Church. But at what cost? He wields the Medici name without scruple, and oils the wheels of his patron's power: when he gives the men of the watch a tip, it is accompanied with a reminder of their, and his, subservience:

> Lord, I'm not angry! Bid your hangdogs go
> Drink out this quarter-florin to the health
> Of the munificent House that harbours me
> (And many more beside, lads! more beside!)
> And all's come square again.   (ll. 27–31)

It is the same with the Church: Lippi chafes at the ignorance of those who commission religious painting merely as an adjunct to piety, but he knows how dangerous it can be to earn one of those 'fatherly rebukes'. 'Hang the fools!' he exclaims at the climax of a tirade against the religious Philistines—and instantly retracts, knowing he has crossed the line:

> —That is—you'll not mistake an idle word
> Spoke in a huff by a poor monk, God wot [. . .]
> Oh, the church knows! don't misreport me, now!   (ll. 335–7, 340)

---

9. 'Epigram on the Grand Duke', *Poems of Browning* iii 474; the missing word, evidently, is 'posteriors'. The lines are reported in a letter of 8 January 1854 from the Brownings' friend Robert Lytton to John Forster, and were presumably composed sometime after Maundy Thursday (24 March) in 1853. The ceremony derives from Jesus's washing of the disciples' feet at the Last Supper (John 13:5–14).

Mid-nineteenth-century Florence (at least for its native inhabitants) has something of this atmosphere, an uneasy, unstable compound of fearful conformity and subversive energy. The poem 'reads' the Risorgimento through the lens of a Renaissance which is not wholly admirable, and whose ideals are mired in contingency. What Lippi does with song, with the *stornelli* that are threaded through his speech, exemplifies his struggle to achieve artistic freedom within a social and political order that fundamentally denies the principle of *libertà*.

If Browning knew the traditional *stornelli* of the Tuscan countryside, either in the original or in Theodosia Garrow Trollope's translations, he would also have known of the radical appropriation of the form by the Italian poet Francesco Dall'Ongaro, who had published a volume of political *stornelli* in 1847. When these poems were reprinted in 1862, the Preface remarked that Italy had few political *stornelli*, or at least few that had survived in the popular memory, and that the love song with which the form was traditionally associated had become overfamiliar and somewhat frigid. Dall'Ongaro, the Preface suggested, had revivified the form: 'al canto politico vibrati le corde dei cuori tese all'unisono; il canto d'amore le sfiora appena'.[10] The poems circulated widely in Italy and further afield—a famous story has Garibaldi chanting one as he embarked for Italy from Montevideo in the spring of 1848. It is true that Dall'Ongaro's *stornelli* are not exact replicas of the traditional form—Browning's abbreviated versions in 'Fra Lippo Lippi' are closer. Dall'Ongaro's *stornelli* are free adaptations, taking the flower motif but turning it a different way, as the following example shows:

Italia libera	*Italy free*
Firenze, 12 settembre 1847	*Florence, 12 September 1847*
E lo vapore se n'è ito a Pisa,	And the steam [train] has gone to Pisa
Portando la canzon de' tre colori:	Carrying the song of the three colours:
I' vo' che me la canti la mia Lisa,	I would like my Lisa to sing it to me,
Il cherubino de' miei primi amori.	The angel of my first loves.
Ma le dirò che nella mia divisa	But I will tell her that on my uniform

10. *Stornelli italiani di Francesco Dall'Ongaro* (Milan: G. Daelli, 1862), p. 6. 'To the political songs all heartstrings vibrated in unison; the song of love barely brushed them.' There are personal connections between Dall'Ongaro and the Brownings, though they post-date 'Fra Lippo Lippi'. They met in September 1859 and the Brownings 'liked him much'; he is frequently mentioned in EBB's letters from this point on. He translated one of her poems, 'A Court Lady', into Italian, and she admired his work: 'Dall'Ongaro is a poet, & has a remarkable command of language' (*Florentine Friends: The Letters of Elizabeth Barrett Browning and Robert Browning to Isa Blagden 1850–1861*, ed. Philip Kelley and Sandra Donaldson [Winfield, KS and Waco, TX: Wedgestone Press and Armstrong Browning Library of Baylor University, 2009], p. 233 n. 6, p. 444).

Il rosso spicchi sopra gli altri fiori.	The red triumphs over the other flowers.
Il rosso è il sangue che versare io voglio,	Red is the blood that I wish to spill,
Ma per la libertà, non per un soglio.	But for freedom, not for a throne.
Lo vo' versar per quella Italia vera,	I want to spill it for that true Italy
Dove non c'è che un Cristo e una bandiera.[11]	Where there is but one Christ and one flag.

Dall'Ongaro's Lisa is clearly not Fra Lippo Lippi's (*'Flower o' the quince, / I let Lisa go, and what good's in life since?'*), though she begins as though she might be. The 'angel of my first loves' is a phrase you can imagine in Lippi's mouth, and later in the poem he scandalously conflates the figure of an angel in one of his paintings with a girl he fancies (ll. 370–87). But Dall'Ongaro wants *his* Lisa to sing him a revolutionary song about the Italian tricolour, and to teach her a lesson about it as well, a lesson about sacrifice and the 'true Italy', united by a single faith and a single flag. None of this applies to Lippi (or would matter to him if it did, I suspect) and there is no suggestion—from him—of any political thread in the 'whiffs of song' he recites. But neither is Lippi Browning's spokesman, and Browning's present—the present of the failed Risorgimento—shadows Lippi's apologia for his own failure to carry through the revolution in painting that he knows will come.

The setting of 'Italia libera' in Florence, and the date, 12 September 1847, connect it to the events described in EBB's *Casa Guidi Windows*, and to Browning's response to his wife's poem. It was the first anniversary of the Brownings' marriage, and, as we have seen, the day on which they witnessed the grand procession of Tuscan dignitaries and delegations to thank the Grand Duke Leopold for granting a Civic Guard.[12] EBB was prepared to go along with popular sentiment to a certain degree, and give the Grand Duke a chance to prove that he really did have the people's interests at heart, but Dall'Ongaro is less concessive. He is willing to shed his blood 'per la libertà, non per un soglio'—for liberty, not for a throne—and he was to maintain this republican intransigence throughout his career: he was a partisan of Mazzini and Garibaldi, and disliked the compromise by which Italian independence was achieved through the establishment of a monarchy.[13] If Browning

---

11. *Stornelli italiani*, p. 19. The first line is topical; the Florence-Pisa railway had only recently opened.
12. See Chapter 2, pp. 37–8.
13. In his poem 'Garibaldi' (1859), Dall'Ongaro addresses Victor Emanuel directly: 'O re Vittorio, chiama i tuoi Sardi, / Grida a Toscani, grida a Lombardi: / —Spezzate i vili patti ribaldi!' [O King Victor, summon your Sardinians, / Call out to the Tuscans, call out to the Lombards / —The vile scoundrelly pacts are broken!] (the 'pacts' are those made by the great powers, France and Austria, who claim the right to decide Italy's

read 'Italia libera', he may or may not have admired its colloquialism, its terseness, and its wit, but he would certainly have approved of its anti-royalist sentiment. Another of the poems of *Men and Women*, 'Old Pictures in Florence', celebrates early Tuscan art—the art that so exasperates Lippi, that paints the soul and ignores or misprizes the body—and connects this art specifically with the period when Florence was a republic. In the concluding part of the poem, the speaker, whom we may identify with Browning, or who is at least much closer to him than Lippi, looks back, as EBB had done in *Casa Guidi Windows*, at the events of 1847 and the disappointment that followed, and hopes that when the time comes the Florentines will do better:

32
When the hour is ripe, and a certain dotard
    Pitched, no parcel that needs invoicing,
To the worse side of the Mont St. Gothard,
    Have, to begin by way of rejoicing,
None of that shooting the sky (blank cartridge),
    No civic guards, all plumes and lacquer,
Hunting Radetzky's soul like a partridge
    Over Morello with squib and cracker.

33
We'll shoot this time better game and bag 'em hot—
    No display at the stone of Dante,
But a sober kind of Witan-agemot
    ("Casa Guidi," quod videas ante)
To ponder Freedom restored to Florence,
    How Art may return that departed with her.[14]

future; Dall'Ongaro is thinking principally of the Treaty of Villafranca). EBB reports Dall'Ongaro's resentment at Garibaldi's having to go to Turin to pay court to King Victor Emanuel in April 1861 (*Florentine Friends* 447).

14. 'Old Pictures in Florence', ll. 249–62, in *Poems of RB* iii 336–9. The 'dotard' is the Austrian general Count Radetzky, aged eighty-nine in 1855; at the battle of Novara in 1849 he defeated the army of Savoy-Piedmont, the only viable force on the side of independence. The speaker imagines Radetzky being unceremoniously dumped onto the Austrian side of the Alps (in contrast to the play-acting of 1847 in which he was figuratively, but not literally, chased 'Over Morello', the name of one of the hills overlooking Florence). The Witanagemot (Browning's hyphen is usual for the period) was the Anglo-Saxon parliament or council of wise men. The allusion is characteristic of a tendency in English radical thought of the period to appeal to the 'ancient liberties' that had supposedly been suppressed by the Normans, but that had eventually re-emerged in the struggle against the divine right of kings in the seventeenth century.

'None of that shooting the sky': the show of force will be replaced by violence with a purpose, and political posturing by serious deliberation. Even Dante must be disavowed if the only use that is made of his memory is for 'display'. In Part One of *Casa Guidi Windows* EBB praised the citizens of Florence for choosing 'the stone of Dante', the spot in the Piazza del Duomo reputed to have been the poet's favourite seat, as their political 'tryst-place' (ll. 600–19), but in Part Two she revoked her praise: Florence is now 'Dante's Florence' with a vengeance (l. 8), the city that sent him into exile and whose blindness and corruption he repeatedly denounced. Browning's specific acknowledgement of his debt to *Casa Guidi Windows* is made in the context of the failure to establish a government which had some claim to represent the people. This is a bit of a stretch, admittedly: if readers did look back to EBB's poem they would find very little about republican or parliamentary forms of government.[15] But Browning's object in setting 'Old Pictures in Florence' as a kind of pendant to *Casa Guidi Windows* has a larger scope. It is the aesthetic turn taken by 'Old Pictures in Florence' that matters; its endorsement, so to speak, of the child's song with which EBB begins: '*O bella libertà*'. 'To ponder Freedom restored to Florence, / How Art may return that departed with her' suggests that political liberty is not just beautiful for its own sake, but that it is the source, the matrix of beauty: 'Pure Art's birth being still the republic's!', as the speaker resoundingly puts it (l. 272). The key image of the poem is that of the Campanile, the bell tower that stands alongside the Duomo, whose design by Giotto was never fulfilled. Florence, and Italy, have lain under the interdict of tyranny, both secular and spiritual; but the speaker looks forward to the completion of the bell tower coinciding with the *re*birth of republican liberty, as though *bella libertà* were to take concrete form:

36
Shall I be alive that morning the scaffold
Is broken away, and the long-pent fire,

15. EBB emphasizes rather the dual need of 'civic spirit' among the people (i 746), and a heroic leader able to wield that spirit effectively: 'some high soul, crowned capable to lead / The conscious people, conscious and advised' (ll. 761–2). The word 'crowned', though it is ostensibly a metaphor here, signals EBB's willingness to envisage a monarchical government. It is a recognizably Carlylean analysis, and though Browning, too, greatly admired Carlyle, he did not subscribe to the 'great man' theory of history that Carlyle had propounded in *On Heroes, Hero-Worship, and the Heroic in History* (1841).

> Like the golden hope of the world unbaffled
>   Springs from its sleep, and up goes the spire—
> As, "God and the People" plain for its motto,
>   Thence the new tricolor flaps at the sky?
> Foreseeing the day that vindicates Giotto
>   And Florence together, the first am I!   (ll. 281–8)[16]

As we shall see, the claim of earliness—*that morning; the first am I*—is the opposite of Lippi's sense of himself as a thwarted figure: he too foresees a revolution, but not one in which he himself will play any part. Browning's thoroughly modern republicanism, expressed in his adoption of the 'new tricolor' with Giuseppe Mazzini's slogan, 'Dio e popolo', is also a regeneration, an awakening; it is not a break with the past but the outbreak of a 'long-pent fire', the fulfilment of 'the golden hope of the world'.[17] But for Lippi this 'long-pent fire' has no meaning. His conception of the past is quite different: it is confined to the past of his own life, the place where he came from, and to which, like the scene of the crime, he obsessively returns.

The historical contexts for the *stornello* help to explain why Browning places it in Lippi's mouth, and why Lippi's appropriation of this street song follows the path it does in the course of his monologue. He recites no other kind of song, which stands in the poem for all the songs with which the carnival season is celebrated in Florence. Why might he be drawn to this one? It has been observed that all the *stornelli* he sings are determinedly secular in outlook, starting with the first—'*Flower o' the broom, / Take away love, and our earth is a tomb!*'— not a Christian sentiment, assuming 'love' means earthly, sexual love. Some are melancholy, evoking lost love or the transience of pleasure. They breathe the spirit of popular wisdom, attached to this world and sceptical about the next—summed up in the last one that Lippi sings, and which appears in the text in a parenthesis, indicating that he is reminded of it by the current of his own thoughts. He explains to the officer of the watch that, while he 'paint[s] to please' his patrons, he is subject to gusts of temptation:

16. 'Tricolor' is Browning's spelling; the 'bandiera tricolore' was a familiar motif in Risorgimento poetry and song. Browning may have known Dall'Ongaro's song 'La Bandiera Tricolore' (*c.*1848): see Chapter 2, n. 11.

17. EBB had a less charitable view of Mazzini's slogan: 'Mazzini writes "God & the people" on a banner, & thinks this enough both for theology & politics' (*Letters to Arabella* i 487).

> For, doing most, there's pretty sure to come
> A turn—some warm eve finds me at my saints—
> A laugh, a cry, the business of the world—
> (*Flower o' the peach,*
> *Death for us all, and his own life for each!*)
> And my whole soul revolves, the cup runs o'er,
> The world and life's too big to pass for a dream,
> And I do these wild things in sheer despite,
> And play the fooleries you catch me at,
> In pure rage!   (ll. 245–54)

'Some warm eve' is the woman as well as the time of day: Eve figures here as temptress, the opposite of the 'saints' whose image Lippi is condemned to replicate, and she also represents 'the business of the world'.[18] At this point, by an involuntary association, sex and death come into conjunction in Lippi's mind. Sex is designated by the peach, whose eroticism features elsewhere in Browning's work,[19] but sex here is not the vehicle of reproduction and companionship, as it is for Eve and Adam, but of a desperate solitary grab at pleasure, an action done 'in pure rage'. What people have in common is death, but death is not a common good; unlike sexual love, it does not bind but loosens fellow-feeling. '*Death for us all, and his own life for each!*' is a way of saying that each person should take possession of his own life, since we are all going to die, but it also a way of saying that each person's own life is of supreme importance to himself, and is inaccessible to anyone else.

Both the poem 'Fra Lippo Lippi' and its central character have a reputation for life-affirming humour and joviality. Readers—I am no exception—feel as though they, too, have 'come up with the fun', with Lippi as their 'hail fellow, well met' companion. We relish his earthiness,

---

18. This is not the first occurrence of the pun in Browning's poems. In *Sordello* (1840), the hero as a child pays regular visits to the mysterious carved font in the vaults of the castle at Goito where he is brought up; the font is upheld by 'shrinking Caryatides / Of just-tinged marble like Eve's lilied flesh / Beneath her Maker's finger when the fresh / First pulse of life shot brightening the snow [. . .] And every eve, Sordello's visit begs / Pardon for them; constant as eve he came' (ll. 412–15, 428–9). The text is that of the first edition (*Poems of RB* i 422).

19. The sculptor Jules, in *Pippa Passes*, expounds his aesthetic and working method to his beloved, Phene: 'With me, each substance tended to one form / Of beauty—to the human archetype. / On every side occurred suggestive germs / Of that—the tree, the flower—or take the fruit,— / Some rosy shape, continuing the peach, / Curved beewise o'er its bough; as rosy limbs, / Depending, nestled in the leaves; and just / From a cleft rose-peach the whole Dryad sprang' (*Poems of RB* ii 85–92).

his humour, his sardonic observation of human foibles, and we relish being
in on his jokes, as when he reports his innocent fellow monks remark-
ing on how lifelike his painting is—'"That woman's like the Prior's
niece who comes / To care about his asthma: it's the life!"' (ll. 170–1)—
knowing, of course, that she is neither niece nor nurse. But the brio of
Lippi's performance masks the fact that it is just that—a performance—
and if we look more closely, we can trace the lineaments of a different
countenance. Looking more closely means reminding ourselves of the
double form of dramatic monologue, which throws author and dramatic character into a contested relationship—a relationship in which
the reader is often uneasily placed, like the best friend of a divorcing
couple.[20] In Lippi the stark equation of desire with lack is so scribbled
over by his energetic flourishes, his verbal arabesques, that it is hard to
see through them; but Browning is an unsparing partner.

The story that Lippi tells is of a starved, abused little boy, growing up
on the streets, and for whom becoming a monk means nothing except
food in his belly and 'day-long blessed idleness' (l. 105). He begins his
artistic career by drawing faces in his prayer books. As for learning,
he has a *stornello* ready to hand to express his scorn:

> Such a to-do! they tried me with their books.
> Lord, they'd have taught me Latin in pure waste!
> *Flower o' the clove,*
> *All the Latin I construe is, "amo" I love!*   (ll. 108–11)

(This is, by the way, the only example of a *stornello* in the poem which
does not contain a perfect rhyme.) Lippi represents himself as completely
self-taught, without a master or any formal training—an impossible
story in fifteenth-century Florence, but it reinforces his sense of himself
as a rebel, like the fallen angels in *Paradise Lost* who deny their maker
and claim, in Satan's words, to be 'self-begot, self-rais'd / By our own
quick'ning power'.[21] But Lippi, unlike Satan, is a compromised figure,
beaten down by necessity, which both gives birth to his art and restricts
its power and scope. One of the *stornelli* he sings enacts the struggle
between his desire to say what he thinks and paint what he likes, and

20. The critical tradition that addresses the doubleness of dramatic monologue begins
   with Robert Langbaum's *The Poetry of Experience* (1957); for a modern reconsideration,
   see Isobel Armstrong, *Victorian Poetry: Poetry, Poetics, Politics* (1993).
21. John Milton, *Paradise Lost* v 860–1. Lippi was in fact influenced, if not taught, by
   Masaccio, and certainly received some training as a painter under the auspices of the
   Carmelite monastery where he was placed as a boy.

his fear of censure—and his turning of this struggle into a joke. 'I'm my own master, paint now as I please', he boasts (l. 226)—and yet—

> And yet the old schooling sticks—the old grave eyes
> Are peeping o'er my shoulder as I work,
> The heads shake still—"It's Art's decline, my son!
> You're not of the true painters, great and old:
> Brother Angelico's the man, you'll find:
> Brother Lorenzo stands his single peer.
> Fag on at flesh, you'll never make the third!"
> *Flower o' the pine,*
> *You keep your mistr . . . manners, and I'll stick to mine!*
> I'm not the third, then: bless us, they must know!
> Don't you think they're the likeliest to know,
> They, with their Latin?   (ll. 231–42)

If we imagine the second line of the *stornello* to have been 'You keep your mistress, and I'll stick to mine!', then Lippi censors himself in the act of reciting it. Alternatively, the stumble in the line may be an intrinsic feature, a deliberate piece of clowning. We can't tell, of course, because Browning has made it up; but in either case Lippi's defiant boast—'I'll *stick* to mine'—is undone by the truth that 'the old schooling *sticks*'. He can keep neither his mistress nor his manners; he has internalized his condition as the 'son' of the Church, he is not 'the man' or his 'single peer', but secondary, dependent, and chafing in his dependence.

Religious orthodoxy is not the only form this dependence takes. In his claim to be his own master, Lippi cannot help acknowledging another kind of bondage:

> I'm my own master, paint now as I please—
> Having a friend, you see, in the Corner-house!
> Lord, it's fast holding by the rings in front—
> Those great rings serve more purposes than just
> To plant a flag in, or tie up a horse!   (ll. 226–9)

The 'friend', as we have seen, is Cosimo de' Medici (the 'Corner-house' is Palazzo Medici). In his first allusion to Cosimo, in line 18 of the poem, Lippi names him as 'Master'; his claim to be *his own* master is undercut by the fact of patronage, and we should recall that Lippi has already described his frustration at being cooped up for three weeks, not painting as he pleased but 'A-painting for the great man'. According to legend, Cosimo, knowing Lippi's propensities, actually had him locked up to ensure that he did his job without distractions. 'Holding fast' to the iron rings bolted onto the front of the palace is therefore as much an image of captivity as security. Here the politics of the poem return with a vengeance: perhaps Lippi's art has no higher purpose than a flag to advertise Cosimo's status, or a horse to do his bidding, and perhaps this is the invariable condition of art produced under the sway of one ideology or another.

As we read through the poem, the *stornelli* become more closely aligned to Lippi's own feelings about his personal and artistic predicament. He deploys them with what looks like conscious intent, as though drawing on this popular art for support against the forces of repression and hypocrisy. Popular song has always had this radical edge, in part because it is anonymous, communal, untraceable; its authors cannot be singled out and persecuted, and it is disseminated in ways that make it almost impossible to censor. Lippi picks up these stones he finds in the street and flings them against his enemies. Yet this reading won't quite do. When Lippi first hears the 'sweep of lute-strings, laughs, and whiffs of song' (l. 52), they come to him from outside, and belong to the men and women who sing them. And they are open-ended, not yet attached, not appropriated to a particular person's use; they are sung by the 'bands / [Who] roam the town and sing out carnival' (ll. 45–6). The sign of this open-endedness is the incomplete *stornello*, the only one that Lippi doesn't finish:

> *Flower o' the broom,*
> *Take away love, and our earth is a tomb!*
> *Flower o' the quince,*
> *I let Lisa go, and what good's in life since?*
> *Flower o' the thyme*—and so on.   (ll. 53–7)[22]

Lippi cuts short his recital, and from this moment on co-opts the *stornelli* into his private narrative. The very next one he sings makes the point:

> I came up with the fun
> Hard by St. Laurence, hail fellow, well met,—
> *Flower o' the rose,*
> *If I've been merry, what matter who knows?*   (ll. 66–9)

22. The name of the flower here puns on 'time', whose flower must be seized before it fades, but which is also cut short. In 1854 Frederick Tennyson, who lived in Florence and was a friend of the Brownings, published 'Mayday' (*Days and Hours*, 1854), in which Love, 'the flower of Time', also wounds its devotees 'With one sharp pang itself cannot redress, / The fear to lose the bliss itself supplies' (ll. 147, 153–4).

This speaks directly to Lippi's current predicament; it is like an appeal to the officer of the watch to use his discretion. The songs lose their impersonal, communal flavour; Lippi might as well be their author.

This 'privatization' of the street song occurs again and again in our literature; it is part of a wider pattern of appropriation, which comes naturally to literary forms in which subjectivity is at a premium. The *stornello* 'occurs' in the poem as it might in real life, fortuitous, rounding a street corner, pursuing its own way; but Lippi 'comes up with the fun'—of course, right outside a church, so that the song is already primed to thumb its nose at organized religion on behalf of the *homme moyen sensuel* whom Lippi claims to represent—'hail fellow well met'. He is one of the gang, but he picks their pocket all the same. He is a con man after all, a street artist in his own right. But the original *stornello* is not his; it has no interest in embellishing the story of his life. The singers are heard in snatches, seen in glimpses, remain unknown and unnamed. This is partly because Lippi is so self-centred, but also because these first songs are genuine folk-songs, the product of an anonymous popular culture, which in turn anonymizes those who circulate it. The 'bands [who] sing out carnival' represent not individuality and autonomy, but a *shared* impulse. Lippi takes and bends the *stornello* to his own use, but on its first fleeting appearance in the poem it speaks with its own voice.

This voice, moreover, has one feature that Lippi can't control, because it belongs not to his design but to that of the poem. This feature is that of the *stornello*'s metre, which intrudes into the iambic pattern of Lippi's speech. It is axiomatic that the speaker of a dramatic mono-logue cannot 'know' that he speaks in verse.[23] As far as Lippi is concerned, the blank verse he utters is simply his normal speech. The technique of dramatic monologue gives us the stage-illusion of a speaking voice, whose diction and rhythms are not those of 'poetry' but of ordinary

23. Hence the joke which Browning gives to the speaker of another of the *Men and Women* poems, 'How It Strikes a Contemporary', which concerns the life and vocation of a poet: 'Well, I could never write a verse—could you?' (l. 114; *Poems of Browning* iii 375). In 'Mr. Sludge, "the Medium"' (*Dramatis Personae*, 1864) Sludge twice finds himself accidentally versifying: 'With Sludge it's too absurd? Fine, draw the line, / Somewhere, but, sir, your somewhere is not mine! // Bless us, I'm turning poet!' (ll. 1182–4); 'Why, when I cheat, / Mean to cheat, do cheat, and am caught in the act, / Are you, or rather am I, sure of the fact? / (There's verse again, but I'm inspired somehow.)' (ll. 1282–5; *Poems of Browning* iv 264, 269). Sludge's first fragment of verse is close to the metrical form of the *stornello* in 'Fra Lippo Lippi'.

conversation. But readers understand how the convention works, and take pleasure in what they know to be an artful 'performance' of natural speech. Lippi's easy, colloquial manner plays with, yet always conforms to, the poem's metrical scheme: 'I am poor brother Lippo, by your leave!' (l. 1); 'He's Judas to a tittle, that man is!' (l. 25); 'Ouf! I leaned out of window for fresh air' (l. 50). The metre flexes but never breaks; only its flow is periodically interrupted by the *stornelli*. All but one of these occupies its own separate space on the page.[24] A strong caesura divides the long line, so that the effect is jolting and *un*-musical. It is hard to 'hear' them as sung.

The *stornelli* draw Lippi into the street, which is where he comes from. The street functions in the poem as the opposite of the cloister, the church, the palace—the enclosed spaces where Lippi does his painting, and where his paintings are displayed. When the night watch arrest him, he is 'at an alley's end / Where sportive ladies leave their doors ajar' (ll. 5–6), and he is exasperated by the watchmen's zeal: 'Zooks, are we pilchards, that they sweep the streets / And count fair prize what comes into their net?' (ll. 23–4). He begins the story of his life in the same place: 'I was a baby when my mother died, / And father died and left me in the street' (ll. 81–2). And the street is the source of his painter's eye:

> when a boy starves in the streets
> Eight years together, as my fortune was,
> Watching folk's faces to know who will fling
> The bit of half-stripped grape-bunch he desires,
> And who will curse or kick him for his pains—
> Which gentleman processional and fine,
> Holding a candle to the Sacrament
> Will wink and let him lift a plate and catch
> The droppings of the wax to sell again,
> Or holla for the Eight and have him whipped,—
> How say I?—nay, which dog bites, which lets drop
> His bone from the heap of offal in the street!
> —The soul and sense of him grow sharp alike,
> He learns the look of things, and none the less
> For admonitions from the hunger-pinch.   (ll. 112–26)

24. Only once—when the *stornello* is itself interrupted—do the two metrical patterns meet in the same line: '*Flower o' the thyme*—and so on. Round they went' (l. 57), and in this line it feels as though the metre, assisted by the smoothly dismissive 'and so on', works to assimilate the *stornello*'s abruptness and restore the iambic status quo.

The general phrase 'starves in the streets' is itself *sharpened* in this passage, in a series of vivid concrete images, culminating in that of the dog letting its bone drop 'from the heap of offal in the street'. Yet Lippi's destiny, in the guise of his redoubtable Aunt Lapaccia, takes him at the age of eight 'along the wall, over the bridge, / By the straight cut to the convent' (ll. 90–1). He is rescued from the street and brought indoors, into comfort, security, and dependence. But the 'straight cut' is actually a devious way, pointing towards a life suppressed, or divided against itself. This division is present from the first in Lippi's art, which begins with the impulse to draw all over his copybooks and cover the walls of the convent with graffiti. His first proper painting, filled with his sharp-eyed and sharp-witted observations of human behaviour, is represented as an unsystematic outpouring, a 'disemburdening' of his 'crammed' head (ll. 140-1). But there is little accidental about it, even in its small details—when the monks crowd round to praise it, for example, one of them exclaims 'Look at the boy who stoops to pat the dog!' (l. 169), and we realize that Lippi has converted the scene of his sordid struggle with the dog over a 'heap of offal' into a benign vignette. The scene in the painting that he spends most time describing is even more suggestive. It is a scene of baffled violence, in which a murderer has sought sanctuary in a church, and cannot therefore be arrested or harmed:

> the breathless fellow at the altar-foot,
> Fresh from his murder, safe and sitting there
> With the little children round him in a row
> Of admiration, half for his beard and half
> For that white anger of his victim's son
> Shaking a fist at him with one fierce arm,
> Signing himself with the other because of Christ
> (Whose sad face on the cross sees only this
> After the passion of a thousand years)
> Till some poor girl, her apron o'er her head
> Which the intense eyes looked through, came at eve
> On tip-toe, said a word, dropped in a loaf,
> Her pair of ear-rings and a bunch of flowers
> The brute took growling, prayed, and then was gone.   (ll. 149–62)

By the end of this passage the sense of its being a *painting* has lapsed: the static image, made up of pose and dumbshow (the seated murderer, the row of children, the victim's son shaking his fist), gives way to the passage of time ('*Till* some poor girl... came at eve') and is animated

by narrative and voice ('said a word . . . the brute took growling'). Lippi
is re-creating an experience, a memory of his own; I envisage him as
one of the children impressed by the murderer's beard and by the
'white anger of his victim's son'; at the same time, the older Lippi overlays
this memory with a complicated thought about the religious function
of art, since the painting or, more likely, sculpture of the crucified Christ
above the altar does nothing except impose, on the victim's son's impulse
of vengeance, the conventional restraint of law and superstition. The
scene of the 'poor girl' (a euphemism for 'prostitute' in the period)
coming to give food and succour to the 'brute', possibly her pimp, to
whom she remains loyal, recycles a stereotype of Victorian popular
fiction, transposing Nancy and Bill Sikes to fifteenth-century Florence;
I find it less credible, less authentic as an emanation of Lippi's inner
life than that extraordinary double gesture of the victim's son, threatening with one arm and crossing himself with the other. Remember
Lippi's claim that he himself is driven by 'pure rage'; the murderer at
the altar-foot is a powerful composite figure for the forces that have
oppressed him, so that he is, again and always, the 'son', orphaned and
secondary: 'It's Art's decline, my son . . . ' He can raise his fist in anger,
but his threat is impotent; it's the bearded, masculine brute, 'fresh from
his murder', who gets the girl.

The street in 'Fra Lippo Lippi' is an ambivalent place. The little boy
starves there, but it is also the place where he learns his trade, his craft;
at the same time, this craft is one of enforced humility, begging,
competing for scraps with a dog. The orphan is rescued from the
streets and given a home in the monastery, and now the street comes
to represent freedom from the prison of conformity. This freedom
incarnates itself as song, seductive, irresistible as the song of the sirens.
But this song can take Lippi only so far, or rather, as he begins his
apologia, it is absorbed, folded into his narrative, changing from a sign
of autonomy to one of self-subjection. In the great painting he envisages
at the end of the poem, the 'Coronation of the Virgin', he cannot help
himself: he will figure in the scene as both master and naughty boy,
creator of an ordered hierarchy of saints and angels and subverter of
that order. An achieved vision of ceremonial stillness is set in motion
by a scandalous irruption of sexual energy. The result, he assures the
officer of the watch, will be a 'pretty picture gained' for the Church;
both sides in this bargain get something in return for a sacrifice of
integrity, but Lippi's sacrifice is the more painful, because he is, after all,

a man and not an institution. In the last, beautifully poised lines of the poem, Lippi's final assertion of autonomy doubles as his gesture of final submission:

> Your hand, sir, and good bye: no lights, no lights!
> The street's hushed, and I know my own way back—
> Don't fear me! There's the grey beginning. Zooks!   (ll. 390–2)

The street's hushed: while Lippi has been talking, the night has worn away, the revellers have gone to bed, and the *stornelli* are no longer being sung. Yet 'hushed' has a hint of coercion; it is not quite the same as saying 'The street is quiet'. The *OED* defines it as 'Reduced to silence; silenced, stilled, quieted'; Lippi acknowledges the power that has imposed silence on the street, and on him, for all his flow of speech. *I know my own way back*: we must remember what Lippi is going back to: 'shut within my mew, / A-painting for the great man'; to go *back* is not to go *home*. *Don't fear me!* But why should Lippi be feared? He means, at the literal level, 'Don't fear that I'll run off; I really am going back to my enforced residence in Palazzo Medici, and you won't get into trouble for letting me go'; beyond that, 'Don't think of me as a dangerous radical, a subversive figure; I know my place, even though I chafe against it'. The *grey beginning* is the dawn of the great age of painting that Lippi foresees, but from which he will be excluded: 'It makes me mad to see what men shall do / And we in our graves' (ll. 312–13); this beginning signals his own ending, marked by his favourite oath, *Zooks*, a contraction of 'Gadzooks'—a mincing term, which can't be taken seriously as an expression of 'pure rage'.[25] The poem ends on a note of exuberance which is also a note of defeat.

---

25. *OED* cites R. H. Barham, 'Lay of St. Cuthbert' (*Ingoldsby Legends*, 2nd Series, 1842): 'And as for that shocking bad habit of swearing,— / In all good society voted past bearing,— / Eschew it! and leave it to dustmen and mobs, / Nor commit yourself much beyond "Zooks!" or "Odsbobs!"' (ll. 369–72). Lippi uses it in ll. 3, 23, 60.

4

The one-legged sailor
and other heroes

S treet songs are surprisingly rare in James Joyce's *Ulysses*, otherwise
so rich in musical motifs and allusions.[1] Even music itself has less of
a presence on Dublin's streets than you might think, with only one
appearance by an organ grinder, for example.[2] The soundscape is predominantly one of urban noise—'a heavy tramcar honking its gong'
('Lotus-Eaters', 5.90), the rumble of carts, the jingling of horses' harness,
the tapping of a blind man's cane—and of urban speech, from civil
exchanges between passers-by to the shouting and swearing of a brawl
in Nighttown. There are hundreds of allusions to song, of course, since
Molly Bloom is a professional singer, and many other characters either
sing themselves, or quote from songs in their conversation, or, in the
case of both Leopold Bloom and Stephen Dedalus, recall snatches of

1. Quotations from *Ulysses* are from the Penguin Twentieth-Century Classics edition
(London: Penguin Books, 1992). This is based on the Bodley Head text of 1960, currently
the conservative choice in view of the debates over the 'corrected' text edited by Hans
Walter Gabler and others (New York: Garland Publishing, 1984). (See Declan Kibberd's
'Short History of the Text' in the Penguin edition, pp. lxxxi–lxxxix.) *Ulysses* is divided
into eighteen chapters or episodes. In the Bodley Head edition followed by Penguin
these are neither numbered nor designated by the 'Homeric' titles which Joyce originally devised for the serialization of the novel in *The Little Review*. Notwithstanding,
these titles have become the standard means of referring to the chapters of the book,
and I use them in my text; and I include chapter numbers in my page references.
2. The organ grinder appears in the 'Hades' episode, as Bloom and his fellow mourners
are making their way to Paddy Dignam's funeral: 'As they turned into Berkeley street a
streetorgan near the Basin sent over and after them a rollicking rattling song of the
halls. Has anybody here seen Kelly? Kay ee double ell wy. Dead March from *Saul*. He's as
bad as old Antonio. He left me on my ownio. Pirouette!' (6.121). The only other allusions
are Bloom's: he associates the stink of garlic with 'Italian organgrinders' ('Lestrygonians',
8.217) and an 'Italian organgrinder' is one of the list of Molly's putative sexual partners
('Ithaca', 17.863), probably more by bawdy verbal association than for any other reason.

song in their internal monologues. Don Gifford's *Ulysses Annotated* lists nearly 400 songs and nursery rhymes, some of which are sung or mentioned many times ('Love's Old Sweet Song', 'The Croppy Boy', 'Seaside Girls', etc.); but you don't hear them on the street.[3] You have to be indoors—in the bar of the Ormond Hotel, to take the obvious example, the setting for the 'Sirens' episode, the book's most deliberate and extended treatment of music and song. In the same way, when characters *remember* performances of music or song (as opposed to hearing them in the 'present time' of the novel), they are almost always remembering a public concert, or a family gathering, or the kind of semi-public musical *soirée* that Joyce had evoked in the final story of *Dubliners*, 'The Dead'.[4]

Eight songs, of varying provenance, are performed on the streets of Dublin in *Ulysses*. A 'onelegged sailor', begging his way around the streets of Dublin, growls out verses from a well-known ballad, 'The Death of Nelson'; he is the main subject of this chapter. The chorus of 'The Boys of Wexford', a ballad of the 1798 rebellion, is sung by a group of newsboys and by a drunken navvy. At the start of the 'Circe' episode, set in Dublin's red-light district, the prostitute Cissy Caffrey 'sings shrill from a lane':

> I gave it to Molly
> Because she was jolly,
> The leg of the duck
> The leg of the duck.   (15.563)

She sings a further two verses of this bawdy song, whose source has not so far been identified. I doubt that Joyce made it up, but I also doubt that the mention of Molly is accidental. Indeed, this is one of the simplest examples of 'appropriation' as I understand it—the song fits the plot of the book, since 'Blazes' Boylan has indeed given Molly Bloom 'the leg of the duck' earlier in the day, and 'jolly' is exactly how he thinks of her.[5] As though in response, Stephen Dedalus 'chants with joy the

---

3. Don Gifford with Robert J. Seidman, *Ulysses Annotated*, 2nd ed. (Berkeley, CA: University of California Press, 2008), pp. 671–2. Hereafter *Gifford*.
4. When Bloom hears Stephen Dedalus singing in the street in his 'phenomenally beautiful tenor voice', he immediately thinks of bringing him indoors: 'It was in fact only a matter of months and he could easily foresee him participating in their musical and artistic *conversaziones* during the festivities of the Christmas season' (16.773).
5. Later in the episode Corny Kelleher uses the phrase 'jolly girls' as a euphemism for prostitutes (p. 700).

introt for paschal time' (15.563).[6] A little later Bloom catches a glimpse of a fire on the south side of the city and hopes it might be Boylan's house. At any rate, he knows it's not Eccles Street, north of the river, where he and Molly live: 'We're safe. *(He hums cheerfully)* London's burning, London's burning! On fire, on fire!' (15.566). The nursery rhyme has popped into his head as songs do in this novel, illustrating here our enjoyment of disaster—when it happens to others. Further on in the episode, Cissy Caffrey reappears, accompanied by Privates Carr and Compton (of whom more later); they pass by Bella Cohen's brothel, 'singing in discord' a fragment of the popular song 'My Girl's a Yorkshire Girl' (15.676). This song has already featured, as a tune, in the viceregal cavalcade at the end of the 'Wandering Rocks' episode; it is then repeated on the pianola inside the brothel.[7] Joyce chose it, I think, not just because it is so markedly, so loudly English, performed for the benefit of the English occupying power, whether the Viceroy or the common soldier, but because its comic plot, in which two men claim that the same girl is *their* Yorkshire girl, only to find that she is in fact married to another, mirrors the way Molly Bloom is perceived by various men in the book. (As Bloom reflects, 'each one who enters imagines himself to be the first to enter whereas he is always the last term of a preceding series even if the first term of a succeeding one' ['Ithaca', 17.863]). Finally, in the 'Eumaeus' episode, as Bloom and Stephen make their way from the cabman's shelter to Bloom's home in Eccles Street, Stephen sings 'Exquisite variations [...] on an air *Youth here has End* by Jans Pieter Sweelinck' and 'an old German song of *Johannes Jeep* about the clear sea and the voices of sirens, sweet murderers of men' (16.772–3).[8] Both songs, especially the second, have affinity with characters and episodes in the book; authorial irony

6. The verses he actually sings, 'Vidi aquam egredientem de templo a latere dextro' and 'Et omnes ad quos pervenit aqua ista' (15.564), are from a different part of the Easter liturgy, an antiphon that accompanies the sprinkling of the congregation with holy water.
7. 'As they drove along Nassau street His Excellency drew the attention of his bowing consort to the programme of music which was being discoursed in College park. Unseen brazen highland laddies blared and drumthumped after the *cortège*: *But though she's a factory lass / And wears no fancy clothes. / Baraabum. / Yet I've a sort of a / Yorkshire relish for / My little Yorkshire rose. / Baraabum*' (10.327). The 'brazen highland laddies' are the band of the 2[d] Battalion of the Seaforth Highlanders, who were playing during the bicycle races in Trinity College Park (*Gifford* 286).
8. The first song is 'Mein junges Leben hat ein End' by the Dutch organist and composer Jan Pieterszoon Sweelinck (1562–1621); the second is 'Dulcia dum loquitur cogitate insidias' by the German composer Johannes Jeep (*c.*1582–1650). Stephen mistranslates Sweelinck's title, which means 'My young life has an end' (*Gifford* 562).

Plate 1 John Everett Millais (1826–96), *Cherry-Ripe*, 1879.

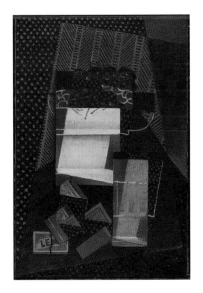

Plate 2 Juan Gris, *Cherries* [*Les cerises*], 1915.

Plate 3 Fra Filippo Lippi (1406–69), self-portrait (detail) in *The Coronation of the Virgin* (1441–7).

Plate 4 Jacopo Pontormo (1494–1557), *Cosimo de' Medici the Elder* (1519–20).

Plate 5 Édouard Manet (1832–83), *Knife Grinder, Rue Mosnier*, 1878.

Plate 6 Kazimir Malevich (1878–1935), *The Knifegrinder: Principle of Scintillation* (1912–13).

allows us, as readers, to penetrate Stephen's self-absorption, for he thinks the allusion to the Sirens concerns him alone, whereas we know that it applies also to Bloom. That completes the tally.[9]

I am going to focus in this chapter on two of these eight songs, 'The Death of Nelson' and 'The Boys of Wexford'—predominantly on the first. They are both patriotic songs, celebrating English and Irish nationalist myths of valour and glory, and subject, in the novel, to satirical appropriation. This makes the technique sound a little facile, but Joyce's attack is not simple-minded. In the case of 'The Death of Nelson' more than one myth is involved, as we shall see. If anything, singer and song illustrate Henry James's dictum: 'Really, universally, relations stop nowhere, and the exquisite problem of the artist is eternally but to draw, by a geometry of his own, the circle within which they shall happily *appear* to do so'.[10] It is also the critic's problem.

In the 'Aeolus' episode, Leopold Bloom is leaving the offices of the *Freeman's Journal*, the locus of windy rhetoric and vain speech which stands for the 'cave of winds' in the *Odyssey*:

He went to the door and, holding it ajar, paused. J. J. O'Molloy slapped the heavy pages over. The noise of two shrill voices, a mouthorgan, echoed in the bare hallway from the newsboys squatted on the doorsteps:

—*We are the boys of Wexford*
Who fought with heart and hand. (7.164)

9. I do not count instances in 'Circe' which belong to the surreal or phantasmagoric dimension of this episode, in which characters hallucinate, undergo comic or grotesque metamorphoses, or take part in elaborate fantasy routines. Some of these are set in public spaces and are accompanied by songs. I differentiate Bloom's humming of 'London's burning', for example, from the 'Distant Voices' which are heard uttering 'Dublin's burning! Dublin's burning' just before Private Carr assaults Stephen (15.694); these 'voices' belong to the parodic or mock-heroic treatment of the episode. Other such instances externalize Bloom's fantasies or unconscious desires: when he thinks about Molly's liking for the racially 'exotic', the 'Bohee brothers', well-known banjoists of African American and Canadian descent, appear and perform a song from their repertoire, 'There's someone in the house with Dina' (15.573); in his burlesque apotheosis, 'Bloom's Boys' sing a verse from a 'wrenbush' chant, a Christmas folk custom: 'The wren, the wren, / The king of all birds, / Saint Stephen's his day, / Was caught in the furze' (p. 604); by contrast, during his equally burlesque degradation, when he is in the pillory, the Artane Orphans taunt him with a street rhyme: 'You hig, you hog, you dirty dog! / You think the ladies love you!' and the girls from the Prison Gate Mission join in with an obscene acrostic: 'If you see kay / Tell him he may / See you in tea / Tell him from me' (pp. 616–17; F-U-C-K and C-U-N-T). All these are interesting but my focus is on songs that are performed in the 'real-world' street.

10. Preface to *Roderick Hudson* in the 'New York Edition' of James's fiction (New York: Charles Scribner's Sons, 1907), vol. I, p. vii.

'The Boys of Wexford' is one of many patriotic ballads which recur, usually with ironic import, in the course of Bloom's wanderings. (The chorus in full: 'We are the boys of Wexford, who fought with heart and hand / To burst in twain the galling chain, and free our native land.') It is a ballad of the 1798 rebellion (the 'United Irishmen' uprising whose most famous leader was Wolfe Tone), written by Robert Dwyer Joyce (1830–83), and first published in his *Ballads of Irish Chivalry* in 1872. It is not, therefore, a contemporary ballad of the rebellion, though R. D. Joyce states in a footnote that 'Two verses of an old song are incorporated in this'—he does not say which, but I will make what I believe to be a plausible guess.[11] The collocation here of the 'newsboys' with the 'boys of Wexford' is bathetic; the next action of these ragged disrespectful urchins is to guy Bloom as he leaves the newspaper offices, to the amusement of his 'friends' Lenehan and J. J. O'Molloy:

A STREET CORTÈGE

Both smiled over the crossblind at the file of capering newsboys in Mr Bloom's wake, the last zigzagging white on the breeze a mocking kite, a tail of white bowknots.

—Look at the young guttersnipe behind him hue and cry, Lenehan said, and you'll kick. O, my rib risible! Taking off his flat spaugs and the walk. Small nines. Steal upon larks.   ('Aeolus', 7.164–5)[12]

Bloom's dignity is compromised many times in *Ulysses*; here the 'capering' children make fun of his flat feet and shifty gait, and also of his dodgy errand, to canvass an advertisement—little better, it would seem, than 'flying the kite': 'In Ireland...a cant phrase for raising money on

---

11. Robert Dwyer Joyce, 'The Boys of Wexford', *Ballads of Irish Chivalry; Songs and Poems* (Boston, MA: Patrick Donahoe, 1872), pp. 404–5. I refer to him as 'R. D. Joyce' to distinguish him from James Joyce (who may well have known that the author of this dubiously authentic text was his namesake).

12. There is some debate as to whether the phrases 'Small nines' and 'Steal upon larks' apply to the newsboys or to Bloom. Don Gifford (*Gifford* 136) takes the former view; I follow Harald Beck's note in *James Joyce Online Notes* (http://www.jjon.org/joyce-s-allusions/larks). Beck points out that Joyce designated Bloom's boots as 'small nines' in one of the notebooks for the 'Aeolus' episode; with the expression 'steal upon larks' he compares Stephen Dedalus's impression of Bloom's catlike walk when their paths cross outside the National Library at the end of the 'Scylla and Charybdis' episode: 'A dark back went before them. Step of a pard...' (9.279). For another quotation from this passage, see below, p. 104.

accommodation bills'.[13] It is another reminder of Bloom's outsider status, his not belonging in his 'native land'; also of his pacifism, his refusal to admire the windy bluster of Irish nationalism.

Bloom is on his way to Dillon's auction rooms in search of the tea merchant Alexander Keyes, the man from whom he is hoping to secure an advertisement in the *Freeman's Journal*. Everyone else is on their way to the pub. This, too—improbable though it may seem—has a connection to 'The Boys of Wexford', which in *Ballads of Irish Chivalry* consists of five verses. The first two may well be the 'verses from an old song' that R. D. Joyce 'incorporated' in his composition; they have the authentic ring of rough metre and narrative illogic:

I.

In comes the captain's daughter, the captain of the Yeos,
Saying, "Brave United man, we'll ne'er again be foes.
A thousand pounds I'll give you, and fly from home with thee,
And dress myself in man's attire, and fight for libertie."
    We are the boys of Wexford, who fought with heart and hand
    To burst in twain the galling chain, and free our native land.

II.

And when we left our cabins, boys, we left with right good will,
To see our friends and neighbors that were at Vinegar Hill;
A young man from our ranks a cannon he let go;
He slapped it into Lord Mountjoy—a tyrant he laid low.
[chorus][14]

These two verses are not connected, but appear as though they were fragments of other songs. The first is founded on the traditional motif of the well-born girl who disguises herself as a man in order to follow her plebeian lover, transgressing social (and, here, political) barriers; but we aren't given the reply of the 'United man' to whom the offer is made,

13. *OED* s.v. 'fly', 5a; citation from *The Sporting Magazine*, 1808, with further instances from 1848 and 1861 ('fly a bill'). Later in the episode, in a section titled 'Raising the Wind', Myles Crawford, the editor of the *Freeman's Journal*, turns down J.J. O'Molloy's request for a loan: 'I'm up to here [...] I was looking for a fellow to back a bill for me no later than last week' (7.186).

14. The 'Yeos' are the 'Yeomen', local Anglo-Irish militia. 'United man' = 'United Irishman', i.e. a member of the movement of that name. The battle of Vinegar Hill, outside the town of Enniscorthy in Co. Wexford, took place on 21 June 1798; the United Irishmen were defeated. Lord Mountjoy was not killed in this battle, but in the battle of New Ross on 5 June.

nor do we find out what happened next.[15] The second verse is cruder and more direct, merely flourishing Lord Mountjoy's scalp. Although the lack of connection between the first and second verses seems odd, it is not untypical of ballads that emerge from an oral tradition. What follows, however, is more disconcerting.

III.

We bravely fought and conquered at Ross and Wexford town,
And if we failed to keep them, 'twas drink that brought us down.
We had no drink beside us on Tubber'neering's day,
Depending on the long, bright pike, and well it worked its way.
[chorus]

IV.

They came into the country, our blood to waste and spill,
But let them weep for Wexford, and think of Oulart Hill.
'Twas drink that still betrayed us,—of them we had no fear,
For every man could do his part, like Forth and Shelmalier.
[chorus]

V.

My curse upon all drinking,—it made our hearts full sore,—
For bravery won each battle, but drink lost evermore;
And if for want of leaders we lost at Vinegar Hill,
We're ready for another fight, and love our country still.
[chorus][16]

A temperance tract has somehow insinuated itself into a ballad about the heroic resistance to tyranny. Such ballads often blame defeat on misfortune, or treachery (there is a trace of that line in the fifth verse which speaks of 'want of leaders'), but it is very unusual to find the failure of a rebellion blamed on the demon drink.[17] It hardly needs

15. Later versions of the ballad do supply an explanatory verse: '"I want no gold, my maiden fair, to fly from home with thee; / Your shining eyes will be my prize—more dear than gold to me. / I want no gold to nerve my arm to do a true man's part; / To free my land I'd gladly give the red drops from my heart"'. But this verse does not appear in *Ballads of Irish Chivalry* and was not written by R. D. Joyce.

16. Tubberneering (modern Toberanierin) near Gorey in Co. Wexford, scene of a successful ambush of a British force by the United Irishmen, 4 June 1798. At Oulart Hill (27 May 1798) several thousand rebels overwhelmed a force of around 100 British troops. 'Forth and Shelmalier' are places in Co. Wexford.

17. Compare the accusation in another famous 'song of '98', 'Kelly the Boy from Killane': 'But the gold sun of freedom grew darkened at Ross / And it set by the Slaney's red waves; / And poor Wexford stripped naked, hung high on a cross / With her heart pierced by traitors and slaves'. Again, later versions of 'The Boys of Wexford' circulate with the references to drink replaced by more conventional sentiments, as in stanza 3:

saying that the references to drink in these three verses do not date from the period of the rebellion itself. They are a product, first, of the Irish temperance movement of the 1830s and 1840s (the period of R. D. Joyce's upbringing) and, perhaps more significantly, the American temperance movement of the 1860s and 1870s. R. D. Joyce had emigrated to America in 1866 and was living in Boston, where the temperance movement was strongly rooted. A good deal of its campaigning targeted the Irish immigrant community, where drunkenness was deemed the main cause of pauperism and criminality. R. D. Joyce, a respected medical practitioner as well as a scholar of Irish folklore, was engaged in a complicated rhetorical balancing act in 'The Boys of Wexford'. The song makes a crude direct appeal to Irish emigrant nationalism and hatred of the British, but also aligns itself with local, Bostonian disapproval of feckless drinking. Drink, the enemy of freedom in the struggle against tyranny in the Old World, threatens the Irish again in the New World.

The attempt to make a hero of the '98 rebellion look back on defeat from the perspective of a mid-nineteenth-century Bostonian teetotaller would have appealed to Joyce. It can't be a coincidence that when the song makes its second appearance on the street, in the 'Circe' episode, it is performed by a drunken navvy in the company of two British soldiers in Dublin's red-light district.[18] The bathos of the earlier scene is soured here by a tang of obscenity. As Bloom

'We bravely fought and conquered / At Ross and Wexford town; / Three Bullet Gate for years to come / Will speak of our renown; / Through Walpole's horse and Walpole's foot / On Tubberneering's day, / Depending on the long, bright pike, / We cut our gory way'. The version recorded by the Irish tenor John McCormack in 1906 omits the second and fourth verses, perhaps because they were thought to be indecorously bloodthirsty, but retains R. D. Joyce's wording in verses 3 and 5. Joyce, who had a fine tenor voice and had thought of becoming a professional singer, shared a platform with McCormack at a concert in 1904 organized by the Irish revival movement. He sang four numbers, among them 'The Croppy Boy'.

18. Prior to this it flashes across Bloom's consciousness during Ben Dollard's performance of another of the 'songs of '98', 'The Croppy Boy': 'All gone. All fallen. At the siege of Ross his father, at Gorey all his brothers fell. To Wexford, we are the boys of Wexford, he would. Last of his name and race. ('Sirens', 11.367). In 'The Croppy Boy' the youth tells the false priest: 'At the siege of Ross did my father fall, / And at Gorey my loving brothers all. I alone am left of my name and race; I will go to Wexford and take their place'. The name 'Wexford' triggers the brief irruption of 'The Boys of Wexford' into Bloom's mind. Even in this minor example the association with drink is maintained, since 'Sirens' takes place in the bar of the Ormond Hotel.

arrives in Nighttown, he is greeted by 'Cheap whores' who 'call from lanes, doors, corners':

THE WHORES:
>Are you going far, queer fellow?
>How's your middle leg?
>Got a match on you?
>Eh, come here till I stiffen it for you.   (15.578)

This, if you like, is the true 'song' of the street—of Mabbot Street, at least. It adds insult to injury as far as 'The Boys of Wexford' is concerned; on its first appearance the song was treated with comic disrespect, but now it is soiled and denatured. As Bloom 'plodges through their [the whores'] sump towards the lighted street beyond', he witnesses 'a shebeenkeeper haggl[ing] with the navvy and the two redcoats':

THE NAVVY: (*Belching*) Where's the bloody house?

THE SHEBEENKEEPER: Purdon street. Shilling a bottle of stout. Respectable woman.

THE NAVVY: (*Gripping the two redcoats, staggers forward with them*) Come on, you British army!

PRIVATE CARR: (*Behind his back*) He aint half balmy.

PRIVATE COMPTON: (*Laughs*) What ho!

PRIVATE CARR: (*To the navvy*) Portobello barracks canteen. You ask for Carr. Just Carr.

THE NAVVY: (*Shouts*)
>We are the boys[.] Of Wexford.

PRIVATE COMPTON: Say! What price the sergeantmajor?

PRIVATE CARR: Bennett? He's my pal. I love old Bennett.

THE NAVVY: (*Shouts*)
>The galling chain.
>And free our native land.

(*He staggers forward, dragging them with him. Bloom stops, at fault. The dog approaches, his tongue lolling, panting.*)

BLOOM: Wildgoose chase this. Disorderly houses.   (15.579)[19]

Bloom is trying to catch up with Stephen Dedalus, whom he will eventually rescue after he is knocked down in a street brawl by Private Carr at the end of the evening—the only martial engagement between

---

19. 'Shebeen': an unlicensed drinking house; 'any low wayside public-house' (*OED*).

the British colonial power and the native Irish that takes place in the book, and one in which Stephen, for his part, embraces the role of Irish patriot without enthusiasm. Bloom's reflection that he is on a 'wildgoose chase' contains a pun (unintended by him) on the 'Wild Geese', the Irish who fled, first in 1691 and then after every unsuccessful uprising, to take service abroad against Britain.[20] Stephen's flight to France at the end of *Portrait of the Artist as a Young Man* was a 'wildgoose chase' from which, when *Ulysses* begins, he has ignominiously returned, baffled but unreconciled. 'Where's the bloody house?' is a resonant question: the navvy has a choice between the 'respectable' establishment in Purdon Street, and Portobello Barracks—both 'disorderly houses' in their own way. That Private Carr should be stationed at Portobello Barracks in 1904 is not surprising in itself—it was one of the principal garrisons of the British Army in the city—but as so often in *Ulysses*, the future looms over the 'present time' of the novel, and to Joyce's Irish readers Portobello Barracks would recall an infamous episode in the Easter Rising of 1916, when three civilians were murdered there by order of Captain Bowen-Colthurst of the Royal Irish Rifles.[21] 'Come on, you British Army!' is not a cry of defiance on the battlefield, but the summons to a drinking bout: "Twas drink that brought us down', and drink is still doing it. Twice the navvy 'staggers forward', physically encumbered with the 'galling chain' of British power. Altogether the atmosphere in which the chorus of 'The Boys of Wexford' is *shouted* (Joyce will not even let it be *sung*) could not be more dishonouring—assuming you take the song seriously to begin with. The problem is not one of insincerity—either as regards the nationalism or the teetotalism—but of false consciousness, the embrace of unreality. Perhaps 'The Boys of Wexford' deserves no better than to end up being circulated by the 'shrill voices' of the newsboys or the drunken navvy's tuneless shout.

---

20. One of the heroes and martyrs of the '98 rebellion, Wolfe Tone, at his trial asked to be executed by firing squad, as he held an officer's commission in the army of the French Republic.

21. The murdered men were two journalists, Thomas Dickson and Patrick MacIntyre, and the radical writer and pacifist Francis Sheehy Skeffington, a close friend of Joyce at University College Dublin (he appears as McCann in *Portrait of the Artist*). Bowen-Colthurst was found guilty of murder but declared insane and sent to Broadmoor. He was released after a year and emigrated to Canada, where he died in 1965. In 1922, the year *Ulysses* was published, Portobello was taken over by the army of the Irish Free State.

Like many of the songs mentioned in *Ulysses*, 'The Boys of Wexford'
turns out to have a depth of association that belies the 'casualness' of
its appearance in the text. But its place in the book's larger design is
relatively narrow. It speaks to Joyce's scepticism about the overblown
rhetoric of Irish nationalism, with its seductive nostalgia for simple-
minded myths of defeat and betrayal; it is a theme that goes far in the
novel, but that is as far as it goes. The second of the songs I am going
to look at is of a different order.

> A onelegged sailor, swinging himself onward by lazy jerks of his crutches,
> growled some notes. He jerked short before the convent of the sisters of char-
> ity and held out a peaked cap for alms towards the very reverend John Conmee
> S. J. Father Conmee blessed him in the sun for his purse held, he knew, one
> silver crown.
> Father Conmee crossed to Mountjoy square. He thought, but not for long,
> of soldiers and sailors, whose legs had been shot off by cannonballs, ending
> their days in some pauper ward, and of cardinal Wolsey's words: *If I had served*
> *my God as I have served my king He would not have abandoned me in my old days.*
>   ('Wandering Rocks', 10.280)

The 'Wandering Rocks' episode of *Ulysses* consists of a series of vignettes
in which characters criss-cross Dublin, crossing each other's paths and
irrupting into each other's narratives, in a complex, paradoxical depiction
of the city's patterned chaos. The episode begins with a Jesuit priest,
Father John Conmee, whom Joyce's readers would remember from *A
Portrait of the Artist as a Young Man* as rector of Clongowes College and
prefect of studies at Belvedere. Now 'superior' of the residence of Saint
Francis Xavier's Church, he is a complacent and compromised figure,
and it may look at first as though Joyce is using this encounter with the
one-legged sailor simply to illustrate the priest's worldly prudence and
smug piety. Faced with an admittedly unprepossessing beggar, Father
Conmee is not prepared to give all that he hath to the poor, and his
reflection on the plight of 'soldiers and sailors, whose legs had been
shot off by cannonballs' is callously brief and conventional. However,
the one-legged sailor has more important work to do than to show up
Father Conmee, and by extension the Irish Roman Catholic establishment he represents.

At this stage we are not told what the one-legged sailor is singing—
he merely 'growl[s] some notes'—but we don't have long to wait: he
reappears a few pages later, in the third section of 'Wandering Rocks',

where his connection with the major characters and themes of the novel becomes clear:

A onelegged sailor crutched himself round MacConnell's corner, skirting Rabaiotti's icecream car, and jerked himself up Eccles street. Towards Larry O'Rourke, in shirtsleeves in his doorway, he growled unamiably:

— *For England . . .*

He swung himself violently forward past Katey and Boody Dedalus, halted and growled:

— *home and beauty.*

J. J. O'Molloy's white careworn face was told that Mr Lambert was in the warehouse with a visitor.

A stout lady stopped, took a copper coin from her purse and dropped it into the cap held out to her. The sailor grumbled thanks and glanced sourly at the unheeding windows, sank his head and swung himself forward four strides.

He halted and growled angrily:

— *For England . . .*

Two barefoot urchins, sucking long liquorice laces, halted near him, gaping at his stump with their yellowslobbered mouths.

He swung himself forward in vigorous jerks, halted, lifted his head towards a window and bayed deeply:

— *home and beauty.*

The gay sweet chirping whistling within went on a bar or two, ceased. The blind of the window was drawn aside. A card *Unfurnished Apartments* slipped from the sash and fell. A plump bare generous arm shone, was seen, held forth from a white petticoatbodice and taut shiftstraps. A woman's hand flung forth a coin over the area railings. It fell on the path.

One of the urchins ran to it, picked it up and dropped it into the minstrel's cap, saying:

— There, sir.   (10.288–9)

The sailor's song can now be identified: it is 'The Death of Nelson', which began life nearly a century earlier as an aria in a long-forgotten opera called *The Americans*, produced in 1811, with music by John Braham and libretto by S. J. Arnold.[22] By the time of Joyce's novel, 'The Death of Nelson' had become a popular number on its own account (Figure 4.1), and I shall have more to say about it later; for now I would only observe

---

22. John Braham (1774–1856) was a successful tenor as well as composer; he was of Jewish origin ('Braham' was a contraction of 'Abraham') and Joyce may well have known of this link with Bloom.

that it elicits a generous response from two women, one a 'stout lady' on the street, the other Molly Bloom, whistling a tune of her own from the window of her bedroom, and that the two 'urchins' are also well-meaning and helpful, despite the sailor's now evident bad temper.[23] Women and children behave better than Father Conmee, and better than the object of their charity.

The one-legged sailor appears twice more in the novel. We glimpse him in section 16 of 'Wandering Rocks', as a narrative intrusion in the conversation between Buck Mulligan and Haines, the English visitor, in the Dublin Bakery Company tearooms. 'O, but you missed Dedalus on *Hamlet*', Mulligan tells Haines, referring to Stephen's exposition of his theory of the play on the steps of the National Library in the preceding episode, 'Scylla and Charybdis'. Haines is dismissive:

— I'm sorry, he said. Shakespeare is the happy huntingground of all minds that have lost their balance.
The onelegged sailor growled at the area of 14 Nelson street:
— *England expects* . . .
Buck Mulligan's primrose waistcoat shook gaily to his laughter.
— You should see him, he said, when his body loses its balance. Wandering Ængus I call him.   (10.320)

On this occasion the phrase cited from the song is not 'England, home and beauty' but 'England expects', that cliché of patriotic sentiment which has become a vehicle for travesty and burlesque. Joyce's interpolation of the figure of the sailor—the subject of whose song, Nelson, now doubles as the name of the street on which he sings it—comments with hostile intent on Haines's patronizing assumption of national and cultural superiority, and on Mulligan's cynical complicity.[24]

The final appearance of the one-legged sailor comes when Molly, going back over the events of the day in 'Penelope', remembers the moment 'when I threw the penny to that lame sailor for England home and beauty when I was whistling there is a charming girl I love' (18.884). Only now do we find out that she was whistling a tune from *The Lily of Killarney*, a light opera based on Dion Boucicault's high Victorian melodrama *The Colleen Bawn* (1860).[25] That song itself

---

23. The 'stout lady' is unidentified but I like to think she is one of the two ladies Father Conmee encounters in section 1, either 'the wife of Mr David Sheehy M. P.' (p. 280) or Mrs M'Guinness, the 'stately, silverhaired' pawnbroker (p. 282).
24. On Mulligan's image of Stephen as Yeats's 'Wandering Ængus', see below, p. 108.
25. Molly slightly misquotes the title, 'It is a charming girl I love'; it occurs in Act I of the opera.

Figure 4.1. John Braham (1774–1856), *The Death of Nelson, Recitative & Song* (Melbourne: L. F. Collin, 1880s)

matters less than Molly's 'gay sweet chirping' of it, her mood of carefree anticipation. She is waiting for her lover, 'Blazes' Boylan; as several critics have remarked, she expects him to do his duty. David G. Wright even sees the 'vigorous jerks' with which the sailor '[swings] himself forward' on his crutches (no longer the 'lazy jerks' witnessed by Father Conmee) as prefiguring Boylan's masculine prowess.[26]

The one-legged sailor therefore appears, as a street singer, four times in *Ulysses*. He is also alluded to in other contexts, without reference to his singing. He is implicated in Mulligan's tirade at the National Maternity Hospital, in 'Oxen of the Sun', about 'the revolting spectacles offered by our streets, hideous publicity posters, religious ministers of all denominations, mutilated soldiers and sailors, exposed scorbutic cardrivers, the suspended carcases of dead animals, paranoic bachelors and unfructified duennas' (14.548). He features in 'Circe', in the wild rout of words and names that follows Stephen's cry, 'Dance of Death', in Bella Cohen's brothel:

(Bang fresh barang bang of lacquey's bell, horse, nag, steer, piglings, Conmee on Christass lame crutch and leg sailor in cockboat armfolded ropepulling hitching stamp hornpipe through and through, Baraabum!)   (15.680)

Last, he figures in another list—the list with which the narrator, in the 'Ithaca' chapter, 'reduces' Bloom 'by cross multiplication of reverses of fortune' to an imagined state of utter destitution. The second stage of this process, entitled 'Mendicancy', includes the 'maimed sailor' as one of the identities Bloom might adopt on his downward path ('Ithaca', 17.855).

The one-legged sailor is a composite figure, each of whose traits (beggar, cripple, singer, sailor) is vital to the meanings with which he is invested in the novel, meanings that go beyond his realistic presence on the streets of Dublin in the early twentieth century. Nevertheless, the realism of the figure also matters: whatever he symbolizes, whatever his place in the plot and patterning of the book, the one-legged sailor remains a closely observed, naturalistically drawn character: tuneless, disagreeable, grudging, repellent. And he has a social and literary history,

---

26. David G. Wright, *Ironies of Ulysses* (Dublin: Gill and Macmillan, 1991), p. 52. Wright reads the connections between the one-legged sailor and the major characters of the novel (Bloom, Stephen, Molly) with great acuteness, though he is himself a little uncharitable in suggesting that Molly's gesture in throwing the sailor a coin is compromised by her approaching adultery.

one aspect of which, at least, suggests a specific, named source, and would account (ironically) for his singing a patriotic English song on the streets of Dublin. It lies several generations back in time from the events of *Ulysses*, but it would be characteristic of Joyce to have dug it up and brought it back.

On Tuesday, 23 June 1832, a one-legged sailor from Co. Cork, Dennis Collins, flung a stone at King William IV at Ascot Races.[27] William's nickname was 'the Sailor King', from his service in the Royal Navy as a young man. The stone struck him on the forehead, but the blow was partly cushioned by the rim of his hat and he was not badly injured. Collins threw another stone which missed its target. He was wrestled to the ground by two onlookers (one of them, inevitably, a Captain in the Royal Navy) and arrested. He was tried for treason, found guilty, and sentenced to the customary punishment, as the judge, Sir John Bosanquet, told him: 'that you be taken to the place from whence you came and from thence to be drawn on a hurdle to the place of execution and that you be there hanged until you are dead, and afterwards that your head be severed from your body, and that your body be divided into four parts to be distributed as his Majesty think fit'. Probably no one really expected this sentence to be carried out. Collins was fifty-seven years old, had lost his leg in the King's service, was wretchedly poor and malnourished, and was widely thought to have been mad at the time, though insanity was not admitted as a plea in his defence. In March 1833 his sentence was commuted to transportation for life. He arrived in the penal colony of Van Diemen's Land in Tasmania on 12 August, and died within three months, on 1 November (Figure 4.2).

A number of details of this case may have caught Joyce's attention, starting with the fact that Collins came from his home district in Ireland, Co. Cork. The incident took place at Ascot, in June, in the week of the Gold Cup meeting. The Gold Cup features throughout *Ulysses*, as several characters are betting heavily on the race—won by the outsider Throwaway, to the chagrin of those who put their money on the horse with the royal name, Sceptre. Newspaper reports stressed Collins's indigence, but also his foul temper. His record contained repeated incidents of 'riotous conduct', including 'violent and improper language'. Some of the details are almost overdetermined in their

27. I am indebted for knowledge of this episode to Cormac F. Lowth, 'The One-Legged Sailor and the King', *Dublin Historical Record* 58.2 (Autumn 2005), pp. 195–207.

Figure 4.2. Dennis Collins

suggestiveness: the principal race of the day was His Majesty's Plate, won by a horse named Conscript; the 'smooth flint stone' that hit the King, and which was produced in court, was described as being 'about the size of a potato'.

I believe it is likely that Joyce knew at least some of this story, and he may even have come across a satirical poem published three weeks after the event in the *Freeman's Journal*—the same newspaper that features in the 'Aeolus' episode. The author, who signs himself '———y, T.C.D.' (i.e. a student of Trinity College Dublin), does not dwell on Collins's wooden leg but on the famous flint. The poem is titled 'A Hard Point Decided':

I.

A group of his Majesty's subjects assembled—
Each heart in the loyal convention had trembled,
To think that a pirate should dare throw a flint
At a head, that had feeling and royalty in't.

II.

When their anger sunk down to a calmer debate,
They started a question of moment and weight—
"Was the flint-stone the traitor exulted to fling
"As hard—or more hard than the head of the King?"

III.

The council was puzzled—till Paddy arose—
On whose head half his hardships were number'd in blows,
A man, who knew well by experience, they said,
The cause and effect of a blow on the head.

IV.

"The granite—the limestone—the Portland—the brown—
"May vex a man sorely—at times knock him down—
"Fling what stone you may please; but believe me, the print"
Quoth Pat—"will be deepest that's made by the flint.

V.

"The scripture—the very best proof of the thing—
"Informs us God hardens the heart of a King;
"But up to this moment, in all I have read,
"I ne'er could discover who hardens his head.

VI.

"The head then remain'd as it had been before,
"As honest and soft as a monarch e'er wore—
"So the question is now, as I clearly have shown,
"Not who harden'd the head but who soften'd the stone.

VII.

"A poet, called Orpheus, mythologists tell,
"Once soften'd the heart of the monarch of hell;
"Rocks lost all their hardness, and oak-trees had hung,
"Enraptur'd, to hear the wild notes that he sung."

VIII.

My opinion is, then, that some voices were singing,
May "God save the King," while the traitor was flinging;
Tho' the flint-stone flew fair, and had caused much alarm,
It lost all its hardness, and did him no harm.[28]

The figure of Orpheus—encountered previously in this book—returns
here in satirical guise (and in the same metre as Wordsworth's 'Power
of Music'), as the fortuitous saviour of a stony-hearted and soft-headed
monarch. 'God save the King' does save the King, but only because the
song is able to soften the flint that is aimed at him—not his heart,
which God has hardened beyond that of the 'monarch of hell'. 'Paddy',
as representative of the Irish common people, rises up in the 'loyal convention' of 'his Majesty's subjects' with a witty recognition that the
'alarm' caused to the King outweighed his own actual and prolonged
sufferings. But the wit is tinged with bitterness. The epithets 'pirate'
and 'traitor' may mock the servile indignation of the 'loyal convention', but they also acknowledge the force of the official narrative of
the event. A counter-narrative is fleetingly voiced in the penultimate
line—'the flint-stone flew fair'—but the 'aim' of political equity is
immediately deflected.

If Joyce's one-legged sailor remembers Dennis Collins, he does so
by inverse analogy. He is, like Collins, wretched and truculent, but
he has been 'transported' not to Van Diemen's Land but to Dublin,
where he is condemned to wander the streets singing the praises of the
British hero with whom (or at the same time as whom) he served, and
whose mutilation brought him not beggary but glory. He no longer
carries a threat to British dominion over Ireland; his deployment in
Ulysses is one of the many shafts that Joyce launches against that
dominion, but these shafts are always double-edged.

In more general terms, the crippled beggar was a feature of all large
towns and cities in the nineteenth and early twentieth century, and a
standard 'type' in journalism and fiction. He (it is mainly he) is not
often treated with sympathy; heartless amusement is a characteristic note,
and so is uncharitable suspicion. 'Visitors should bear in mind—what
residents should know already—that the impostorship of street-beggars
is the one rule to which, as yet, there has been no known exception',

---

28. The poem is reprinted in Lowth (*art. cit.* 199–200) but the transcription contains some
    errors; I have taken this version from the journal itself.

Charles Dickens's son asserted in 1879. 'London beggardom is a close corporation, and allows of no non-professional interlopers'.[29] There is no evidence that Joyce's one-legged sailor is a fraud, though readers familiar with Irish folklore might identify him with the 'boccough' or 'lame beggar', said to belong to a criminal fraternity with its own hier-archy and language. Charles Lamb, writing in 1822, is exceptional in opposing campaigns such as that waged by the recently formed Society for the Suppression of Mendicity (1818) to 'extirpate the last fluttering tatters of the bugbear MENDICITY from the metropolis', and in urging unconditional charity: 'Reader, do not be frightened at the hard words, imposition, imposture—*give, and ask no questions*'.[30] But Lamb's gener-osity is perhaps not as unconditional as it looks. He sees the beggar as a necessary figure in the urban landscape, whose 'decay' he mourns on aesthetic or even environmental grounds:

> The Mendicants of this great city were so many of her sights, her lions. I can no more spare them than I could the Cries of London. No corner of a street is complete without them. They are as indispensable as the Ballad Singer; and in their picturesque attire as ornamental as the Signs of old London.   (p. 133)

Lamb's collocation of 'Mendicants' with 'the Cries of London' and 'the Ballad Singer' is suggestive, but Joyce takes it a step further. In making his one-legged sailor both beggar and singer, he conflates two conven-tional categories. The crippled beggar's disability usually spoke for itself; I have found no literary or visual tradition of lame beggars who were also professional street singers.[31] The 'typical' disability of the

---

29. Charles Dickens, Jr, *Dickens's Dictionary of London: An Unconventional Handbook* (1879).
30. Charles Lamb, 'A Complaint of the Decay of Begging in the Metropolis', in *Elia and The Last Essays of Elia*, ed. Jonathan Bate (Oxford: Oxford University Press, 1987), p. 137. The essay was first published in the *London Magazine* in May 1822 and included in *Elia* (1823).
31. There is, however, a literary precursor in the character of Silas Wegg, the one-legged comic villain in Dickens's novel *Our Mutual Friend* (1865). Joyce is likely to have read this novel, whose title phrase turns up in *Ulysses* in a suggestive context (see n. 48). Wegg, who like the one-legged sailor is hard-featured and gruff-voiced, has a stall on a street corner from which he sells ballads and cheap sweets. He is befriended by the newly rich but illiterate Mr Boffin, who notices him not just selling his ballads but singing them to prospective customers. Boffin is naively impressed by this 'literary man—with a wooden leg', and employs Wegg to read to him in the evenings. Wegg, who exploits Boffin's good nature and ends by attempting to blackmail and ruin him, lards his conversation with references to the ballads and popular songs he sells, bend-ing them to his own purposes; one of these is the 'The Death of Nelson', the song the one-legged sailor sings. See Jay Clayton, 'Londublin: Dickens's London in Joyce's Dublin', *NOVEL: A Forum on Fiction* 28.3 (Spring 1995), pp. 327–42. For a more

street singer or musician was blindness, as with Wordsworth's fiddler in 'Power of Music'.[32] The fact that the sailor is not blind means that he can be set in motion around the city; blind musicians almost always occupied a single station, at any rate for a good portion of each day. Having one leg was no bar to mobility, as an article in *Fraser's Magazine* in 1846 mockingly remarked: 'One would suppose that the best reason for a beggar being stationary would be the loss of both legs; but it may be asserted, that a beggar with one leg is always more locomotive than a beggar with two; and that a beggar with no legs, is more locomotive than all'. The writer goes on to make fun of the same jerky movement that Joyce describes:

The one-legged beggar [...] hangs himself, as it were, on the pivot centre of two crutches under his shoulders, and swings forward in vast segments to the wonder of the pavement beneath him. [...] He presents, in fact, a most lively instance of a moving tripod of two-to-one-progressive-power; and of an activity only matched by those surprising monkeys which make a fifth limb of their tail; or that celebrated hero, the Devil upon two Sticks.[33]

Joyce's sailor is not dehumanized in this way, but nor does 'swinging himself onward by lazy jerks of his crutches' breathe fellow feeling.

What, then, of his profession? The mutilated soldier or sailor is another urban 'type', as Wordsworth observes in book 7 of *The Prelude* ('Residence in London'). The narrator, wandering through the bewildering and cacophonous city, encounters

> a face hard and strong
> In lineaments, and red with over-toil.
> 'Tis one encountered here and everywhere;
> A travelling cripple, by the trunk cut short,
> And stumping on his arms. In sailor's garb

detailed account of Wegg's performances, see Wilfred P. Dvorak, 'Dickens and Popular Culture: Silas Wegg's Ballads in *Our Mutual Friend*', *The Dickensian* 86 (1990), pp. 142–57.

32. See Chapter 1, p. 15 and n. 3. In *Ulysses* this role is given to the nameless 'blind stripling', a piano tuner—not a beggar, but still a frail, precarious, marginal figure. He first appears in 'Lestrygonians' when Bloom helps him across the road (8.231–2); he is jostled on the street by Cashel Boyle O'Connor Fitzmaurice Tisdall Farrell in 'Wandering Rocks', and curses him: 'You're blinder nor I am, you bitch's bastard!' (10.322); Miss Douce praises his touch on the piano in 'Sirens' (11.338); in 'Ithaca' he follows the 'maimed sailor' in the list of degrees of misery to which Bloom might be reduced (17.855).

33. 'On Beggars', *Frazer's Magazine* xxxiii (January–June 1846), pp. 669–70.

> Another lies at length, beside a range
> Of well-formed characters, with chalk inscribed
> Upon the smooth flint stones...[34]

'In sailor's garb' registers a slight but distinct withholding of trust. Perhaps this beggar was never really a sailor; by the mid-century, Henry Mayhew's collaborator Andrew Halliday was reporting on a regular racket, featuring the 'turnpike sailor' who is 'generally the offspring of some inhabitant of the most notorious haunts of a seaport town, and has seldom been at sea', whose 'face bears the stamp of diabolically low cunning', and who speaks 'in a gruff voice, intended to convey the idea of hardships, storms, shipwrecks, battles, and privations'. But even Halliday concedes 'that at times a begging sailor may be met, who has really been a seaman, and who is a proper object of benevolence'.[35] Again, it must be emphasized that Joyce makes no authorial judgement as to the one-legged sailor's authenticity. It is more a question of what readers at the time would assume. For what it is worth, it does not occur to Father Conmee that this particular beggar is a fraud; and Father Conmee is a worldly man. In the 'Eumaeus' episode, Bloom and Stephen encounter another sailor whose veracity is more questionable, and who, indeed, fulfils another of the stereotypes associated with sailors, that of Sinbad, or the Ancient Mariner, as a teller of tall tales.[36]

Binding all these sailor-figures together is of course the hero, sailor, and wanderer who gives his name to the book, Ulysses, and his author, Homer. The sailor is a mutilated parody of the bard, but recognizable nonetheless. As the old rhyme has it: 'Seven wealthy Towns contend for HOMER Dead / Through which the Living HOMER begged his Bread'.[37] He is called a 'minstrel', though he plays no instrument, but figuratively he carries Homer's lyre. He is also Homer's hero, Ulysses, who disguises himself as a beggar when he returns to Ithaca, and is

---

34. William Wordsworth, *The Prelude* (1850) vii 199–207. In the street where the narrator meets this familiar sight, 'files of ballads dangle from dead walls' (l. 193); he has just left a neighbourhood whose 'sights and sounds' include 'a minstrel band / Of Savoyards' and 'An English ballad-singer' (ll. 173, 178, 180).

35. Andrew Halliday, 'Naval and Military Beggars', in volume 4 ('Those That Will Not Work') of Henry Mayhew's *London Labour and the London Poor* (London: Charles Griffin, 1861), pp. 415–17. Halliday remarks that 'At times the turnpike sailor roars out a song in praise of British valour by sea; but of late this "lay" has been unfrequent'.

36. See below, pp. 112–13.

37. One of a number of versions of this epigram; this one is attributed to the clergyman and man of letters Thomas Seward (1708–90).

therefore one of the many doubles of Bloom in his wanderings around the city. Sailors are famously proverbially and indiscriminate; when Buck Mulligan catches sight of Bloom leaving the National Library at the end of the 'Scylla and Charybdis' episode, he mockingly casts him in this role:

—The wandering jew, Buck Mulligan whispered with clown's awe. Did you see his eye? He looked upon you to lust after you. I fear thee, ancient mariner. O, Kinch, thou art in peril. Get thee a breechpad.   (9.279)

The sailor's appetite for casual, rough, impersonal sex also occurs to Molly Bloom: 'by the Lord God I was thinking would I go around by the quays there some dark evening where nobodyd know me and pick up a sailor off the sea thatd be hot on for it and not care a pin whose I was only to do it off up in a gate somewhere' ('Circe', 18.925). Molly, who grew up in Gibraltar, also remembers 'the sailors playing all birds fly and I say stoop and washing up dishes they called it on the pier' (18.932); her first lover, Harry Mulvey, was a lieutenant in the Royal Navy.[38] In 'Wandering Rocks' Stephen Dedalus, too, conjures up this stereotype, as a fantasy of 'exotic' arousal, masked by disgust, passes through his brain:

She dances in a foul gloom where gum burns with garlic. A sailorman, rust-bearded, sips from a beaker rum and eyes her. A long and seafed silent rut. She dances, capers, wagging her sowish haunches and her hips, on her gross belly flapping a ruby egg.   (10.310)

His being a cripple aligns him with Nelson, the hero of whom he sings, and whose statue, standing on its pillar in the centre of Dublin, is the focus of the 'Parable of the Plums', the story that Stephen relates to his

---

38. 'All birds fly' and 'I say stoop' are games in which the players have to follow the commands of a leader, under penalty of forfeit; Iona Opie comments on 'All birds fly' that it is 'typical of games played by sailors, in which alertness is the chief requirement and inattention is punished with the strap'. 'Washing up dishes' may be a slang euphemism for urinating (*Gifford* 633). Bloom first mentions Mulvey in 'Nausicaa', in the context of first love: 'Molly, lieutenant Mulvey that kissed her under the Moorish wall beside the gardens' (13.483); in 'Ithaca' he assumes Mulvey to be 'the first term of [the] series' of Molly's lovers (17.863). Mulvey is threaded through Molly's monologue, right to the end of the book where she remembers Bloom's proposal of marriage and the sailors' games just mentioned: 'I was thinking of so many things he didnt know of Mulvey and Mr Stanhope and Hester and father and old Captain Groves and the sailors playing all birds fly [etc.]'. Note that Mulvey is the first of this 'series' too.

uncomprehending listeners in 'Aeolus' (7.183–9). In this crafty anecdote, two old women climb laboriously to the top of the pillar to enjoy the famous view. It makes them giddy (again, the theme of loss of balance), so they hitch up their skirts and sit down, 'peering up at the statue of the onehandled adulterer' (7.187). But this gives them a crick in the neck, so they end up simply eating the twenty-four plums they have brought with them and spitting the stones over the railings. Nelson is a cripple like the one-legged sailor, like him a dubious figure of imperial power and sexual potency, but also of frustration and lack. Admired and resented, he is an inescapable presence, and an irresistible target. The song the one-legged sailor is growling out, 'The Death of Nelson', measures the degree to which Ireland remains in thrall to England, enthralled by England, though England may also be disfigured and degraded.

No song is quoted in its complete textual form in *Ulysses*; even songs that are sung from beginning to end, such as 'M'appari' or 'The Croppy Boy' in 'Sirens', are rendered by paraphrase as much as direct citation. 'The Death of Nelson' is represented by two key phrases, one a recycling of the famous signal at Trafalgar, 'England expects that every man will do his duty', the other an allusion to the three traditional spurs to courage in battle: 'England, home and beauty'. But I think Joyce had in mind the odd way in which these phrases function in the song as a whole; the song serves his purpose so well because the England of 'England expects' and the England of 'England, home and beauty' are not quite the same.

Here, then, is the full text of 'The Death of Nelson':

> 'Twas in Trafalgar's bay
> We saw the Frenchman lay,
> Each heart was bounding then.
> We scorned the foreign yoke,
> For our Ships were British Oak,
> And hearts of oak our men!
> Our Nelson mark'd them on the wave,
> Three cheers our gallant Seamen gave,
> Nor thought of home or beauty.
> Along the line this signal ran,
> England expects that ev'ry man
> This day will do his duty!
>
> And now the cannons roar
> Along th'affrighted shore,

Our Nelson led the way,
His Ship the Vict'ry nam'd!
Long be that Vict'ry famed,
For Vict'ry crowned the day!
But dearly was that conquest bought,
Too well the gallant Hero fought,
For England, home and beauty.
He cried as 'midst the fire he ran,
"England shall find that ev'ry man
This day will do his duty!"

At last the fatal wound,
Which spread dismay around,
The Hero's breast received;
"Heav'n fights on our side,
The day's our own," he cried!
"Now long enough I've lived!
In honour's cause my life was past,
In honour's cause I fell at last,
For England, home and beauty."
Thus ending life as he began,
England confessed that ev'ry man,
That day had done his duty!

In the first stanza 'home and beauty' are not associated with 'England', and are *not* to be thought of; they evoke sentiments which might distract men from concentrating on the matter in hand, 'doing their duty'. In the second stanza, however, the phrase 'England, home and beauty' has become the motivation for fighting well—'too well', it is oddly said, in Nelson's case, as though excess of zeal led to his death. At any rate, 'England' now has two meanings: it is the authority licensed to demand of every man that he do his duty, and that which every man is doing his duty to preserve. In the third stanza Nelson himself endorses this conjunction: 'In honour's cause my life was past, / In honour's cause I fell at last, / For England, home and beauty'. And yet the last three lines— 'Thus ending life as he began, / England confessed that ev'ry man, / That day had done his duty!'—are grammatically incoherent, and suggest an impossible conflation of Nelson's personal sacrifice with the behaviour of the entire fleet.

It does not seem unjust or unkind to say that 'The Death of Nelson' is a bad poem, but a bad poem may be of interest if it catches the attention of a great artist. What caught Joyce's attention, I think, was precisely the incoherence and instability of the poem's terms. We must remember that it was written only six years after Trafalgar, when Nelson's legend was still not fixed and, in particular, the nature of his relations to 'home and beauty' was a matter of continuing scandal. If Lady Hamilton was the 'beauty' in Nelson's life, she could stand neither for 'honour' nor 'home'; on the other hand, the song covertly acknowledges Nelson's sexual appetite as appropriate to his vocation, since sailors are types of sexual license; the 'fatal wound' which the hero receives in his 'breast' is a common trope of sexual passion, and the 'gallant Hero' is a conqueror in more than one sense. To 'do one's duty' carries a sexual meaning, as in the phrase 'conjugal duty', though in Nelson's case the duty lay outside wedlock. Victory is allied to adultery; the odd term out, the losing term so to speak, is 'home'. In *Ulysses*, Bloom's home is violated by adultery; Molly's lover, Blazes Boylan—vain, boastful, gallant—stands in for Nelson, and both are travestied in the figure of the one-legged sailor, who is also the bard who chants their conquests. That Molly should throw him a coin is apt: as a sailor, he stimulates her sexual appetite; as a bard, he is rewarded for telling her what she wants to hear. Her generosity is specifically seen as an aspect of her body, and her disembodied arm responds to the sailor's missing leg by suggesting a kind of surplus of fleshiness, all the more erotic for being constrained: 'A plump bare generous arm shone, was seen, held forth from a white petticoatbodice and taut shiftstraps'.

The pointed, specific allusions to the plot of the novel contained in the figure of the one-legged sailor don't exhaust his significance. For a start, his song, 'The Death of Nelson', pops up in other places in the novel in the form of travesty or burlesque. It is there from the very first episode, 'Telemachus', in which Buck Mulligan presses Stephen for money:

— Seriously, Dedalus. I'm stony. Hurry out to your school kip and bring us back some money. Today the bards must drink and junket. Ireland expects that every man this day will do his duty.
— That reminds me, Haines said, rising, that I have to visit your national library today.   (1.17–18)[39]

---

39. The association of the song with a demand for money takes us back to Dickens's *Our Mutual Friend* (see n. 31) and to Silas Wegg's (mis)appropriations of the ballads and songs from which he made his living; when Wegg has (or thinks he has) Mr Boffin under his thumb, he boasts of his power to extort money from him: "'I've got him under inspection, and I'll inspect him. // *Along the line the signal ran / England*

We know that Mulligan is not parodying Nelson's signal itself, but its version in 'The Death of Nelson', because the original signal simply read 'England expects that every man will do his duty'; the phrase 'England expects that every man *this day* will do his duty' was dictated by the lilting metre of S. J. Arnold's song-lyric. Mulligan's joke reduces the concept of 'duty' to performance in a drinking bout; but mock-epic has a double edge, since it may be that this, after all, is what Irish heroism amounts to. Haines's response obliquely acknowledges the point: Mulligan's insistence on 'today' ('Today the bards must drink and junket... this day') prompts him to remember that he '[has] to visit your national library today'. He *has to* do it today because it is on his schedule, presumably; but the form of words also suggests that it's his duty. What Haines is looking for in the national library is Ireland's Celtic past, an English fantasy to which Joyce believed the Irish themselves were addicted. When Haines misses Stephen's improvised lecture on *Hamlet*, he misses something that turns the tables on him, an Irish myth of Shakespeare rather than an English myth of the Irish bards. Mulligan both plays up to Haines's notions and makes fun of them, by calling Stephen 'Wandering Ængus', alluding to Yeats's 'Song of Wandering Ængus', one of his earliest reworkings of Celtic myth, exactly the kind of facile lyric that would appeal to Haines, as it had done to a generation of *fin-de-siècle* English readers.[40] But Stephen Dedalus, if he ever resembled Yeats's Wandering Ængus, abandoned the search for the silver apples of the moon and the golden apples of the sun at the end of *Portrait of the Artist* and set out on a different journey. He is deaf to Ireland's call to be one of her 'bards', or to conform to her expectation that he will do his 'duty'. He has no intention of being entombed in the national library. Against this fate the one-legged sailor utters a kind of protest on his behalf.[41]

Mulligan is not the only character to transform 'England expects' into 'Ireland expects'. 'Lifeboat Sunday', Mr Bloom thinks in 'Eumaeus',

---

expects as this present man / Will keep Boffin to his duty. // —Boffin, I'll see you home"' (bk. iv, ch. 3).

40. W. B. Yeats, 'The Song of Wandering Ængus', *The Wind Among the Reeds* (1899).

41. As David Wright points out, Stephen is also linked to the one-legged sailor through Haines's and Mulligan's remarks about his loss of balance (*Ironies of Ulysses*, p. 51). See also Brook Thomas, 'The Balance of History', *James Joyce Quarterly* 23.3 (Spring 1986), pp. 359–61. In 'Circe' Stephen 'falls' in the sexual sense, becomes unbalanced in his behaviour, physically staggers and totters, and is finally 'felled' by Private Carr. It is not Mulligan who helps him to his feet, but Bloom.

was a very laudable institution to which the public at large, no matter where living, inland or seaside, as the case might be, having it brought home to them like that, should extend its gratitude also to the harbourmasters and coastguard service who had to man the rigging and push off and out amid the elements, whatever the season, when duty called *Ireland expects that every man* and so on, and sometimes had a terrible time of it in the wintertime not forgetting the Irish lights, Kish and others, liable to capsize at any moment rounding which he once with his daughter had experienced some remarkably choppy, not to say stormy, weather.   (16.728)[42]

It is typical of Bloom's pacifism that when he thinks of heroism at sea, he thinks of life-saving, not killing: *Ireland expects* men to risk their lives on behalf of others. His mundane, clichéd train of thought is subject to bathos, but has a human aspect missing from Mulligan's jaunty wit.

Bloom's reflections here have been prompted by the encounter with the sailor in the cabman's shelter, who calls himself 'W. B. Murphy', and whom I'll come to shortly. But this is not the first occasion in the novel in which he thinks about the lives of sailors. In 'Nausicaa', Bloom's reverie on Sandymount strand takes him from bats and the language of birds and their migratory flights to a meditation on the sailor's lot:

> Ba. Who knows what they're always flying for. Insects? That bee last week got into the room playing with his shadow on the ceiling. Might be the one bit me, come back to see. Birds too never find out what they say. Like our small talk. And says she and says he. Nerve they have to fly over the ocean and back. Lot must be killed in storms, telegraph wires. Dreadful life sailors have too. Big brutes of ocean-going steamers floundering along in the dark, lowing out like seacows. *Faugh a ballagh*. Out of that, bloody curse to you. Others in vessels, bit of a handkerchief sail, pitched about like snuff at a wake when the stormy winds do blow. Married too. Sometimes away for years at the ends of the earth somewhere. No ends really because it's round. Wife in every port they say. She has a good job if she minds it till Johnny comes marching home again. If ever

---

42. Songs run in Bloom's head as much as in that of any other character in the novel, and it is at least plausible that he, like Mulligan, is recalling 'The Death of Nelson' rather than just the phrase 'England expects…'. He certainly knows the song; he 'quotes' it in one of the transformations he undergoes during the 'Circe' chapter: 'MRS BREEN: You were the lion of the night with your seriocomic recitation and you looked the part. You were always a favourite with the ladies. // BLOOM: *(Squire of dames, in dinner jacket, with watered-silk facings, blue masonic badge in his buttonhole, black bow and mother-of-pearl studs, a prismatic champagne glass tilted in his hand)* Ladies and gentlemen, I give you Ireland, home and beauty. // MRS BREEN: The dear dead days beyond recall. Love's old sweet song' ('Circe', 15.574). Note that Mrs Breen responds to Bloom's 'toast' by quoting two lines from 'Love's Old Sweet Song', another of the key songs in the novel.

he does. Smelling the tail end of ports. How can they like the sea? Yet they do.
The anchor's weighed. Off he sails with a scapular or a medal on him for luck.
                    (13.493–4; I have altered 'Nerve they have' from 'Nerve?
                                      they have' in the source text.)

As always, Bloom's thoughts are threaded by songs; there are four in
this short extract, and they touch on politics, seafaring, war, and love.[43]
'*Faugh a ballagh*' was, with the title 'Fag a Bealaċ', a nationalist song by
Charles Gavan Duffy, who notes that the phrase, which means 'Clear
the road', began as 'the cry with which the clans of Connaught and
Munster used in faction fights to come through a fair with high hearts
and smashing shillelahs' and was then taken up as a battle cry by Irish
regiments in the Napoleonic Wars.[44] Again, it is characteristic of
Bloom's dislike of swagger and bullying to apply this phrase to the way
in which 'Big brutes of oceangoing steamers' shouldered their way past
smaller craft. 'When the stormy winds do blow' is from the chorus of
an eighteenth-century ballad, 'The Mermaid'; the 'fair pretty maid /
With a comb and a glass in her hand' is an omen of death to the mari-
ners that encounter her:

> The up starts the captain of our gallant ship,
>   And a brave young man was he:
> 'I've a wife and a child in fair Bristol town,
>   But a widow I fear she'll be.'
> [Chorus]
> For the raging seas did roar,
>   And the stormy winds did blow [etc.][45]

The mermaid or siren combing her hair in the mirror is one of many
images of Molly Bloom, whose sexuality is double, connoting, as
befits a goddess, both death and life. 'When Johnny comes marching
home again' was a Union army marching song in the American Civil

---

43. Information from *Gifford* 401.
44. Charles Gavan Duffy (1816–1903) wrote the song in 1842 when editor of *The Nation*
and published it in *The Spirit of the Nation* (1843), with the title 'Fag a Bealaċ' and the
subtitle 'A National Hymn, chaunted in full chorus at the Symposiacs of the Editors
and Contributors of *The Nation*'. In subsequent reprintings of *The Spirit of the Nation*
the title phrase became 'Fág an Beallach'.
45. 'The Mermaid' is Child #289 (*English and Scottish Popular Ballads*, ed. Francis James
Child, 5 vols. [Boston, MA and New York: Houghton, Mifflin and Company, 1882–98]
v 148–52). Child records six versions, the earliest conjecturally dated 1765; the text
varies widely, but the mermaid is always a fatal sign. My quotation is from version B,
whose source is a Victorian collection, *Popular Music of the Olden Time*, ed. William
Chappell (London: Cramer, Beale & Chappell, n.d. [1855–6]).

War; it evidently has nothing to do with seafaring, and seems comically incongruous here, but it was written by the Irish-American Patrick Gilmore, one of the most famous bandleaders of the nineteenth century, and it, too, is taken by Bloom not in the context of war and glory, but of a doubtful homecoming and dubious welcome.[46] Last, and most significant for my purpose, is 'The Anchor's Weighed', the title of a song by S. J. Arnold and John Braham—the same duo who wrote 'The Death of Nelson'.

> The tear fell gently from her eye
> When last we parted on the shore;
> My bosom heav'd with many a sigh,
> To think I ne'er might see her more.
> 'Dear youth,' she cried,
> 'And canst thou haste away.
> My heart will break,—a little moment stay;
> Alas, I cannot, I cannot part from thee.'
> 'The anchor's weigh'd, the anchor's weigh'd,
> Farewell! farewell! remember me.'
>
> 'Weep not, my love,' I trembling said,
> 'Doubt not a constant heart like mine;
> I ne'er can meet another maid
> Whose charms can fix that heart like thine!'
> 'Go, then,' she cried,
> 'But let thy constant mind
> Oft think of her you leave in tears behind.'
> 'Dear maid, this last embrace my pledge shall be!
> The anchor's weigh'd, the anchor's weigh'd,
> Farewell! farewell! remember me.'[47]

The sentiment here is on the side of the woman, who is likely to be abandoned and betrayed by her departing lover, whatever his protestations. The repetition of 'last', as an indicator of time ('When last we parted') and of finality ('This last embrace'), tells us as much. The sailor himself is doubtful as to his homecoming—as Bloom was sceptical that Johnny would ever come marching home again. The sailor with a wife in every port is more crudely represented as 'Smelling

---

46. The song itself adapts an Irish lyric, 'Johnny I hardly knew ye'.
47. The line 'Farewell! farewell! remember me' may have been influenced by the Ghost in *Hamlet* ('Adieu, adieu! Hamlet, remember me' [I v 91]).

the tail end of ports', the red-light districts where the sailor spends his wages before rejoining his true love, and true home, the sea.

By the time Bloom and Stephen meet W. B. Murphy in the cabman's shelter, then, Joyce has already set up a number of associations with seafaring and the sea, and Murphy resumes these associations. He has 'circumnavigated a bit', like Ulysses, like Bloom; his red hair denotes him as a sexual adventurer and man of violence; he is the father of a lost son, and claims, like many compulsive voyagers, to be weary of the sea; he is even 'a bit of a literary cove in his own small way'; above all he is a teller of tall tales, both about himself and others: my favourite is the delightful vignette of Stephen's father, Simon Dedalus, as a crack shot touring the world with Hengler's Royal Circus and shooting eggs off the tops of bottles at fifty yards.[48] But this shifty character affirms his own identity with circumstantial detail:

— Murphy's my name, the sailor continued, W. B. Murphy, of Carrigaloe. Know where that is?
— Queenstown Harbour, Stephen replied.
— That's right, the sailor said. Fort Camden and Fort Carlisle. That's where I hails from. My little woman's down there. She's waiting for me, I know. *For England, home and beauty.* She's my own true wife I haven't seen for seven years now, sailing about.   ('Eumaeus', 16.719)

The connection between W. B. Murphy and the one-legged sailor is made via the quotation from 'The Death of Nelson', which seems even more at odds with its Irish setting than on its previous appearances. Yet the sailor who affirms his Irishness with such geographical precision is linked to Nelson by his name, since 'Murphy' is the 'Anglicized form of Gael[ic] "Ó Murchadha", "descendant of *Murchadh*", a personal name composed of the elements *muir* sea + *cadh* warrior'.[49] Murphy's

---

48. Circumnavigation, pp. 720–1; red hair and beard, *passim*; sex, pp. 721 and 766 (where Bloom imagines him spending time in 'some sponger's bawdy-house of retired beauties off Sheriff street lower', telling 'sixchamber revolver anecdotes' to the 'mermaids' and 'mauling their largesized charms betweenwhiles with rough and tumble gusto'); violence, pp. 725 and 735 (where Bloom suspects him of being a released convict, who had perhaps 'done for his man'); fatherhood, p. 728; weariness, pp. 727, 728; literature, pp. 767–8 (where he declares that his favourite books are *The Arabian Nights' Entertainment* and *Red as a Rose is She*); Simon Dedalus as crack shot, p. 718; tall tales, p. 734 (where Bloom remarks to Stephen: '— Our mutual friend's stories are like himself [...] Do you think they are genuine?' Note the occurrence of the title phrase of Dickens's novel).

49. *The Oxford Names Companion*, ed. Patrick Hanks, Flavia Hodges, A. D. Mills, and Adrian Room (Oxford: Oxford University Press, 2002), p. 443. The exact locations

other affirmation—that his 'little woman' is 'waiting for him' at home and that she is 'his own true wife'—rings the changes on Bloom's complex fate as Ulysses, the wanderer who returns to find himself betrayed, yet not supplanted. Murphy again casts himself as Nelson, motivated by 'England, home and beauty', but the identification is preposterous and Bloom will have none of it. His response to Murphy's declaration is to think of stories about sailors returning home to find that their wives have given them up for dead—stories such as Tennyson's 'Enoch Arden'—and this will not be his fate. Molly remains his 'own true wife' despite the lovers she has taken. Boylan, the most recent, resembles Nelson in being a 'onehandled adulterer'—not physically crippled but humanly lacking. He is able to penetrate Molly but not, so to speak, to enter in to her. Molly's gesture in throwing the coin to the one-legged sailor 'for England, home and beauty', while she sits at her window preparing for Boylan's visit, is deeply ironic; it is Bloom whose return really matters to her, and to whom, in turn, 'home and beauty'—if not England—really matter.

The sailor in the cabman's shelter therefore both sums up Bloom as Ulysses, and falls short of him; just as Bloom, the unseamanlike sailor, the cuckolded Ulysses, the unconquering hero, falls short of the models of sexual prowess or military glory against which he is measured, yet in doing so fulfils the purpose of the novel more completely, more humanly, than he could ever do as epic protagonist. After all, 'The Death of Nelson' is a song that exalts death and sacrifice over the very qualities it supposedly cherishes. If Bloom cannot match the 'onehandled adulterer's' glamour, he can avoid his fate. At the end of 'Ithaca', it is another sailor with whom he is identified, as he falls asleep rocked by cadences that are like the swell of the waves, with

> Sinbad the Sailor and Tinbad the Tailor and Jinbad the Jailer and Whinbad the Whaler and Ninbad the Nailer and Finbad the Failer and Binbad the Bailer and Pinbad the Pailer and Minbad the Mailer and Hinbad the Hailer and Rinbad the Railer and Dinbad the Kailer and Vinbad the Quailer and Linbad the Yailer and Xinbad the Phthailer [...]   (17.871)

Some of the rhyme words for 'Sailor' can be attached to Bloom himself, or to the people he has encountered during the day: 'Tailor' is shared

given by the sailor are in the vicinity of Cork, which is where the Dedalus family 'hails from'.

by Boylan and Bloom ('Sirens', 11.360–1; 'Circe', 15.617); 'Failer' recalls
Bloom's money troubles and his impotence; 'Mailer' his letter writing;
'Hailer' the many instances of characters 'hailing' each other (or a cab),
along with the 'Hail Mary' prayer, and so on. But in the end the rhythm
of the sentence carries all before it. In this children's chanting game, or
lullaby, the figure of Sinbad, derived both from the Arabian Nights and
a Dublin pantomime, is transformed by alphabet magic into nonsensical forms, as Bloom's consciousness fragments and dissolves.

5

The voice of an ancient spring

The following episode takes place in Virginia Woolf's novel *Mrs. Dalloway*, published in 1925. *Mrs. Dalloway* has no chapters, but we can locate the episode a little under half-way through the novel, and it occurs around midday. Clarissa Dalloway's old friend Peter Walsh is waiting to cross the Marylebone Road opposite Regent's Park underground station; close behind him are Rezia Smith and her husband Septimus, on their way to Harley Street to see the nerve specialist Sir William Bradshaw, who is going, Rezia believes, to make Septimus better (Figure 5.1).

It is Peter Walsh's train of thought that the old woman's song interrupts, though when the passage begins he is not sure what is being sung or who is singing it:

> A sound interrupted him; a frail quivering sound, a voice bubbling up without direction, vigour, beginning or end, running weakly and shrilly and with an absence of all human meaning into
>
> ee um fah um so
> foo swee too eem oo—
>
> the voice of no age or sex, the voice of an ancient spring spouting from the earth; which issued, just opposite Regent's Park Tube Station, from a tall quivering shape, like a funnel, like a rusty pump, like a wind-beaten tree for ever barren of leaves which lets the wind run up and down its branches singing
>
> ee um fah um so
> foo swee too eem oo,
>
> and rocks and creaks and moans in the eternal breeze.
> Through all ages—when the pavement was grass, when it was swamp, through the age of tusk and mammoth, through the age of silent sunrise—the battered woman—for she wore a skirt—with her right hand exposed,

Figure 5.1. Regent's Park underground station entrance, 1921

her left clutching at her side, stood singing of love—love which has lasted
a million years, she sang, love which prevails, and millions of years ago,
her lover, who had been dead these centuries, had walked, she crooned,
with her in May; but in the course of ages, long as summer days, and
flaming, she remembered, with nothing but red asters, he had gone;
death's enormous sickle had swept those tremendous hills, and when at
last she laid her hoary and immensely aged head on the earth, now
become a mere cinder of ice, she implored the Gods to lay by her side a
bunch of purple heather, there on her high burial place which the last
rays of the last sun caressed; for then the pageant of the universe would
be over.

As the ancient song bubbled up opposite Regent's Park Tube Station,
still the earth seemed green and flowery; still, though it issued from so
rude a mouth, a mere hole in the earth, muddy too, matted with root
fibres and tangled grasses, still the old bubbling burbling song, soaking
through the knotted roots of infinite ages, and skeletons and treasure,
streamed away in rivulets over the pavement and all along the Marylebone
Road, and down towards Euston, fertilising, leaving a damp stain.

Still remembering how once in some primeval May she had walked
with her lover, this rusty pump, this battered old woman with one hand
exposed for coppers, the other clutching her side, would still be there in
ten million years, remembering how once she had walked in May, where
the sea flows now, with whom it did not matter—he was a man, oh yes,
a man who had loved her. But the passage of ages had blurred the clarity
of that ancient May day; the bright petalled flowers were hoar and silver

frosted; and she no longer saw, when she implored him (as she did now quite clearly) "look in my eyes with thy sweet eyes intently," she no longer saw brown eyes, black whiskers or sunburnt face, but only a looming shape, a shadow shape, to which, with the bird-like freshness of the very aged, she still twittered "give me your hand and let me press it gently" (Peter Walsh couldn't help giving the poor creature a coin as he stepped into his taxi), "and if some one should see, what matter they?" she demanded; and her fist clutched at her side, and she smiled, pocketing her shilling, and all peering inquisitive eyes seemed blotted out, and the passing generations—the pavement was crowded with bustling middle-class people—vanished, like leaves, to be trodden under, to be soaked and steeped and made mould of by that eternal spring—

> ee um fah um so
> foo swee too eem oo.

"Poor old woman," said Rezia Warren Smith.

Oh poor old wretch! she said, waiting to cross.

Suppose it was a wet night? Suppose one's father, or somebody who had known one in better days had happened to pass, and saw one standing there in the gutter? And where did she sleep at night?

Cheerfully, almost gaily, the invincible thread of sound wound up into the air like the smoke from a cottage chimney, winding up clean beech trees and issuing in a tuft of blue smoke among the topmost leaves. "And if some one should see, what matter they?"

Since she was so unhappy, for weeks and weeks now, Rezia had given meanings to things that happened, almost felt sometimes that she must stop people in the street, if they looked good, kind people, just to say to them "I am unhappy"; and this old woman singing in the street "if some one should see, what matter they?" made her suddenly quite sure that everything was going to be right. They were going to Sir William Bradshaw; she thought his name sounded nice; he would cure Septimus at once. And then there was a brewer's cart, and the grey horses had upright bristles of straw in their tails; there were newspaper placards. It was a silly, silly dream, being unhappy.[1]

In *Ulysses*, the one-legged sailor who sings verses from 'The Death of Nelson' is not, taken in isolation, a conspicuous figure. His brief appearances—the longest is barely a page—might pass unnoticed in the novel's vast landscape, or be read as incidental urban scene painting. His significance emerges only when we 'read' the presence on the streets of Dublin of a wandering sailor who is also a beggar who is also

---

1. Virginia Woolf, *Mrs. Dalloway* [1925], ed. Anne E. Fernald (Cambridge: Cambridge University Press, 2015), pp. 72–5.

a singer as part of a larger pattern, which tells us that wandering sailors, beggars, and singers are indeed central to the novel's design. Virginia Woolf presents her street singer in diametrical opposition to this allusive patterning. The old woman is a singular, emblematic, powerful (and stationary) figure in the novel in which she appears; her song is not a fragment of a popular ballad, but something altogether less familiar and more complicated. She appears only once in the novel, and is neither anticipated by any other character or episode, nor subsequently remembered or cited. She is, as the very first words of the episode tell us, an *interruption* in the story.

What happens before and after this interruption, the perspective from which it is narrated, the characters to whom it relates—all this is of interest, and I will come to it in due course. But I begin with the street song itself, and its singer, apart from their significance in the novel's design.

On 8 June 1920 Virginia Woolf made the following entry in her diary:

My drive to Waterloo on top of a bus [was] very vivid. [...] An old beggar woman, blind, sat against a stone wall in Kingsway holding a brown mongrel in her arms and sang aloud. There was a recklessness about her; much in the spirit of London. Defiant—almost gay, clasping her dog as if for warmth. How many Junes has she sat there, in the heart of London? How she came to be there, what scenes she can go through, I can't imagine. O damn it all, I say, why can't I know all that too? Perhaps it was the song at night that seemed strange; she was singing shrilly, but for her own amusement, not begging. Then the fire engines came by—shrill too; with their helmets pale yellow in the moonlight. Sometimes everything gets into the same mood; how to define this one I don't know—It was gay, and yet terrible and fearfully vivid.[2]

She made use of this figure in *Jacob's Room*, published in 1922; it is one of the vignettes of urban life recorded in chapter 5:

Long past sunset an old blind woman sat on a camp-stool with her back to the stone wall of the Union of London and Smith's Bank, clasping a brown mongrel tight in her arms and singing out loud, not for coppers, no, from the depths of her gay wild heart—her sinful, tanned heart—for the child who fetches her is the fruit of sin, and should have been in bed, curtained, asleep, instead of hearing in the lamplight her mother's wild song, where she sits against the Bank, singing not for coppers, with her dog against her breast.[3]

2. *A Moment's Liberty: The Shorter Diary [of] Virginia Woolf*, ed. Anne Olivier Bell (London: Hogarth Press, 1990), pp. 108–9.
3. Virginia Woolf, *Jacob's Room*, ed. Kate Flint (Oxford: Oxford University Press, 2008), p. 89.

Neither in the diary entry nor *Jacob's Room* is the song identified, or quoted. In *Mrs. Dalloway*, the old woman is not blind, and has lost her dog. The dog is a conventional appendage of the metropolitan beggar; its being designated a *mongrel* makes it into a kind of symbolic attribute, like those carried by saints, and the transferred epithet *tanned*, though applied here to *heart* and not *skin*, suggests that the woman is a Gipsy, again, a conventional figure of the London street scene. The old woman in *Jacob's Room* is also encumbered, improbably, with a young daughter who is given the conventional role of caring for her presumably drunken parent; this child, too, disappears from the scene in *Mrs. Dalloway*, in part perhaps because the time of day has shifted from evening to noon. The fact that the original scene took place in the evening allows Woolf to speculate that the old woman, though at first clearly designated a *beggar*, is not in fact begging, but singing 'for her own amusement', or 'from the depths of her gay wild heart'.[4] In *Mrs. Dalloway*, by contrast, the old woman is not called a beggar, yet she is begging and Peter Walsh gives her a shilling—more than the 'coppers' she might usually expect.

There were, as indicated in earlier chapters, several kinds of street singer in London in the late nineteenth and early twentieth centuries. Some were professional entertainers, who made a living by singing ballads and popular songs, and who might either have their own regular 'pitch', or travel in a circuit from one location to another, depending on the season or time of day. Some accompanied themselves on a musical instrument, or had a partner who accompanied them; occasionally (though this was rarer) singers went about in groups. The old woman is not a professional singer in any of these senses; she is plainly a beggar, whose song, Mayhew and other reporters of street life tell us, serves as a pretext to avoid the charge of mendicancy. Yet this classification doesn't quite fit, or rather it stops short at the surface of things. It is a realistic observation, but realism is satisfied with conventional ways of seeing.

---

4. Woolf mentions this element of delight in one of her earliest published essays: 'I have seen violinists who were obviously using their instrument to express something in their own hearts as they swayed by the kerb in Fleet Street; and the copper, though rags make it acceptable, was, as it is to all who love their work, a perfectly incongruous payment' ('Street Music' [1905], in *The Essays of Virginia Woolf*, vol. I (1904–1912), ed. Andrew McNeillie (London: The Hogarth Press, 1986), p. 28. For another quotation from this essay, see below, p. 125.

As to the song itself, this is given to us first in the guise of gibberish: 'ee um fah um so / foo swee too eem oo'. The closest analogy I can think of for this is the 'transcription' of birdsong, which attempts to render syllabic phrases without semantic content. Walter Garstang, for example, in a book called *Songs of the Birds* published in 1922, gives this notation of a skylark's song:

> *Swee! Swee! Swee! Swee!*
> *Zwée-o! Zwée-o! Zwée-o! Zwée-o!*
> *Sís-is-is- Swée! Sís-is-is- Swée!*
> *Joo! Joo! Joo! Joo!*[5]

On the one hand, these 'words' are recognizable as human language, since they can be pronounced, but on the other hand, they don't make sense. They translate the bird's vocal performance into something we can reproduce, but without fully appropriating it, unlike many traditional renderings of a bird's song or call, such as Woolf uses elsewhere.[6] I don't know whether Woolf came across Garstang's book, or whether her use of the syllable 'swee' is coincidental; I do, however, think that both she and Garstang were influenced by the way in which 'swee' falls teasingly short of the definite word 'sweet'. But the difference is that 'ee um fah um so / foo swee too eem oo' represents a failure to render intelligible something which, we assume, *was* intelligible to begin with, and could be recovered if we had the key. The old woman is not singing nonsense; the transliteration makes nonsense of what she sings, like the defective copying by an ignorant scribe of a damaged manuscript. At the same time, this transliteration generates its own meaning, not as a sequence of words governed by grammatical and syntactical order, but as a sequence of sounds. Two of these happen to be spelled in the same way as English words—'so' and 'too'—but they can't be construed as 'meaning' what 'so' and 'too' mean in their ordinary usage. Of the ten sounds, three are repeated—*ee*, *um*, and *oo*—and two are not—*fah* and *so*. Of the repeated sounds, only the first, *ee*, occurs in both lines;

---

5. Walter Garstang, *Songs of the Birds* (London: Curwen Press, 1923), p. 63 (a 'revised and enlarged' edition of the work published in 1922). I discuss Garstang's book in relation to nineteenth-century poems about birdsong in *The Figure of the Singer* (Oxford: Oxford University Press, 2013), p. 78.

6. The cooing of a wood pigeon, for example, heard at intervals in *The Years*: 'Take two coos, Taffy. Take two coos...Tak' (Virginia Woolf, *The Years* [1937], ed. Anna Snaith [Cambridge: Cambridge University Press, 2012], pp. 66 ['1880'], 159, 169 ['1910'], 390 ['The Present Day']).

um occurs only in the first, and *oo* only in the second. Both the non-repeated sounds occur in the first line. Arguably *ee* and *um* merge in the second line to form *eem*, but apart from this tenuous connection, there is no link between the two lines, which don't rhyme and don't form a recognizable metrical unit. Each line has five separate syllables; you can fit them into a rough trochaic pattern ('<u>ee</u> um <u>fah</u> um <u>so</u> / <u>foo</u> swee <u>too</u> eem <u>oo</u>') or alternatively a dactylic pattern with catalexis ('<u>ee</u> um fah <u>um</u> so / <u>foo</u> swee too <u>eem</u> oo').[7] But then the sounds slur into each other: 'eeyum', 'sweetoo', 'eemoo'. The more you think about it, the more cunning it looks: an artefact of language which is neither speech, nor verse, nor song lyric, still less 'pure sound'—itself a nonsensical notion, at least in the medium of writing.

Virginia Woolf returned to this teasing formulation in the final pages of *The Years*, when the caretaker's children appear in Delia's drawing room and sing their incomprehensible song. Here is the first verse:

> Etho passo tanno hai,
> Fai donk to tu do,
> Mai to, kai to, lai to see
> Toh dom to tuh do —[8]

The nonsense language here, though it looks at first glance like that of the old woman in *Mrs. Dalloway*, is in fact fundamentally different. It is not monosyllabic, and the verse scans: it is common measure, the alternating four and three beats of innumerable ballads, hymns, popular songs, and nursery rhymes, from 'Sumer is acumen in / Lhude sing cuccu' and 'Mary had a little lamb, / Its fleece was white as snow' to 'O God, our help in ages past, / Our hope for years to come'.[9] The children's song in *The Years*, in other words, is connected to English literature and song in a way that is, I think, quite as deliberate on Virginia Woolf's part as is the absence of any such connection in the case of the old woman's song in *Mrs. Dalloway*.

The question of what the old woman is singing is hard to answer, and not simply because the phrases 'ee um fah um so / foo swee too

---

7. Imagine the line made up of 'proper' words: '<u>beat</u> some <u>far</u> drum <u>so</u> / <u>fool</u> sweet <u>too</u> seem <u>you</u>', or '<u>beat</u> some far <u>drum</u> so / <u>fool</u> sweet too <u>seem</u> you'.

8. *The Years*, p. 386. The scene takes place towards the end of the section called 'The Present Day'.

9. It is also one of the standard metres of lyric verse, as in many of Emily Dickinson's poems.

eem oo' are not reducible to semantic or metrical order. The 'song'
consists of sounds, but has not been composed by anyone; it is 'the
voice of no age or sex, the voice of an ancient spring spouting from
the earth'. Its 'absence of all human meaning' is linked to the indeter-
minate 'tall quivering shape' from which it comes; this 'shape' is then
successively compared to a 'funnel', a 'rusty pump', and a 'wind-beaten
tree for ever barren of leaves which lets the wind run up and down its
branches'. That last image is of the Aeolian harp, a type in Romantic
poetry of natural music, the wind in the trees being a form of breath,
of ideal inspiration, purged of human design. But the small word *lets* is
carefully chosen: the fact that the tree is 'barren of leaves' *lets* the wind
run up and down its branches; at the same time, the tree *lets* this happen, as though by its own volition. This trace of ambiguity is followed
by a kind of acoustic memory of Wordsworth: the tree 'rocks and
creaks and moans in the eternal breeze': 'rocks and creaks and moans'
are verbs here, but they can also be nouns, and together with the
vowel sound of 'breeze' they take us to the last verse of 'A slumber did
my spirit seal':

> No motion has she now, no force;
>   She neither hears nor sees;
> Rolled round in earth's diurnal course,
>   With rocks, and stones, and trees.[10]

These lines constitute one of the most resonant silences, or more properly silencings, in our literature; I hear in Woolf's sentence a challenge
to Wordsworth's natural sublimity, with its tremendous coercive power;
one form of the sublime answers another, *eternal breeze* against *diurnal
course*. The woman here is not silenced but singing.

She *is* a woman now, we learn: this is the second phase of Woolf's
evocation of the song. The 'wind-beaten tree' becomes a 'battered
woman', whose gender is indicated simply by the skirt she wears, and
simultaneously the song which was devoid of 'human meaning' has
acquired this meaning—acquired it in profusion. The old woman is
'singing of love', the power of Eros which, in ancient physics and
philosophy and poetry, holds the universe together, and is stronger
than death. It seems as though this primitive, rhapsodic form of love is

10. William Wordsworth, 'A Slumber Did My Spirit Seal', ll. 5–8, in *The Poems*, ed.
John O. Hayden, 2 vols. (Harmondsworth: Penguin Books, 1977), i 364; first published
in the second edition of *Lyrical Ballads* (1800).

timeless and general, but the long sentence that begins with 'Through all ages' and ends with 'the pageant of the universe would be over' contains the seeds of the third phase, the definite attribution of the song to a particular lyric and musical setting.

Starting with references to 'May', to 'red asters' and 'purple heather', and culminating in three quoted phrases—' "look in my eyes with thy sweet eyes intently" ', ' "give me your hand and let me press it gently" ', ' "and if some one should see, what matter they?" '—an actual song takes shape, an English translation of 'Allerseelen', or 'All Souls' Day', by the Austrian poet Hermann von Gilm, published in 1864 and set to music by a number of composers in the late nineteenth century and early twentieth century (Figure 5.2). The most famous setting is by Richard Strauss, and Virginia Woolf almost certainly knew it, but the English translation she uses, by Mrs Malcolm Lawson, was made to accompany a setting by the Belgian composer Eduard Lassen.[11] Here are the first two stanzas, transcribed from sheet music published in 1899:

> Stell' auf den Tisch die duftenden Reseden,
>> Die letzten rothen Astern trag' herbei,
> Und lass' uns wieder von der Liebe reden,
>> Wie einst im Mai, wie einst im Mai.
>
> Gieb mir die Hand, dass ich sie heimlich drücke,
>> Und wenn man's sieht, mir ist es einerlei.
> Gieb mir nur einen deiner süssen Blicke,
>> Wie einst im Mai, wie einst im Mai.
>
> Lay by my side your bunch of purple heather,
>> The last red asters of an autumn day,
> And let us sit and talk of love together,
>> As once in May, as once in May.
>
> Give me your hand, that I may press it gently,
>> And if the others see, what matter they?
> Look in mine eyes with your sweet eyes intently,
>> As once in May, as once in May.[12]

11. The LiederNet Archive (http://www.lieder.net/lieder/get_text.html?TextId=6190) lists eighteen settings between 1878 and 1914, the majority in the 1890s. Strauss's version is op. 10 (*Acht Gedichte aus 'Letzte Blätter' von Hermann von Gilm*) no. 8 (1882–3). Lassen's is op. 85 (*Sechs Lieder für 1 Singstimme mit Pianofortebegleitung*) no. 3 (1886).

12. *All Souls Day and Resolution* | *Songs* | *With original English version by Mrs. Malcolm Lawson* | *Music by Eduard Lassen* (London: Bosworth & Co., 1899), pp. 3–4. The German title 'Allerseelen' appears below the English 'All Souls Day' on p. 3, with attribution to

Figure 5.2. Eduard Lassen (1830–1904), 'All Souls Day' ('Allerseelen'), Op. 85, no. 3, in *All Souls Day and Resolution: Songs* (London: Bosworth & Co., 1899)

Hermann von Gilm; in contrast to the phrase 'original English version' on the cover, the phrase used here is 'English adaptation by Mrs. Malcolm Lawson'. Lawson's translation is indeed not exact: a more literal rendition of the first two lines, for example, would be: 'Place on the table the fragrant mignonette, bring hither the last red asters'; in the fifth line, 'that I may press it gently' should be 'that I may press it secretly'; the

A great deal has been written on the significance of Woolf's choice of this song about All Souls' Day, the day of the dead, which touches on the past, present, and future of several of the main characters in the book; but my immediate concern is with something more mundane, namely the improbability of its being performed by a beggar outside a London tube station in 1925. Very few if any of the numerous critics who have written on this episode of the novel, some of them at great length and in intensive detail, seem troubled by this incongruity.[13] It seems to be taken for granted, as though it were no more than a literary or dramatic convention—like Oliver Twist being brought up in a workhouse and speaking standard English. But the unreality of this third version of the song seems to me to be essential to any reading of it.

Virginia Woolf knew perfectly well what she was doing. She knew the kinds of song performed by street singers and musicians in London at any time from her childhood in the 1880s to the date of the novel, because she heard them first-hand and recorded them in her fiction and non-fiction. In the early essay 'Street Music' she mentions the 'crude melody' of 'German band[s]' and 'Italian organ grinders', and concludes with a self-confessed fantasy—that 'instead of libraries, philanthropists would bestow free music upon the poor, so that at each street corner the melodies of Beethoven and Brahms and Mozart could be heard'.[14] That was evidently not the case in the London she knew. Ballads, hymns, popular songs, music-hall numbers, light opera—you could hear all of these on a London street, but you wouldn't be hearing a melancholy German *lied* set by a modern composer of

seventh line should read 'Give me just one of your sweet looks'. Bosworth & Co. had published the song in 1896 with a more faithful translation by C. Valery (though misspelling Gilm's name as 'Hilm'). I have adjusted the layout as verse; in the sheet music the lyrics conform to the musical score. In Gilm's original poem, the refrain 'Wie einst in Mai' in the last line of each stanza is not repeated.

13. For example: 'Elegiac aspects aside, and these have been wonderfully useful in interpretation, what is remarkable is this reversal of the high and low or popular art continuum [...] Strauss's words [sic] are not just filtered through this popular, oral form, they are remade as a feminized British folk culture—an international, or read in this context, a European, high art fragment recirculates through the old woman, a sexing of the metropole' (Jennifer Wicke, '"Mrs. Dalloway" Goes to Market: Woolf, Keynes, and Modern Markets', *NOVEL: A Forum on Fiction* 28.1 [Autumn 1994], p. 18).

14. 'Street Music' (1905; see above, n. 4), pp. 27, 31–2.

high-art music—the kind of music performed indoors, whether in a
drawing room or concert hall. Woolf's exact knowledge of the street
music scene is on show in *The Years*, which covers the period of her
own life from '1880' to 'The Present Day' of the 1930s. In '1880' we read
of an 'elderly street singer, who had been swaying along the kerb, with
a fisherman's cap stuck jauntily on the back of his head, lustily chanting "Count your blessings, Count your blessings —" [...] "Count your
blessings. Every One"'—the chorus of a popular American hymn.[15] In
'1891', Eleanor hears a barrel-organ playing 'Sur le pont d'Avignon';[16]
in '1907' a popular waltz, 'After the Ball', becomes the craze of the city,
and is described with humorous exasperation as 'the eternal waltz [...]
like a serpent that swallowed its own tail, since the ring was complete
from Hammersmith to Shoreditch'.[17] In '1914' another barrel-organ,
'fluting its merry little jig further down the street', gets intertwined
with Martin's humming of an old nursery rhyme, 'I had a little nut
tree'.[18] These instances, whatever their symbolic import in the novel,
are grounded in realistic observation; they correspond to what readers
might themselves have experienced. The old woman in *Mrs. Dalloway*
does not belong in their company.

   The question of what the old woman was 'really' singing turns out
to be a red herring. We can't 'translate' 'ee um fah um so / foo swee
too eem oo' into 'Give me your hand, that I may press it gently, / And
if the others see, what matter they?' On the contrary, Woolf has set up
an impassable barrier between her transliteration of those initial
monosyllables and the lilting, rhyming phrases that follow. If the three
versions of the song that I have identified—a primitive wellspring of
sound, a timeless song of 'love which prevails', and a contemporary

---

15. *The Years*, pp. 8–9. The hymn, 'When Upon Life's Billows You Are Tempest-Tossed', is
    by Johnson Oatman, Jr (1856–1922), music by Edwin O. Excell (1851–1921); its
    appearance in '1880' is an anachronism, as it dates from 1897. The text is given in a
    simplified form; the chorus runs: 'Count your blessings, name them one by one; /
    Count your blessings, see what God hath done; / Count your blessings, name them
    one by one, / And it will surprise you what the Lord hath done'.

16. *The Years*, p. 81.

17. *The Years*, p. 115. The passage continues: 'Over and over again it was repeated by
    trombones outside public houses; errand boys whistled it; bands inside private rooms
    where people were dancing played it. There they sat at little tables at Wapping in
    the romantic Inn that overhung the river, between timber warehouses where barges
    were moored; and here again in Mayfair.'

18. *The Years*, p. 203.

art-song—are related to each other, it is not linguistically, or as components of a 'realist' fiction. The scene is 'impossible', incoherent, at the level of representation. We have to go *behind* the scene to understand what is taking place on the verbal stage.

Even if it cannot be pinned down to a singular, definite form, the old woman's song has an 'aura', not of originality but authenticity. Indeed, the originality of most street songs is beside the point. Authenticity belongs to the collective, the impersonal, the anonymous. Looked at in this light, street song is one branch of folk-song, considered not as a local, historical phenomenon but as a product of the 'deep time' of human creativity, before writing, before agricultural settlement. In an unfinished essay, 'Anon', written not long before her death in 1941, Woolf evokes the immense prestige of such early, anonymous song for the sophisticated writer and critic of the twentieth century. The first paragraph sets the scene in the 'untamed forest' of prehistoric Britain, in which the song of 'innumerable birds' was heard 'by a few skin clad hunters in the clearings':

> Did the desire to sing come to one of those huntsmen because he heard the birds sing, and so rested his axe against the tree for a moment? But the tree had to be felled; and a hut made from its branches before the human voice sang too.

> > By a bank as I lay
> > > Musing myself alone, hey ho!
> > A birdes voice
> > Did me rejoice,
> > > Singing before the day;
> > And me thought in her lay
> > She said, winter was past, hey ho!

> The voice that broke the silence of the forest was the voice of Anon. Some one heard the song and remembered it for it was later written down, beautifully, on parchment. Thus the singer had his audience, but the audience was so little interested in his name that he never thought to give it. The audience was itself the singer; "Terly, terlow" they sang; and "By, by lullay" filling in the pauses, helping out with a chorus. Every body shared in the emotion of Anons song, and supplied the story. Anon sang because spring has come; or winter is gone; because he loves; because he is hungry, or lustful; or merry: or because he adores some God. Anon is sometimes man; sometimes woman. He is the common voice singing out of doors, He has no house. He lives a roaming life

crossing the fields, mounting the hills, lying under the hawthorn to listen to the nightingale.[19]

It is an unscholarly leap from the primeval forest to a polished sixteenth-century lyric; but Woolf is concerned with myth, not history.[20] And with the magical facility of myth, 'Anon' is transported from the forest to the Anglo-Norman manor house; history and social class enter the picture, and we find the singers

> singing their songs at the back door to the farm hands and the maid servants in the uncouth jargon of their native tongue.
>
> > Icham for woing al forwake
> > Wery no water in wore
>
> Up stairs they spoke French. [...] Anon singing at the back door was despised. He had no name; he had no place.   (*Anon* 383)[21]

It is tempting for the non-specialist to remark that the language of this song is closer than 'By a bank as I lay' to the old woman's 'ee um fah um so / foo swee too eem oo', but we should resist the temptation; Woolf was not pastiching medieval English any more than she was giving a garbled version of 'Allerseelen'. But the low social status of Anon is another matter. Here again, in disguise, is the divinity, whose 'uncouth jargon' is holy, and constitutes the oral foundation of the sacred texts of our 'native tongue'. Without Anon, no Shakespeare— and no Virginia Woolf. But more than this: Anon incarnates the system of beliefs of the common people, expressed in 'pagan' rites and ceremonies that signify not just an abstract worship of 'Nature' but our embodiment in the natural world:

> It was Anon who gave voice to the old stories, who incited the peasants when he came to the back door to put off their working clothes and deck themselves in green leaves. [...] He taught them the songs they sung at Christmas and at midsummer. He led them to the haunted tree; to the well; to the old

19. '"Anon" and "The Reader": Virginia Woolf's Last Essays', ed. Brenda R. Silver, *Twentieth Century Literature* 25.3/4 (Autumn–Winter 1979), pp. 356–441 (p. 382). Hereafter *Anon*. Errors of spelling and punctuation are as transcribed. Silver identifies the song as No. XXXIII in *Early English Lyrics*, ed. E. K. Chambers and F. Sidgwick (London: Sidgwick & Jackson, 1926 [first publ. 1907]); the picture of the 'untamed forest' derives from G. M. Trevelyan's *History of England* (London: Longmans, Green, 1926), p. 3. In Woolf's first drafts the 'huntsmen' were 'savages' (*Anon* 402 n. 4).

20. 'By the bank as I lay' is first recorded in 1565.

21. The song is no. IV in *Early English Lyrics* (see n. 19). Woolf has 'woing' for 'wowing' and 'no water' for 'so water'.

burial place where they did homage to the pagan gods. [. . .] The old Gods lay hidden beneath the new. It was to them led by Anon that they did worship, in their coats of green leaves, bearing swords in their hands, dancing through the houses, enacting their ancient parts.   (*Anon* 383–4)[22]

In this light, Woolf's old woman has a generic standing which transcends her actual social or personal identity. She is a figure, first, of natural expressiveness—non-human, non-gendered, 'an ancient spring'; next, by the pun which English allows, a goddess of spring, eternally recurring, eternally youthful beneath her bent and withered aspect; last, she is a modern artist, chanting the melancholy cadences that evoke the return of the dead. To encounter her outside Regent's Park tube station, in the press of 'bustling, middle-class people', is to be put back in touch with ancient rites of fertility, and with the pagan myths that underlie English folk-song and lyric, but also to be subjected to a peculiarly modern kind of haunting.

The problem with projecting 'Anon' back onto the old woman in *Mrs. Dalloway* is the problem of audience. In Woolf's idealized summary of the origins of song, the bond between singer and audience is more than social, it constitutes the 'poetics' of song itself. Woolf goes well beyond Wordsworth's formulation, in the Preface to *Lyrical Ballads*, of 'a man speaking to men' (the poet being different from his fellows not in kind but in degree); she emphasizes the co-creation of song by Anon and his hearers.[23] Moreover, she traces the evolution of Anon from ballad singer to playwright, and as Brenda Silver observes, she had already argued, in 'Notes on an Elizabethan Play' (*The Common Reader*,

22. The theme of divinity, and of paganism, is already present in the early essay 'Street Music' (1905; see n. 4), in which Woolf plays with the popular fancy that 'the gods who went into exile when the first Christian altars rose will come back to enjoy their own again. Many writers have tried to trace these old pagans, and have professed to find them in the disguise of animals and in the shelter of far-away woods and mountains; but it is not fantastic to suppose that while every one is searching for them they are working their charms in the midst of us, and that those strange heathens who do the bidding of no man and are inspired by a voice that is other than human in their ears are not really as other people, but are either the very gods themselves or their priests and prophets upon earth' (p. 29).

23. William Wordsworth, Preface to *Lyrical Ballads*: 'He [the poet] is a man speaking to men: a man, it is true, endued with more lively sensibility, more enthusiasm and tenderness, who has a greater knowledge of human nature, and a more comprehensive soul, than are supposed to be common among mankind [. . .] Among the qualities which I have enumerated as principally conducting to form a Poet, is implied nothing differing in kind from other men, but only in degree' (*Lyrical Ballads*, ed. Michael Mason [Harlow: Longman, 1992], pp. 71, 78).

1925), that 'half the work of the dramatists, one feels, was done in the Elizabethan age by the public'.[24] The fall from song to writing is measured by the separation of poet and audience, exemplified in the case of Spenser, who is 'separate from the minstrel' and whose audience 'no longer joined in the song and added their own verses to the poem' (*Anon* 389). Neither Peter Walsh nor Rezia Smith experience the old woman's song as co-creators; that faculty has been irretrievably lost.[25] It is supplemented, ironically enough, by the *textual* intervention of the author, whose interpretative 'hearing' of the song posits a relationship which is grounded in nothing, and can have no continuance. What, then, of our position, as readers? Woolf herself was aware of the paradoxical role that print plays in the destruction and preservation of oral culture. 'It was the printing press that finally was to kill Anon', she declares. 'But it was the press also that preserved him' (*Anon* 384). On the page the old woman's song cannot be heard directly, whether or not we recognize the allusion to 'Allerseelen' (and indeed to the particular setting and translation). What *can* be heard is Woolf's voice, which both mediates the old woman's and transforms it, so that our initial impression of 'an absence of all human meaning' is comprehensively reversed.

This appropriation of 'Anon's' voice is not the only irony at play in the episode. The ancient, early, primitive song, an impersonal vocal spring, emanates from an industrial artefact, a 'rusty pump' or a 'funnel'; the timeless song of love is also the occasion of a dubious urban transaction, so that the gesture of desire—'Give me your hand and let me press it gently'—is also the gesture of begging, to which Peter Walsh responds, either appropriately or ignorantly, by 'giving the poor creature a coin'. And that phrase 'poor creature' itself suggests a further

---

24. *Anon* 380. It is true that she immediately adds that 'the influence of the public was in many respects detestable'.

25. In an earlier draft of the episode, the old woman's song *does* involve 'everybody who passed'; this was cut from the published version. The sentence beginning 'Still remembering how once in some primeval May she had walked with her lover' reads as follows in the manuscript: 'How once in May on some flowering [coast] headland, she, [then it seemed] had walked with—[some youth, whose features were all dim, & well, it was not important to remember] with whom. So that everybody who passed could supply for themselves a hero or a heroine' ('*The Hours*': *The British Museum Manuscript of Mrs. Dalloway*, ed. Helen M. Wussow [New York: Pace University Press, 1997], p. 99; cited in Kathryn Van Wert, 'The Early Life of Septimus Smith', *Journal of Modern Literature* 36.1 [Fall 2012], p. 80). Compare, in *Anon*, 'Every body shared in the emotion of Anons song, and supplied the story'.

irony, one to which Virginia Woolf is perhaps not so attuned. The prestige of 'Anon' comes at another kind of cost. In the vision of high art, the lower orders are given a status they are not accorded in life. Alison Light, in *Mrs Woolf and the Servants*, aligns the old woman with her predecessor in *Jacob's Room*, and with 'the women at the street corners with their arms akimbo, and the rings embedded in their fat swollen fingers, talking with a gesticulation like the swing of Shakespeare's words' from *A Room of One's Own*, or with Mrs McNab, the char-woman in the 'Time Passes' section of *To the Lighthouse*, who, as she spring-cleans the Ramsays' house, sings to herself a song 'robbed of meaning, like the voice of witlessness, humour, persistency itself, trod-den down but springing up again'. Such figures, Light remarks, were 'safely removed' from Woolf's private life, 'figures of romance', members of an 'archetypal species'—' "the poor", the eternal poor'.[26] They are available for appropriation, in part at least because they can't answer back, and are not readers of the fictions in which they are co-opted. The image of 'Anon' singing at the back door to 'the farm hands and the maid servants' is circumscribed, framed, by a knowing, an educated artist.

The old woman's song is a complicated thing, and I intend to com-plicate it further. We come now to the question of who hears the song, and who is responsible for the reflections on it. Two main characters— Peter Walsh and Rezia Smith—are in play here, along with the narra-tor, whom I shall call, without prejudice, Virginia Woolf. It seems clear enough that the first perception of the old woman is Peter's. His train of thought is 'interrupted' by the sound of the song, and it is rational to infer that he looks around, identifies the source of the sound, is momentarily uncertain as to the singer's gender, then 'places' her as an old woman, a beggar. The opening series of similes—'a tall quivering shape, like a funnel, like a rusty pump, like a wind-beaten tree'—might be his, and he is certainly moved in some sense by her song, or her plight, but the flight of imagination in which she is re-figured as a timeless incarnation of sexual love isn't 'in character', and he is given no specific reflection other than the perfunctory phrase 'poor creature' as he gets into his taxi and departs. At this point he hands the baton of consciousness to Rezia, so to speak. But Rezia cannot possibly be the source of the description of the old woman as mythic archetype. Her

26. Alison Light, *Mrs Woolf and the Servants* (London: Penguin Books, 2008), pp. 199–200.

response to the singer is one of sympathy, mingled with a personal dread Peter Walsh couldn't share, since her social position is precarious as his is not; Rezia shivers with the horror of respectability confronted by destitution. She wonders, as her author had wondered on top of the bus on the way to Waterloo, about the lives such women lead (Woolf: 'How she came to be there, what scenes she can go through, I can't imagine.'—Rezia: 'And where did she sleep at night?'), but Rezia doesn't have Woolf's desire. 'O damn it all, I say, why can't I know all that too?' That's the writer, greedy for experience, wanting to know everything, understand everything from the inside. It's not Rezia; her response is equally self-centred, perhaps, but shaped by a kind of pragmatic superstition: she gives 'meanings to things that happened', but not like an artist; these meanings are signs and omens, in this case a poignant and deluded form of wish fulfilment: 'this old woman singing in the street "if some one should see, what matter they?" made her suddenly quite sure that everything was going to be right'.

I am driven to the conclusion, then, that the old woman's poetic and symbolic attributes are the author's work, and that Woolf is telling us, as readers, something to which the characters in the scene have no access. It is an exercise of authorial power, like the dramatic irony which shadows Rezia's pathetic misjudgement about Sir William Bradshaw's healing powers and even the niceness of his name. It is Woolf who sees London dissolved into a primeval swamp, its hard pavement soaked and stained, its 'skeletons and treasure' made of no account. She is drawing on a long tradition of literary and artistic representations of the city as a wilderness, or ruin, situated either in the past or the future; such representations were especially popular in the late nineteenth century, for example Richard Jefferies' *After London* (1885) and H. G. Wells's *The Time Machine* (1895); Gustave Doré's 'New Zealander', sketching a ruined St Paul's in a post-imperial future, exemplifies the curious mixture of anxiety and relish with which London has been so often imagined as a landscape of ruins.[27] Standing at the entrance to the underground, or underworld, the old woman is also a figure poised between

27. Doré's image was published in his and Blanchard Jerrold's *London: A Pilgrimage* (1872). It alludes to a remark in a review essay by Thomas Babington Macaulay ('On Ranke's *History of the Popes*', 1840), imagining a time 'when some traveller from New Zealand shall, in the midst of a vast solitude, take his stand on a broken arch of London Bridge to sketch the ruins of St Paul's'; Macaulay himself was recycling an image which dates to the eighteenth century at least.

death and rebirth. Seeing the urban crowd as a figure for the 'passing generations ... vanished, like leaves, to be trodden under, to be soaked and steeped and made mould of by that eternal spring', Woolf enters into conversation with her peers, all poets: Dante, Milton, T. S. Eliot.[28] For this episode is a prose poem, an interlude in the novel, whose thread is only resumed when Peter Walsh gets into his taxi and the focus of the narrative shifts to Rezia Smith.

I see the depiction of the old woman, therefore, as a kind of parenthesis, or authorial 'aside'. But an aside is not a sideshow; on the contrary, it bears on the action, and that is the case here. The vision of the old woman belongs neither to Peter nor Rezia, but comments on them both—specifically on their broken or strained relationship to their 'partners', Clarissa and Septimus.

Peter Walsh, after his bittersweet visit to Clarissa Dalloway, has walked from her house to Regent's Park. He falls asleep on a bench, then wakes up and walks out of the Park, passing Septimus Smith and Rezia, whom he mistakenly thinks are having a conventional lovers' tiff. On the way, Peter thinks about Clarissa; he reviews the trajectory of their friendship, more bitter to him now than sweet, and passes judgement not only on her but on her sex.

That was what tortured him, that was what came over him when he saw Clarissa so calm, so cold, so intent on her dress or whatever it was; realizing what she might have spared him, what she had reduced him to—a whimpering, snivelling old ass. But women, he thought, shutting his pocket-knife, don't know what passion is. They don't know the meaning of it to men. Clarissa was as cold as an icicle. There she would sit on the sofa by his side, let him take her hand, give him one kiss on the cheek——Here he was at the crossing.
A sound interrupted him...

What the old woman's song *interrupts* is therefore Peter's outburst of ill-feeling, directed at himself, at Clarissa, at women in general. The argument that the old woman's song is meant to undermine Peter's male chauvinism by showing that women are, indeed, passionate seems to me to impoverish the episode, and to say something demeaning

28. Dante sees the souls of the damned fling themselves into Charon's ferry: 'Come d'autunno si levan le foglie / l'una appresso dell'altra' [As the leaves of autumn fall off one after the other] (*Inferno* iii 112–13; transl. J. A. Carlyle); the rebel angels in *Paradise Lost* lie 'Thick as autumnal leaves that strew the brooks / In Vallombrosa' (i 302–3); in the opening lines of pt. 3 of *The Waste Land*, 'The Fire Sermon', 'The river's tent is broken: the last fingers of leaf / Clutch and sink into the wet bank' (ll. 173–4).

about the author, as though she were petty enough to triumph over her own creation. The old woman is not less like Peter than she is like Clarissa, or indeed Rezia; if she transcends one, she transcends all; her being female gives the women who pass her in the street no special privilege of affinity. Her song does not deny the justice of Peter's self-loathing and self-pity, or his construction of Clarissa as a descendant of Tennyson's Maud, with her 'Passionless, pale, cold face'.[29] But it is a corrective vision nonetheless. It places Peter's relationship with Clarissa in a different frame; it generalizes on a scale beyond his grasp. He remembers the scene of his break-up with Clarissa in the garden at Bourton—'The final scene, the terrible scene which he believed had mattered more than anything in the whole of his life'—taking place by a fountain:

> The fountain was in the middle of a little shrubbery, far from the house, with shrubs and trees all round it. There she came, even before the time, and they stood with the fountain between them, the spout (it was broken) dribbling water incessantly. How sights fix themselves upon the mind! For example, the vivid green moss.[30]

The fountain 'dribbling water incessantly' from its broken spout anticipates the perpetual bubbling spring of the old woman's song, and the 'vivid green moss' is the 'fertilizing stain' it leaves; but this analogy is lost on Peter. *How sights fix themselves upon the mind!*—but the sight of the fountain remains, for him, an isolated point of anguish. The connection between the two images of flowing, fertilizing water is made not by the character, as it might be in Proust, but by the author. Just as Peter perceives the old woman first as a 'tall quivering shape', so he now becomes for her, as he takes the place of her lost lover, 'only a looming shape, a shadow shape', and he leaves her without recognition. The banal transaction in which he gives her a shilling and steps into his taxi is as portentous as paying the ferryman on the banks of the Styx. It is a moment of obliviousness, like one of those moments in fairytale or myth in which the hero fails to recognize a god.

As Peter leaves, Rezia and Septimus, who are a little behind him, have reached Marylebone Road and are waiting to cross. Rezia now becomes aware of the old woman. Her initial exclamation, 'Poor old woman',

29. Alfred Tennyson, *Maud* (1855) I iii 90, in *The Poems of Tennyson*, ed. Christopher Ricks, 3 vols. (Harlow: Longman, 1987), vol. 2, p. 527.
30. *Mrs. Dalloway*, p. 58.

is in quotation marks, which implies it is said aloud, presumably to Septimus; 'Oh poor old wretch!' is not in quotation marks but is marked by the phrase 'she said'; then, from the next paragraph, 'Suppose it was a wet night?', she is not speaking to Septimus but thinking to herself. 'Poor old woman' and 'Poor old wretch' connect Rezia to Peter, who thinks of the old woman as 'the poor creature'; 'poor' has the double function, thoroughly conventional in this usage, of stating a fact—a beggar is poor—and expressing sympathy. It's a condescending phrase, though Rezia's condescension differs from Peter's, as I've suggested, because her own social position is not as secure. Nevertheless, she is as oblivious, as uncomprehending as he; her response is first conventional ('how awful to be like that'), then selfishly personal ('perhaps it's a good omen'). What she doesn't do is properly listen.

Unlike Peter, Rezia doesn't seem to have a problem hearing the words of the song—the impossible words, we should remember, the words of the art-song which the old woman cannot, 'realistically', be singing. Rezia doesn't hear 'ee um fah um so / foo swee too eem oo' but hears, distinctly, the phrase 'And if some one should see, what matter they?' At this point a pastoral scene emerges, an English genre scene which incongruously presents itself to Rezia's Italian mind's eye:

> Cheerfully, almost gaily, the invincible thread of sound wound up into the air like the smoke from a cottage chimney, winding up clean beech trees and issuing in a tuft of blue smoke among the topmost leaves. "And if some one should see, what matter they?"

'Cheerfully, almost gaily' takes us back to Woolf's diary: 'Defiant— almost gay'; and again, 'It was gay, and yet terrible and fearfully vivid'; and in *Jacob's Room*, 'her gay wild heart'. But the context of this gaiety is quite different. The 'cottage chimney', the 'clean beech trees', the 'tuft of blue smoke' are picturesque stereotypes of English rural landscape.[31] The beech trees are *clean* because the beech is an elegant tree, with 'clean lines', and because they are free from urban grime; the 'cottage chimney' is not in coal-burning London. In this scene the phrase 'And if some one should see, what matter they?' has connotations

---

31. A passage from Wordsworth's 'Lines Composed a Few Miles above Tintern Abbey' may have been at the back of Woolf's mind: 'These plots of cottage-ground, these orchard-tufts...wreaths of smoke / Sent up, in silence, from among the trees!' (ll. 11, 17–18).

of pastoral lyric—a bold shepherd wooing his lass, or, less benignly, a master stealing a kiss from a servant.

But the actual connotations are not those of some idealized genre scene. The question of *seeing* is central to Septimus's mental condition, and to Rezia's incomprehension of it. She is fearful of people in the street noticing Septimus, realizing that he is suicidal: 'People must notice; people must see. [. . .] Septimus had said, "I will kill myself"; an awful thing to say. Suppose they had heard him?' (p. 14). Yet she is constantly exhorting *him* to notice things, to 'see' with normal eyes. In the park 'She could not sit beside him when he stared so and did not see her and made everything terrible' (p. 21); following Dr Holmes's idiotic advice, she keeps on pointing, urging him to see:

> "Look," she implored him, pointing at a little troop of boys carrying cricket stumps, and one shuffled, spun round on his heel and shuffled, as if he were acting a clown at the music hall.
> "Look," she implored him, for Dr. Holmes had told her to make him notice real things, go to a music hall, play cricket—that was the very game, Dr. Holmes said, a nice out-of-door game, the very game for her husband.
> "Look," she repeated.   (p. 23)

But looking is just what Septimus doesn't want to do; if he looks he will see the dead, and in particular the figure of Evans, his officer, his friend, whose return Septimus dreads the more because his dread is so mixed with desire. So Rezia's innocent insistence is horribly ill-timed; it comes as Septimus sits on the bench listening to the sparrow singing

> freshly and piercingly in Greek words how there is no crime and, joined by another sparrow, they sang in voices prolonged and piercing in Greek words, from trees in the meadow of life beyond a river where the dead walk, how there is no death.
> There was his hand; there the dead. White things were assembling behind the railings opposite. But he dared not look. Evans was behind the railings!   (p. 22)[32]

He dared not look: and later in this scene, again, 'he could not look upon the dead'. The phrase that triggers Rezia's consoling fantasy, 'And if someone should see, what matter they?', would seem to Septimus—if he heard it—a callous reflection on his predicament. But there is no

---

32. The sparrow is both an ancient and modern emblem: Venus' bird, and the 'Cockney sparrer' whose 'street song' is a cliché of London's soundscape.

indication that the old woman's song gets through to Septimus; the sharp point of its irony is directed at the reader, who is also in a position to understand what has been left out, the third verse of the poem which Woolf does not quote, the one which speaks of the return of the dead on All Souls' Day:

> Es blüht und funkelt heut' auf jedem Grabe,
>   Ein Tag im Jahre ist den Todten frei:
> Komm' an mein Herz, dass ich dich wieder habe,
>   Wie einst im Mai, wie einst im Mai.
>
> On ev'ry grave are flowers all red and golden,
>   In death's dark valley this is Holy Day.
> Come to my heart, be in mine arms enfolden,
>   As once in May, as once in May.[33]

Julia Briggs connects this theme with 'a sense that, for Clarissa and her friends, passion is confined to the past—it can only be voiced by someone free of social inhibitions'.[34] This is true, but not the whole truth; the 'day of the dead' belongs as much to Septimus as to Clarissa or Peter—perhaps even more so. And none of these characters 'owns' the insight that the author has into their predicament. The old woman outside Regent's Park tube station, like a classical goddess, is the more powerful, the more numinous, for being in disguise.

---

33. Lawson's translation, or 'adaptation' (see n. 12). More exactly: 'Today each grave is blooming and sparkling, on one day in the year the dead are free; come to my heart, that I may have you again, as once in May, as once in May'; 'dass ich dich wieder habe' might be rendered 'that I may again possess you (sexually)'.
34. Julia Briggs, *Virginia Woolf: An Inner Life* (London: Allen Lane, 2005), p. 151.

6

Voulez ouyr les cris de Paris?

In *La Prisonnière*, the sixth volume of Marcel Proust's *À la recherche du temps perdu*, the narrator, whom I am going to call Marcel, listens in the early morning to the cries of the street-vendors of Paris.[1] Like the 'cries of London', with one of which—'Cherry-Ripe'—I began this book, the *cris de Paris* had been studied and interpreted as musical performances, and had featured in stage plays and operas, long before Proust took hold of them. One opera in particular, Gustave Charpentier's *Louise*, first produced in 1900, stages the *cris de Paris* as an emblem of the city itself, and may have served Proust as a provocation and foil.[2] In the course of the episode in *La Prisonnière*, Marcel hears or mentions a score of cries relating to food—winkles, snails, artichokes, biscuits, goat's milk, oysters, shrimps, skate, mackerel, mussels, lettuces, asparagus, oranges, onions, leeks, carrots, green beans, cream cheese, grapes, and tripe; and the cries of a dozen tradespeople: the man who

1. All quotations from *La Prisonnière* [The Captive] are from the edition by Pierre-Edmond Robert in volume 3 of *À la recherche du temps perdu*, gen. ed. Jean-Yves Tadié (Paris: Gallimard, 1988 [Bibliothèque de la Pléiade]); the episode I discuss begins on p. 623 ('Le lendemain de cette soirée ...'). Critics are undecided as to what to call the anonymous first-person narrator of *À la recherche*. His first name is not Marcel, but that name is used on occasion as a meta-fictional equivalent, as when he describes Albertine's manner of waking from sleep: 'Elle retrouvait la parole, elle disait: "Mon" ou "Mon chéri", suivis l'un ou l'autre de mon nom de baptême, ce qui, en donnant au narrateur le même prénom qu'à l'auteur de ce livre, eût fait: "Mon Marcel", "Mon chéri Marcel"' [As soon as she was able to speak she said: 'My ――' or 'My dearest ――' followed by my Christian name, which, if we give the narrator the same name as the author of this book, would be 'My Marcel', or 'My dearest Marcel'] (*La Prisonnière*, p. 583). He is usually referred to as 'the narrator'; some French critics follow Roland Barthes in capitalizing the word (the Narrator—le Narrateur); others vary the appellation according to the context, e.g. using 'hero' (*le héros du roman*, meaning the protagonist).
2. See Cécile Leblanc, 'De Charpentier à Wagner: transfigurations musicales dans les cris de Paris chez Proust', *Revue d'histoire littéraire de la France* 107.4 (2007), pp. 903–21.

grooms dogs and trims the ears and tails of cats, the old-clothes man, the knife-grinder, saw-setter, tinker, cooper, and glazier, the ragman, the sweet-seller, the toy-seller, and the mender of porcelain. These are a fraction of the 'cries' that Proust could have used; hundreds of them have been documented since the Middle Ages. Each has a plain, literal meaning, rooted in the social and economic conditions of pre-industrial cities, and which still survived—though in attenuated form—in the early years of the twentieth century. People still bought food and goods and services of all kinds on the streets from itinerant sellers, whose cries were part of the urban soundscape, and Proust's depiction of them has nothing fanciful about it. Yet this depiction is not 'atmospheric', and the *cris de Paris* aren't there to provide local colour or enhance the verisimilitude of a realist fiction. Proust appropriates them for a different purpose. In doing so he responds to something in the compressed form of the street cry itself, which so readily suggests that it means more than it says (Figure 6.1).

When *La Prisonnière* opens, Marcel has returned to Paris, in the company of his girlfriend Albertine, from the seaside town of Balbec

Figure 6.1. Anonymous, *Paris qui s'éveille* (*Scènes et Moeurs de Paris*). Lithograph. French School, nineteenth century

in Normandy. They are living in his parents' apartment, part of a large mansion, the *Hôtel de Guermantes*, which is located in one of the 'old aristocratic quarters' of the city. His parents are conveniently absent, though the old family servant, Françoise, keeps a baleful eye on the unseemly goings-on. It is of course an irregular arrangement in an ultra-respectable bourgeois family such as Marcel's that a young unmarried girl should live in the same house as her boyfriend, even if they are, supposedly, engaged. Marcel's mother allows it to happen because Marcel has convinced her that he is desperately unhappy and in need of Albertine's company, that he intends to marry her, and that his decision to spend the rest of his life with her is absolute and irrevocable. What Marcel's mother does not know is that Albertine is the cause, as well as the remedy, of Marcel's suffering. He has brought her to Paris not out of love but pathological jealousy. Having discovered at Balbec that Albertine is a lesbian, he determines to prevent her, as far as he is able, from satisfying her desire for other women, a desire which horrifies him for reasons which are fascinating to explore but which are not my concern here. All that needs to be said is that he keeps her a virtual prisoner in his apartment—not an actual prisoner, since she is perfectly free to go out, and does indeed go out almost every day, and could leave him whenever she wanted—but in the sense that he keeps her presence a secret from his friends, tracks her every movement, torments her, and himself, with a continuous inquisition about her past, and plays a hopeless, compulsive game in which he tries to baffle her every attempt to elude his surveillance. And all through the time in which he and Albertine live together, Marcel deludes himself that what he actually wants is to be free of her; it is *she* who has enslaved *him*, not the other way round; if only she would take it into her head to abandon him! Or perhaps, one fine day, he will give her the slip; at a time of his own choosing, when he does not feel so oppressed by the thoughts of her 'vice', he will leave for Venice and Albertine's hold on him will weaken, until indifference and oblivion complete his cure. Meanwhile, however, he cannot relax his guard; at any moment Albertine might be planning a rendezvous with a former lover, or making an assignation with a girl she has picked up in a shop. For though Albertine claims to love him and to enjoy her life with him, it is clear to Marcel, and to the reader, that she is lying to him in the exact measure that he is lying to her when he claims to love her for herself. She betrays him, we later learn, at every opportunity, and those whom he trusts to watch over her and inform him of her actions turn out to be in league with her and as treacherous as she.

It is crucial to the plot of *La Prisonnière* as a whole, and of the particular episode I am going to discuss, that Marcel doesn't do the tracking and watching and listening himself. He is an invalid, a prey to his asthma and his nerves; he rarely leaves the apartment, and has only second-hand knowledge of what Albertine does when she is out shopping, or visiting a gallery, or on an excursion to Versailles. Alone in his room, his imagination and his memory are busy, not on the great work which we are reading but which he does not yet know he is going to write, but on a kind of sickly tragedy, or morbid romance, the tale of his love for Albertine, whose potency is paradoxically a form of impotence, since it is kept alive by his inability to possess her fully, to govern her desire. To say that Marcel does not cut a heroic figure in this part of the novel is an understatement. He may be on his way to becoming the great artist who will one day write *À la recherche du temps perdu*, but when we encounter him in this book he is a figure of almost unendurable anguish, pitiable and repellent in equal measure. And yet this monster of suffering egotism has a twin, a recording angel, comprehensive, exact, unflinching, an artist whose impressions, whether of external or psychological phenomena, have the stamp not so much of truth as necessity.

One word more, about translation. Unless otherwise indicated, I use the first English translation of *À la recherche* by Charles Scott Moncrieff, published under the title *Remembrance of Things Past* by Chatto and Windus between 1922 and 1931. *The Captive*, Scott Moncrieff's translation of the title *La Prisonnière*, appeared in 1929. I haven't done this out of a preference for Scott Moncrieff's version as such—it is often less accurate than more modern translations—but because of the particular decision he made with regard to the *cris de Paris*, namely that they remain in French. More recent translations, beginning with Terence Kilmartin's revision of Scott Moncrieff, published in 1981, translate the 'cries', sometimes literally and sometimes into English equivalents. However accurate or ingenious these translations may be, they do violence to the native wit and historical context of the *cris de Paris*, let alone their verbal texture, and too often they produce incongruity or absurdity.[3]

---

3. A Parisian fishmonger turns into Molly Malone, crying cockles and mussels alive, alive-oh; or Steptoe and Son pass by the hôtel de Guermantes singing 'any old iron'. I discuss

The episode of the *cris de Paris* is a late addition to the novel: as Jean Milly has shown, it does not feature in the fair copy of the manuscript produced between 1915 and 1917, and develops gradually in the successive typescripts, and additions to these typescripts, of 1921–2.[4] Yet Milly's careful documentary work supports the view of critics such as Emily Eells and Martine Gantrel that, despite the lateness of these additions, they are far from being random digressions or interruptions.[5] The episode unfolds in three stages. In the first, Marcel is on his own, describing his enjoyment of the sounds he hears; this stage concludes with Albertine's entry into his room. She asks him whether the cries from the street bother him, since he is so light a sleeper, and his reply— delayed by a long excursus on sleep, which has its own part to play in the episode but which lies outside the scope of this book—initiates the second stage, in which the cries are both heard directly and quoted by Albertine. This stage climaxes in a celebrated set piece, a long speech by Albertine about her appetite for the sophisticated presentation and consumption of luxury ice cream, and which is also a pastiche by Proust of his own style. It offers a deliberate contrast to the appetite she has for food bought on the street, as the gourmet ice-sorbet sculptures she describes are sold in the most fashionable and expensive shops and hotels in Paris. After she delivers this speech, Albertine leaves, and in the final stage we have a brief reprise of the narrator's solitary observation and reflection on the *cris de Paris*. What connects these three phases is, as we shall see, the question of Albertine's taste—of what she enjoys, of what gives her pleasure—but this theme is developed with an element of misdirection, disguised by Marcel's seeming preoccupation, not with the meaning of the street cries, but with their form and style. This in itself is a kind of auto-pastiche; it is what Proust was persistently accused of, and it is as though he invites or provokes his critics to think of him as no more than a phrase-maker and colourist in words.

The episode begins with Marcel waking up early and realizing 'qu'il y avait, interpolé dans l'hiver, un jour de printemps' [that there was,

---

the problem of translation of the *cris* in 'Traduire les cris de Paris dans *La Prisonnière*', *Son et traduction dans l'oeuvre de Proust*, ed. Emily Eells and Naomi Toth (Paris: Honoré Champion, 2018).

4. Jean Milly, 'Glaces et cris de Paris dans *La Prisonnière* de Proust', in *Mélanges littéraires offerts à Pierre Larthomas*, Collection de l'École Normale Supérieure de Jeunes Filles, n° 26 (1985), p. 333–44.

5. Emily Eells, 'Proust à sa manière', *Littérature* 46 (1982), pp. 105–23; Martine Gantrel, 'Albertine ou l'étrangère: une nouvelle interprétation des "Cris de Paris" dans *La Prisonnière*', *Revue d'histoire littéraire de la France* 1 (2000), pp. 3–25.

interpolated in the winter, a day of spring] (p. 623). He makes this discovery not by sight, since he is lying in bed with the curtains and shutters closed, but by hearing, and what he hears is the music of the streets:

Dehors, des thèmes populaires finement écrits pour des instruments variés, depuis la corne du raccommodeur de porcelaine, ou la trompette du rempailleur de chaises, jusqu'à la flûte du chevrier qui paraissait dans un beau jour être un pâtre de Sicile, orchestraient légèrement l'air matinal, en une "Ouverture pour un jour de fête". L'ouïe, ce sens délicieux, nous apporte la compagnie de la rue dont elle nous retrace toutes les lignes, dessine toutes les formes qui y passent, nous en montrant la couleur.[6]

Had he been living in a different part of Paris, Marcel goes on, this concert might have consisted in nothing more than the noise of iron shutters being lifted, because in the modern city the itinerant street traders have given way to shops, and their cries have been drowned out by the noise of motorized traffic. Street trading is associated with the poor, and Marcel is therefore lucky to live in a neighbourhood where the poor and the rich still live cheek by jowl: 'C'est l'enchantement des vieux quartiers aristocratiques d'être, à côté de cela, populaires' (p. 623).[7] 'Enchantement' contains the word 'chant', or song, so that the phrase 'chant populaire', popular song, lurks in the impression Marcel is conveying. He repeats the point later in the episode, this time with a more explicit notation of the social and economic forces at play:

Et il me semblait que, si jamais je devais quitter ce quartier aristocratique—à moins que ce ne fût pour un tout à fait populaire—les rues et boulevards du centre (où la fruiterie, la poissonnerie, etc. stabilisées dans de grandes maisons d'alimentation, rendraient inutiles les cris des marchands qui n'eussent pas, du reste, réussi à se faire entendre) me sembleraient bien mornes, bien inhabitables, dépouillés, décantés de toutes ces litanies des petits métiers et des ambulantes mangeailles, privés de l'orchestre qui venait de me charmer dès le matin.   (p. 643)[8]

---

6. 'Outside, popular themes skilfully transposed for various instruments, from the horn of the mender of porcelain, or the trumpet of the chair weaver, to the flute of the goat driver who seemed, on a fine morning, to be a Sicilian goatherd, were lightly orchestrating the matutinal air, with an "Overture for a Public Holiday." Our hearing, that delicious sense, brings us the company of the street, every line of which it traces for us, sketches all the figures that pass along it, shewing us their colours.'
7. 'It is the magic charm of the old aristocratic quarters that they are at the same time plebeian.'
8. 'And I felt that, should I ever have to leave this aristocratic quarter—unless it were to move to one that was entirely plebeian—the streets and boulevards of central Paris (where the fruit, fish and other trades, stabilised in huge stores, rendered superfluous the

Such observations seem, at first sight, to belong to an aestheticizing impulse on Marcel's part, combined with a form of nostalgia for the old ways which is very much of its time. Modernity, as so often in À la recherche, is interpreted as loss, a loss which is here figured as the stripping or emptying-out of an aesthetic pleasure that is itself figured as unified and harmonious—the playing of an 'orchestra'. For though Proust's account of the *cris* allows for competition between the street-vendors, and for the overlapping of sounds which they produce, they nevertheless form a composition, a work of art.

We know from many written and graphic accounts, some of which have been cited in this book, how differently the noise of the streets could be represented—as cacophony, as chaos, as emblem of disorder, whether joyful or threatening. The impulse to arrange the *cris de Paris* into a concert, a unified performance, did not of course originate with Proust; it dates back at least three centuries, to a famous song by Clément Janequin, 'Voulez ouyr les cris de Paris' [Would you like to hear the cries of Paris], published in 1530, whose four unaccompanied voices mimic the overlapping and competing of the cries, in a *tour de force* of musical appropriation.[9] But Janequin's work lacks the element of nostalgia which infiltrates most nineteenth-century treatments. As the *cris de Paris* began to disappear from the urban soundscape during the nineteenth century, antiquarian interest in them increased, and Marcel's reaction might be that of a collector of folk-songs, or village customs, or other aspects of popular culture whose intellectual or aesthetic value rises as their actual practice declines.

Even though he doesn't leave his bed, Marcel may be thought of as a kind of aural *flâneur*, enjoying and consuming the sounds of the city as they are brought to his ears, and finding a series of ingenious metaphors and analogies by which he can appropriate them for his own aesthetic purpose. The first of these analogies is with the juxtaposition of 'high' and 'low' culture in medieval Christianity; and contained within it is a further analogy with contemporary opera:

> cries of the street hawkers, who for that matter would not have been able to make themselves heard) would seem to me very dreary, quite uninhabitable, stripped, drained of all these litanies of the small trades and peripatetic victuals, deprived of the orchestra that had come to charm me as soon as the day began.' The last phrase is my translation, replacing 'that returned every morning to charm me'.

9. Janequin was a priest before he was a secular songwriter, and he died in Paris; his music was still being performed in the nineteenth century.

Comme parfois les cathédrales en eurent non loin de leur portail (à qui il
arriva même d'en garder le nom, comme celui de la cathédrale de Rouen,
appelé des "Libraires", parce que contre lui ceux-ci exposaient en plein vent
leur marchandise), divers petits métiers, mais ambulants, passaient devant le
noble hôtel de Guermantes, et faisaient penser par moments à la France ecclé-
siastique d'autrefois. Car l'appel qu'ils lançaient aux petites maisons voisines
n'avait, à de rares exceptions près, rien d'une chanson. Il en différait autant que
la déclamation—à peine colorée par des variations insensibles—de *Boris
Godounov* et de *Pelléas*; mais d'autre part rappelait la psalmodie d'un prêtre au
cours d'offices dont ces scènes de la rue ne sont que la contrepartie bon
enfant, foraine, pourtant à demi liturgique.   (p. 623)[10]

Against the interpretation of the *cris* in musical terms, in hearing them
as songs, Proust suggests, on the one hand, that they correspond to an
older liturgical tradition, and on the other that they resemble the
'spoken' discourse of modern Russian and French opera. I have neither
the room nor the expertise to pause over these analogies, but their
purpose seems clear: by associating the *cris de Paris* with the old Latin
liturgy and with the music of Mussorgsky and Debussy, and by associating those two things with each other, Proust combines sacred and
secular, aristocratic and popular, ancient and modern, in a way that
suggests the fundamental technique of his own style. Proust's key term
for this style is *composite*—it is a mixture of different elements, not
dissolved or fused together, but set alongside each other. It is an art of
proximity, as the 'peripatetic' street traders 'pass in front of the noble
Hôtel de Guermantes'; it is also an art of allusion, as when the old-clothes
man intones his cry, ' "Habits, marchand d'habits, ha...bits" avec la
même pause entre les deux dernières syllabes d'habits que s'il eût
entonné en plain-chant: "*Per omnia saecula saeculo...rum*" ou: "*Requiescat
in pa...ce*", bien qu'il ne dût pas croire à l'éternité de ses habits et ne

---

10. 'Just as, sometimes, cathedrals used to have them [*sc.* "trades"] within a stone's throw
of their porches (which have even preserved the name, like the porch of Rouen styled
"the Booksellers", because these latter used to expose their merchandise in the open
air against its walls), so various minor trades, but peripatetic, used to pass in front of
the noble Hôtel de Guermantes, and made one think at times of the ecclesiastical
France of long ago. For the appeal which they launched at the little houses on either
side had, with rare exceptions, nothing of a song. It differed from song as much as the
declamation—barely coloured by imperceptible modulations—of *Boris Godounov* and
Pelléas; but on the other hand recalled the psalmody of a priest chanting his office of
which these street scenes are but the good-humoured, secular, and yet half liturgical
counterpart.'

les offrît pas non plus comme linceuls pour le suprême repos dans la paix' (p. 625).[11]

The playfulness here has a note of condescension, and of course it is only possible to bring high and low forms of culture together if you have access to both; Marcel is privileged in all kinds of ways to lie in his bed and convert the vocal currency of the streets into his own artistic denomination. He is not at street level: his perspective places him at a distance, literally and metaphorically; his room is high up in the building, and he takes possession of the soundscape, which he re-creates according to his fancy. Moreover, the economic basis of the scene that Marcel's hearing 'traces' for him seems not to matter: even though all the 'cries' are about possible transactions, and several of them name their price, this aspect of the scene, too, is brought into the domain of the aesthetic. Here, for example, is Marcel's elaborate disquisition on the musical contours of the cry of the snail-seller:

Ici, c'était bien encore à la déclamation à peine lyrique de Moussorgsky que faisait penser le marchand, mais pas à elle seulement. Car après avoir presque "parlé": "Les escargots, ils sont frais, ils sont beaux", c'était avec la tristesse et le vague de Maeterlinck, musicalement transposés par Debussy, que le marchand d'escargots, dans un de ces douloureux finales par où l'auteur de *Pelléas* s'apparente à Rameau ("Si je dois être vaincue, est-ce à toi d'être mon vainqueur?"), ajoutait avec une chantante mélancolie: "On les vend six sous la douzaine…"

Il m'a toujours été difficile de comprendre pourquoi ces mots fort clairs étaient soupirés sur un ton si peu approprié, mystérieux, comme le secret qui fait que tout le monde a l'air triste dans le vieux palais où Mélisande n'a pas réussi à apporter la joie, et profond comme une pensée du vieillard Arkel qui cherche à proférer dans des mots très simples toute la sagesse et la destinée. Les notes mêmes sur lesquelles s'élève avec une douceur grandissante la voix du vieux roi d'Allemonde ou de Golaud, pour dire: "On ne sait pas ce qu'il y a ici. Cela peut paraître étrange. Il n'y a peut-être pas d'événements inutiles", ou bien: "Il ne faut pas s'effrayer… C'était un pauvre petit être mystérieux, comme tout le monde", étaient celles qui servaient au marchand d'escargots pour reprendre, en une cantilène indéfinie: "On les vend six sous la douzaine…"[12]

11. 'with the same pause between the final syllables as if he had been intoning in plain chant: "*Per omnia saecula saeculo… rum*" or "*requiescat in pa… ce*" albeit he had no reason to believe in the immortality of his clothes, nor did he offer them as cerements for the supreme repose in peace.'
12. 'Here again it was of the barely lyrical declamation of Mussorgsky that the vendor reminded me, but not of it alone. For after having almost "spoken": "Les escargots, ils sont frais, ils sont beaux," it was with the vague melancholy of Maeterlinck, transposed into music by Debussy, that the snail vendor, in one of those pathetic finales in which

The price of snails isn't really an issue here. The street-seller's cry is divided into two parts, each attributed to a different composer: the first reminds Marcel of Mussorgsky, the second of Debussy, or rather of Maeterlinck musically transposed by Debussy; and this latter comparison is then itself the subject of a further comparison, in which Debussy is said to be akin to his Baroque precursor Jean-Philippe Rameau. At this point the reader may feel some sympathy with Proust's early critics, who accused him of wilfully indulging every caprice of thought, sacrificing clarity of outline for density of texture, losing story and character in a maze of impressions; a subordinate clause, we might say, was for him the fatal Cleopatra for which he lost the world, and was content to lose it.[13]

We might say this; but we would be wrong. It is true that Proust's method is intricate, but it is not haphazard. A clue is given, as so often when one writer quotes another, by a mistake. Debussy may or may not be akin to Rameau, but the line that Marcel cites is not from one of Rameau's operas, and is itself misquoted. It comes from the libretto for *Armide*, an opera by Lully first produced in 1686; the same libretto, by Philippe Quinault, was then used by Gluck in 1777, in a deliberate act of appropriation and renovation of a French classic for modern musical tastes. *Armide* is based on one of the most famous stories in Tasso's *Gerusalemme Liberata*, in which the Saracen sorceress Armida holds the Christian knight Rinaldo captive. In Quinault's tragedy, Armide is torn between her love for Renaud and her desire to exact vengeance on him. She places a spell on him to make him love her, but at the climax of the opera the spell is broken and Renaud escapes,

the composer of Pelléas shews his kinship with Rameau: "If vanquished I must be, is it for thee to be my vanquisher?" added with a singsong melancholy: "On les vend six sous la douzaine..." // I have always found it difficult to understand why these perfectly simple words were sighed in a tone so far from appropriate, mysterious, like the secret which makes everyone look sad in the old palace to which Mélisande has not succeeded in bringing joy, and profound as one of the thoughts of the aged Arkel who seeks to utter, in the simplest words, the whole lore of wisdom and destiny. The very notes upon which rises with an increasing sweetness the voice of the old King of Allemonde or that of Golaud, to say: "We know not what is happening here, it may seem strange, maybe nought that happens is in vain," or else: "No cause here for alarm, 'twas a poor little mysterious creature, like all the world," were those which served the snail vendor to resume, in an endless cadenza: "On les vend six sous la douzaine..."'. I have substituted 'Golaud' for the misprinted 'Goland' in Scott Moncrieff's text.

13. Adapting Samuel Johnson's criticism of Shakespeare's fondness for puns in his *Preface to Shakespeare*: 'A quibble was for him...'.

leaving Armide desolate. The line Marcel misremembers begins not 'Si je dois être vaincue' [If vanquished I must be] but 'Ah! si la liberté me doit être ravie' [If liberty must be torn from me]. It occurs in the aria sung by Armide at the start of Act III, for although she holds Renaud captive, he in turn has captivated her: they are each other's prisoner, as Marcel and Albertine are in *La Prisonnière*; either of them might ask that rhetorical question. The plot of *Armide*, in which a woman attempts to compel a man to love her, hates both him and herself, and ultimately loses him, is reinscribed in Proust's novel: the fact that Marcel is cast in the female role of Armide reinforces the connection, since it takes its place among the innumerable transpositions of gender in *À la recherche*.[14]

The aesthetic surface of Marcel's enjoyment of the *cris de Paris* is real enough, but it is also a false front, behind which something more psychologically complex is going on. The snail-seller's melancholy cadence recalls to the narrator his own predicament: 'the old palace to which Mélisande has not succeeded in bringing joy' is, after all, a good image of his apartment, his life with Albertine, and his state of mind. And when you look again at the way Marcel frames and interprets the cries that he hears, they all reveal this other aspect. His jealous desire colours everything he sees and hears: each cry is an offer, each transaction a seduction; the city's mobile, changing, overlapping voices speak to him of Albertine's sexual nature and appetite, of his fear that he cannot keep hold of her, or rather of his *knowledge*, ever-present and suppressed, of her inevitable flight.

The connection between the urban setting of the *cris de Paris* and the drama of Marcel's relationship with Albertine is made by Marcel

---

14. It is not certain whether the buried allusion to *Armide* relates to Lully's opera or Gluck's; both composers were the subject of renewed interest at the turn of the century, and their respective versions of *Armide* were performed in Paris. If I had to choose, I would point to Gluck, because *Armide* is mentioned in the poem which Proust addressed to him, the second of the 'Portraits de musiciens' in *Les Plaisirs et les jours* (1896), and, in particular, because of the praise he gives to his recitatives in his essay 'Journées de lecture' (*Pastiches et mélanges*, 1919): 'Je ne crois pas que l'essence particulière de la musique de Gluck se trahisse autant dans tel air sublime que dans telle cadence de ses récitatifs où l'harmonie est comme le son même de la voix de son génie' [I do not believe that the peculiar essence of Gluck's music betrays itself so much in any sublime tune as in the cadence of his recitatives, in which the harmony is, as it were, the very sound of the voice of his genius] (*Contre Sainte-Beuve*, précédé de *Pastiches et mélanges* et suivi de *Essais et articles*, ed. Pierre Clairac and Yves Sandre [Paris: Gallimard, 1971; Bibliothèque de la Pléiade], author's note on pp. 192–3).

himself. He speaks of the 'cries' as a phenomenon 'où nous est rendue sensible la vie circulante des métiers, des nourritures de Paris' (p. 633).[15] Scott Moncrieff translates *la vie circulante des métiers, des nourritures de Paris* as 'the peripatetic life of the tradesmen, the victuallers of Paris', which both loses the vital term *circulating* and replaces Proust's deliberate abstractions, which invest the *trades* and *foodstuffs* themselves with life, with a banal and condescending interest in the lives of the little people. There may be a learned pun on *circulante*, because *circulator* in Latin means a street-vendor,[16] but in any case it matters because it is immediately repeated and applied to Albertine herself and to the power that Marcel presumes he has over her movements:

En plus du plaisir de savoir le goût qu'Albertine avait pour eux et de sortir moi-même tout en restant couché, j'entendais en eux comme le symbole de l'atmosphère du dehors, de la dangereuse vie remuante au sein de laquelle je ne la laissais circuler que sous ma tutelle, dans un prolongement extérieur de la séquestration, et d'où je la retirais à l'heure que je voulais pour rentrer auprès de moi.[17]

The benign 'circulating life' of the streets transforms into the 'dangerous stirring life' in which Albertine 'circulates': *circulante* is first converted from a kind of autonomous ordered motion, like that of the planets, to one of turmoil, like the heaving of the ocean, and then brought back under the sign of authority and surveillance. A whole history of the efforts made by the state to control the movement of crowds in nineteenth-century cities, and to track suspect individuals in the flux of urban life, is condensed and, so to speak, privatized in this passage.

The life of the streets is *dangerous* because it offers Albertine so many opportunities to satisfy her desire; the *cris de Paris* symbolize these

---

15. 'in which is rendered tangible to us the circulating life of the trades, of the foodstuffs of Paris' [my translation].
16. See Claire Holleran, 'Representations of Food Hawkers in Ancient Rome', in *Food Hawkers: Selling in the Streets from Antiquity to the Present*, ed. Melissa Calaresu and Danielle van den Heuvel (London: Routledge, 2016), pp. 24, 26–7; Holleran points out that 'circulator' could 'refer to both hawkers and street performers'.
17. 'Besides the pleasure of knowing Albertine's relish for them [the street cries] and of going out myself while remaining in bed, I heard in them as it were the symbol of the outside atmosphere, of the dangerous stirring life in whose midst I did not allow her to circulate except under my tutelage, prolonging outdoors her [indoor] sequestration, from which I could withdraw her at the hour I wished for her to return to my side' [my translation].

opportunities, their sheer number is in itself a sign of promiscuity, and each 'cry' is capable of bearing a double meaning. Such double meanings have always formed part of the representation of street cries, especially in popular song and visual art, and many of Proust's readers would have been familiar with the bawdy suggestion of the tinker who offers to fill your hole, or the asparagus-seller's priapic flourish. The erotic subtext is not always so obvious. The first 'cry' that Marcel records is that of the artichoke-seller:

> À la tendresse, à la verduresse
> Artichauts tendres et beaux
> Arti-chauts   (p. 625)[18]

Marcel tells us that he is struck by the resemblance of this cry to Gregorian chant, but Léo Spitzer, in an article of 1959 on its etymology, traces it to an even more ancient form of song, the 'renverdie', which celebrates the return of spring and its green growth, and is associated with the dances of young girls.[19] The narrator's fear of Albertine's orgiastic sexuality is therefore encoded in this cry, whose images of greenness and tenderness she herself picks up later in the episode, when she tells Marcel how much she looks forward to the season when green beans will be cried in the street:

> Et dire qu'il faut attendre encore deux mois pour que nous entendions: "Haricots verts et tendres haricots, v'là l'haricot vert." Comme c'est bien dit: Tendres haricots! vous savez que je les veux tout fins, tout fins, ruisselants de vinaigrette, on ne dirait pas qu'on les mange, c'est frais comme une rosée.
>
> (p. 635)[20]

Of the other cries to do with food, the ones that stand out are those that recall Albertine's association with the sea, and also the seaside: from his first encounter with her at Balbec, in Normandy, in *A l'ombre des jeunes filles en fleurs*, she incarnates for Marcel both the ocean's ungraspable fluidity, its alternations of terror and bliss, and at the same

---

18. 'Tenderness, greenness, / Lovely tender artichokes, / Arti-chokes' [my translation].
19. Léo Spitzer, 'L'Étymologie d'un cri de Paris', in *Études de style* (Paris: Gallimard, 1970), pp. 474–81.
20. 'And to think that we shall have to wait two whole months before we hear: "*Haricots verts et tendres haricots, v'là l'haricot vert.*" How true that is: tender haricots; you know I like them as soft as soft, dripping with vinegar sauce, you wouldn't think you were eating, they melt in the mouth like drops of dew.' The cry translates as: 'Green beans and tender beans, here are the green beans'.

time the frivolity, vulgarity, and promiscuity of a seaside resort. As he and Albertine listen together to the fishmonger's cries, his fearful jealousy transmutes them into signs and wonders:

"À la barque, les huîtres, à la barque."—"Oh! des huîtres, j'en ai si envie!" Heureusement, Albertine, moitié inconstance, moitié docilité, oubliait vite ce qu'elle avait désiré, et avant que j'eusse eu le temps de lui dire qu'elle les aurait meilleures chez Prunier, elle voulait successivement tout ce qu'elle entendait crier par la marchande de poisson: "À la crevette, à la bonne crevette, j'ai de la raie toute en vie, toute en vie.—Merlans à frire, à frire.—Il arrive le maquereau, maquereau frais, maquereau nouveau.—Voilà le maquereau, Mesdames, il est beau le maquereau.—À la moule fraîche et bonne, à la moule!"—Malgré moi, l'avertissement: "Il arrive le maquereau" me faisait frémir. Mais comme cet avertissement ne pouvait s'appliquer, me semblait-il, à mon chauffeur, je ne songeais qu'au poisson que je détestais, mon inquiétude ne durait pas. "Ah! des moules, dit Albertine, j'aimerais tant manger des moules."   (p. 633)[21]

Two double meanings in this passage need explaining. The first is a play on words: Marcel shudders at the ladies being told that fresh mackerel has arrived because 'maquereau' is slang for 'pimp', and he half suspects his chauffeur of being in Albertine's pay. The second depends on the phrase Albertine uses to declare how much she would like to eat oysters: 'Oh! des huîtres, j'en ai si envie!' The word *envie* is then echoed by the fishmonger a few lines further on: *J'ai de la raie toute en vie, toute en vie*, so that the word *envie*, meaning desire, has been split open, like an oyster, to mean 'alive', and together these sum up Albertine's longing, not just for sexual pleasure but to be *toute en vie*, all alive, as she cannot be under Marcel's regime.

---

21. '"*À la barque, les huîtres, à la barque!*" [Straight from the boat, oysters, from the boat!]. "Oh, oysters! I've been simply longing for some!" Fortunately Albertine, partly from inconsistency, partly from docility, quickly forgot the things for which she had been longing, and before I had time to tell her that she would find better oysters at Prunier's, she wanted in succession all the things that she heard cried by the fish hawker: "*À la crevette, à la bonne crevette, j'ai de la raie toute en vie, toute en vie.—Merlans à frire, à frire.—Il arrive le maquereau, maquereau frais, maquereau nouveau.—Voilà le maquereau, Mesdames, il est beau le maquereau.—À la moule fraîche et bonne, à la moule!*" [Shrimp, fine shrimp, I have skate all alive, all alive.—Whiting to fry, to fry.—Mackerel's arrived, fresh mackerel, new mackerel.—Here's mackerel, ladies, beautiful mackerel!—Mussels, fresh and fine, mussels!"] In spite of myself, the warning: "*Il arrive le maquereau*" made me shudder. But as this warning could not, I felt, apply to our chauffeur, I thought only of the fish of that name, which I detested, and my uneasiness did not last. "Ah! Mussels," said Albertine, "I should so like some mussels."' 'Straight from the boat' is Terence Kilmartin's translation; all other translations are mine.

The life that Albertine craves is embodied and articulated by the whole of the *cris de Paris*, which collectively sum up the life of the streets, a life open to infinite suggestions and transactions, free from the stifling atmosphere of the apartment where she has not succeeded in bringing joy. Proust was not the first artist to make this link between the *cris de Paris* and the life of the city, and more particularly its pleasures. The imprint of at least one of these works is visible in *La Prisonnière*, as the critic and music historian Cécile Leblanc has shown: this is Gustave Charpentier's opera *Louise*.[22] Act II begins with a scene in which the young Bohemian artist Julien, in love with the seamstress Louise, comes to her poor neighbourhood hoping to persuade her to elope with him. 'Painfully agitated', as the libretto has it, he is pacing up and down, wondering if she will agree to follow him: 'What must I say to her? How to persuade her?' He ends, 'with anguish', by asking, 'Who will come to my aid?' In answer come the *Marchands de la Rue*, the street-vendors, who give a musical performance of the *cris de Paris*. Several will reappear in *La Prisonnière*, including the chair-mender, the ragman, the cooper, and the artichoke-seller, with exactly the same cry, 'à la tendress', la verduress'!' *Verts et tendres* also features—in Charpentier it is applied to peas, not haricots, but the appeal is the same. Julien listens 'with growing emotion' to the street-vendors' chorus; this is the help he has prayed for, as he exclaims 'with enthusiasm': 'Ah! song of Paris, where my soul vibrates and palpitates! [. . .] Naïve and ancient refrain of the street that awakens, sound of dawn that rejoices my ear! Cries of Paris. . . voices of the street: Are you the victory song of our triumphant love?'

Louise was phenomenally successful—it was Charpentier's one great hit, and is still performed today—and Proust was one of thousands of Parisians who saw it during its long run at the Opéra Comique. He didn't think much of it, admittedly—he referred to it in a letter to a friend as a 'stupid opera'—but Cécile Leblanc convincingly argues that he took what he needed from it in *La Prisonnière*.[23] He gave a dark turn to the identification of the *cris de Paris* with the erotic energy of

---

22. See above, n. 2.
23. Letter to Daniel Halévy of January 1908 (*Correspondance*, ed. Philip Kolb, vol. 22 [Paris: Plon, 1993], p. 632). He made a further disparaging remark in a letter to Jean Cocteau in July 1919, to the effect that although Saint-Saëns was overrated, 'je trouve tout de même dur de le mettre dans le même sac que Charpentier ou Bruneau' [I do think it's harsh to put him in the same bag as Charpentier or Bruneau] (ibid., vol. 18 [1990], p. 267).

the great city, a force Julien interprets as unproblematically (and hetero-
sexually) joyful and liberating. Of course things are more complicated,
as Charpentier acknowledges. Julien believes that the choice he is offering Louise, a choice between sexual passion and domestic drudgery,
whether in her parents' home or within the confines of a 'respectable'
marriage, is no choice at all. But though the outcome is not really in
doubt, Charpentier makes the final scene of the opera, in which Louise
wrenches herself away from her parents, painfully difficult and moving
in its recognition of the cost of her choice.

As Leblanc points out, the denouement formally resembles that of
La Prisonnière in that a young woman escapes from a life of unhappiness
and repression in order to seek her pleasure. This escape is marked by
the return, in the opera, of one of the most symbolically charged of all
the *cris de Paris*, which Proust makes use of in *La Prisonnière*. It is uttered
by Louise's father, in a kind of savage mockery of Julien's celebration
of the 'cries' as the 'victory song of triumphant love'. The cry itself,
when we hear it in Act II, is 'Régalez-vous, mesdames, v'la le plaisir';
now, in this climactic scene, Louise's father seizes his daughter's hands
and, as the stage direction puts it, 'shows her Paris', meaning that he
points to the view of the city they can see from their window; '"Voilà
l'Plaisir, mesdam's!"' he cries, and when Louise breaks away and moves
towards the door he repeats it: '"Voilà l'Plaisir, mesdam's!"' This 'cry'
translates literally as 'Here's pleasure, ladies!', but the 'pleasure' in question
is not what you might think.

Plaisir is one of the keywords of *À la recherche*: it can mean sexual
pleasure, of course, but it can also be used in more neutral or apparently innocuous phrases. So, for example, in the passage in which he
first mentions the *cris de Paris*, Marcel declares: 'Jamais je n'y avais pris
tant de plaisir que depuis qu'Albertine habitait avec moi' (p. 623): the
word *plaisir* is vital here, not just because of its resonance in the book
as a whole, but because of the local connotation which Proust goes on
to evoke.[24] The last 'cry' that he mentions in the first phase of the
episode—when he is on his own, before Albertine comes to join
him—is that of 'de petits Italiens, portant de grandes boîtes de fer
peintes en rouge où les numéros—perdants et gagnants—étaient

24. 'Never had I taken such pleasure in them as since Albertine had come to live with
me'; I have altered Scott Moncrieff's translation, which has 'Never had I so delighted
in them'.

marqués, et jouant d'une crécelle, proposaient: "Amusez-vous, Mesdames, v'là le plaisir"' (p. 626).[25]

The allusion to gambling is at first sight very puzzling, because *le plaisir* in this context is actually a small biscuit or thin pastry, also known as an *oublie*. They were cooked like waffles between two hot plates, and could either be flat or shaped into cones. Their manufacture goes back to medieval times, and the story of how they came to be associated with gambling is a long and complex one, but the fact is that in the nineteenth century, on the streets of Paris, you could indeed encounter street-vendors carrying these pastries in cylindrical boxes, on top of which was a primitive form of roulette wheel. Customers would pay a fixed amount and then spin the wheel, and if one of the winning numbers came up, they got the biscuits (Figure 6.2).[26]

Figure 6.2. *Fête du Palais-Royal: costume 1830 marchande de plaisir*

25. 'young Italians carrying big iron boxes painted red, upon which the numbers—winning and losing—were marked, and [who,] springing their rattles, gave the invitation: "Have fun, ladies, here comes pleasure".'
26. A variant of this practice was that the number that came up was the number of biscuits you won, but Proust has 'winning and losing numbers', so this is definitely a form of gambling.

Proust has altered the wording of the cry—it is usually, as it is in Charpentier, *Régalez-vous, mesdames, v'la le plaisir*—the word 'régalez' having a strong association with food, so that it may be translated 'Treat yourselves'. *Amusez-vous, mesdames* has a different connotation; it means 'Have fun', and lessens the emphasis on taste; it directs our attention more to the element of chance, as though these little Italians were selling something intangible, immaterial, incomestible—not a foodstuff or a service but the *chance* of pleasure, the chance that the narrator is so desperate to deny to Albertine.

Proust's choice of the *petits Italiens* as vendors of *le plaisir* may be, like the mention of Rameau, a kind of deliberate mistake. Italian children or youths were well known as street-vendors, but their wares were not biscuits but little statuettes—and as it happens they appear in their rightful guise later on in the episode, when Marcel is on his own again. He records the vivacious cry of the toy-seller, and then observes: 'De petits Italiens, coiffés d'un béret, n'essayaient pas de lutter avec cet *aria vivace*, et c'est sans rien dire qu'ils offraient de petites statuettes' (p. 644).[27] These Italian boys are the only figures to appear twice in the episode, once vocal, once mute. Why are they given the unlikely role of 'crying' a quintessentially French pastry? I think that Proust is deliberately disguising the fact that, although both men and women could undertake this trade, the vendors of *le plaisir* in nineteenth-century Paris were predominantly women. Georges Kastner, in his 1857 treatise *Les Voix de Paris* [The Voices of Paris], is effusive in his praise of 'l'exclamation vive et joyeuse qui échappe à la marchande de plaisir: *Voilà l'plaisir, mesdames! voilà l'plaisir!* Ici la mélodie s'envole, tourne, pivote sur elle-même, fait la roue, et s'épanouit sur un dernier son joyeux comme une fleur ouvrant tout à coup son calice pour recevoir les baisers du soleil'—a rhapsody that reads like a pastiche of Proust written half a century in advance.[28] Proust may well have known Kastner's work, but even if he didn't, this association of *le plaisir* with female street-vendors would have been familiar to him; it is a woman's

27. 'Some Italian boys in felt bérets made no attempt to compete with this lively aria, and it was without a word that they offered their little statuettes'.
28. Georges Kastner, *Les Voix de Paris: Essai d'une histoire littéraire et musicale des cris populaires de la capitale depuis le moyen age jusqu'à nos jours* (Paris: G. Brandus, Dufour and Jules Renouard, 1857), pp. 84–5. ['the lively and joyous exclamation uttered by the *marchande de plaisir. Here's pleasure, ladies! Here's pleasure!* Here the melody takes flight, turns, pivots on itself, wheels round, and unfurls itself in a final joyful sound like a flower suddenly opening its calix to receive the sun's kisses'; my translation].

voice that Albertine would be most likely to hear on the streets, 'crying' the pleasure she craves.

The pun on this particular cry, 'voilà *le plaisir*', is in one sense obvious, but it also conceals something, or holds something back, and in this it is typical of the way the *cris de Paris* are represented in *La Prisonnière*. This is true of Marcel as narrator, but also of Proust as author. I am wary of biographical readings, but I am going to conclude with a sound from the street which, I think, Proust placed in this episode for his own reasons. It is not in fact a *cri* but a *sifflet*, a whistle, and so is not transcribed but evoked. After Albertine leaves for her outing, Marcel engages in a series of anguished reflections on her possible infidelity. Then the narrative shifts gear:

Laissant ces pensées, maintenant qu'Albertine était sortie, j'allai me mettre un instant à la fenêtre. Il y eut d'abord un silence où le sifflet du marchand de tripes et la corne du tramway firent résonner l'air à des octaves différentes, comme un accordeur de piano aveugle. Puis peu à peu devinrent distincts les motifs entrecroisés auxquels de nouveaux s'ajoutaient. Il y avait aussi un autre sifflet, appel d'un marchand dont je n'ai jamais su ce qu'il vendait, sifflet qui, lui, était exactement pareil à celui d'un tramway, et comme il n'était pas emporté par la vitesse on croyait à un seul tramway, non doué de mouvement, ou en panne, immobilisé, criant à petits intervalles, comme un animal qui meurt.

Et il me semblait que, si jamais je devais quitter ce quartier aristocratique—à moins que ce ne fût pour un tout à fait populaire—les rues et boulevards du centre (où la fruiterie, la poissonnerie, etc. stabilisées dans de grandes maisons d'alimentation, rendraient inutiles les cris des marchands qui n'eussent pas, du reste, réussi à se faire entendre) me sembleraient bien mornes, bien inhabitables, dépouillés, décantés de toutes ces litanies des petits métiers et des ambulantes mangeailles, privés de l'orchestre qui venait de me charmer dès le matin.   (p. 643)[29]

29. 'Dismissing these reflexions, now that Albertine had gone out, I went and took my stand for a moment at the window. There was at first a silence, amid which the whistle of the tripe-vendor and the horn of the tramcar made the air ring in different octaves, like a blind piano-tuner. Then gradually the interwoven motifs became distinct, and others were combined with them. There was also another whistle, the call of a vendor selling something, but what it was I have never discovered, a whistle that was itself exactly like that of a tram and, as it was not carried out of earshot by its own velocity, one thought of a single tram, not endowed with motion, or broken down, immobilized, crying out at short intervals like a dying animal. And I felt that, should I ever have to leave this aristocratic quarter—unless it were to move to one that was entirely plebeian—the streets and boulevards of central Paris (where the fruit, fish, and other trades, stabilized in huge stores, rendered superfluous the cries of the street hawkers, who for that matter would not have been able to make themselves heard) would seem to me very dreary, quite uninhabitable, stripped, drained of all these litanies of the small trades and peripatetic victuals, deprived of the orchestra that had come to charm me as soon as the day began.'

I have repeated a passage I cited earlier—the one about the difference between the 'aristocratic quarter' where Marcel lives and central Paris—in order to emphasize how jarring, how incongruous, the description of this 'other whistle' appears. The sequence of Marcel's impressions would be much smoother if the sentence beginning 'Il y avait aussi un autre sifflet' were removed. It feels like an interpolation, the more powerful for being so arbitrary. Something is being offered, but we can't know what it is; its 'call' is compared to the whistle of a stalled tram, which is itself compared to the cry of a dying animal. That last image hauntingly echoes the one Marcel had used to describe his grandmother on her deathbed, looking as though a beast had decked itself out in her hair and were lying in her sheets.[30] To understand why it should be a tram which undergoes this metamorphosis you have to remember all the Proustian associations of the humble word *tramway*, imported from English and whose pronunciation is not fully assimilable into French. I am thinking, for example, of the celebrated passage in *Le Côté de Guermantes* in which Marcel imagines a sick person, rendered temporarily deaf by having his ears stuffed with cotton, who is restored to the world of sound when the cotton wool is removed: 'on assiste, comme si elles étaient psalmodiées par des anges musiciens, à la résurrection des voix. Les rues vides sont remplies pour un instant par les ailes rapides et successives des tramways chanteurs'.[31] The tramway also has another kind of poetry, nothing to do with choirs of angels but with M. de Charlus's scandalously funny account of cruising the streets of Paris, catching a glimpse of a fanciable tram conductor, and stalking his quarry from one tram line to another.[32] The tram is a sign of mobility and interchange, which is why it is so apt that the church at Balbec, which Marcel had imagined buffeted by the waves on a clifftop in Normandy, should actually be located on a square where two tramway lines intersect.[33] But in *La Prisonnière* the analogy between the street-vendor's call and the whistle of a tram portends the opposite of movement. The whistle of a tram should be heard disappearing, diminishing in the distance, 'carried out of earshot by its own velocity'. But this

30. *Le Côté de Guermantes II*, ch. 1 (*Pléiade* edition, ii 631–2).
31. *Le Côté de Guermantes I* (*Pléiade* ii 375). 'we are present, as though it were the chanting of choirs of angels, at the resurrection of the voice. The empty streets are filled for a moment with the whirr of the swift, consecutive wings of the singing tramway-cars.'
32. *Sodome et Gomorrhe I* (*Pléiade* edition, iii 12–13).
33. *À l'ombre des jeunes filles en fleurs II* (*Pléiade* ii 19).

machine—'not endowed with motion, or broken down, immobilized, crying out at short intervals like a dying animal'—is Proust himself, in the last days of his life. Like a painter, he has placed a self-portrait in this crowded urban scene. In the autumn of 1922 he was working on *La Prisonnière* with '[une] espèce d'acharnement' [a kind of furious determination], he told his publisher Gaston Gallimard, finishing the revisions for the book and preparing advance extracts from the early section of the novel which could be published in magazines. I quote from the *Pléiade* edition notes: 'Dans sa dernière lettre à Gaston Gallimard, du 30 octobre ou du 1er novembre 1922, Proust exprime le sentiment d'en avoir terminé avec son œuvre [...] Sinon le sentiment de l'avoir achevée, du moins celui de ne pouvoir aller plus loin, d'être allé au bout de ses forces' (p. 1667).[34] I believe this exhaustion, the sense of having ground to a halt, is embodied in the image of the stalled tram whose cry is that of a dying animal. Proust speaks of 'the call of a vendor selling something, but what it was I have never discovered'. He cannot know, of course, until he has bought what this merchant is selling; and after that he will not remember.

34. 'In his last letter to Gaston Gallimard, of 30 October or 1 November 1922, Proust expresses the sense of having finished with his work [...] If not the feeling of having completed it, at least that of not being able to go further, of having come to the end of his strength' [my translation].

7

The poet and the knife-grinder

In the course of this book I have been considering examples of literary works which appropriate the songs and 'cries' of the city streets. But street songs and street cries are only part of an urban soundscape filled with other kinds of music—or noise, depending on your point of view. In Hogarth's 'Enrag'd Musician', not only the musician of the title, but the ones in the street, including the ballad singer, are competing with a dozen other noise-makers, and as we have seen, there are many passages of writing about the city which represent music and song drowned out, or overwhelmed, by other urban sounds. But another way of interpreting the noises of the city is to think of them all as songs—to extend the definition of the term into the realm of metaphor, or analogy, so that the sounds of machinery, or of traffic, are heard *as* song. Proust's reference to 'the whirr of the swift, consecutive wings of the singing tramway-cars' is one such transposition of sound into song.[1] In this last chapter I will go a step further and extend the definition of street song to something seen as well as heard.

The following poem by Walt Whitman was first published in the 1871 edition of *Leaves of Grass*.

Sparkles from the Wheel

Where the city's ceaseless crowd moves on the livelong day,
Withdrawn I join a group of children watching, I pause aside with them.

By the curb toward the edge of the flagging,
A knife-grinder works at his wheel sharpening a great knife,
Bending over he carefully holds it to the stone, by foot and knee,
With measur'd tread he turns rapidly, as he presses with light but firm hand,

---

1. See Chapter 6, p. 157 n. 31.

Forth issue then in copious golden jets,
Sparkles from the wheel.

The scene and all its belongings, how they seize and affect me,
The sad sharp-chinn'd old man with worn clothes and broad shoulder-
    band of leather,
Myself effusing and fluid, a phantom curiously floating, now here absorb'd
    and arrested,
The group, (an unminded point set in a vast surrounding,)
The attentive, quiet children, the loud, proud, restive base of the streets,
The low hoarse purr of the whirling stone, the light-press'd blade,
Diffusing, dropping, sideways-darting, in tiny showers of gold,
Sparkles from the wheel.[2]

There is a first reading that remains, preserving its power through the
complications of successive rereadings, especially when that first reading
belongs to our childhood, or to some formative time of life. I first read
'Sparkles from the Wheel' over forty years ago, when I knew very little
about Whitman, and had no interest in street traders in general, or the
knife-grinder in particular. The textual history of the poem was as blank
to me as the social history of its subject, or the kind of machine it
describes. The mechanism of a treadle-operated grinding wheel seems
to have come into use in the fifteenth century; the machine could be
mounted on a wheelbarrow or small cart, and its portability allowed
the knife-grinder to become an itinerant craftsman who could move
from village to village, or neighbourhood to neighbourhood of a large
city; but I had only the vaguest idea of this technology, let alone of the
knife-grinder's literary and artistic affiliations. The poem enchanted
me; so often Whitman's magic is bound up with song; he repeatedly
uses the word *chant* as both noun and verb to describe his poems.[3] The
formal properties of song—notably repetition and refrain—shape the
poem both on the page and when read aloud. It is itself a wheel, turning
on itself from title to last line. What seem to be plain prosaic units carry
expressive weight: in the first two lines, for example, the poet places

2. Walt Whitman, 'Sparkles from the Wheel', *Leaves of Grass*, 1891–2 (the so-called 'deathbed
   edition'), in *Walt Whitman: Complete Poetry and Collected Prose* (New York: Library of America,
   1982), pp. 514–15. All page references are to this volume unless otherwise indicated.
3. There are over a hundred occurrences of 'chant' and its cognates (e.g. 'chanter') in the
   edition of 1891–2, including prose prefaces and afterwords. A small example, from a
   little-known poem, 'Then Last of All' (from *First Annex: Sands at Seventy* [1888]): 'Then
   last of all, caught from these shores, this hill, / Of you O tides, the mystic human
   meaning: / Only by law of you, your swell and ebb, enclosing me the same, / The
   brain that shapes, the voice that chants this song' (p. 620).

himself in the scene by a graduated process marked by shorter and shorter phrases: 'Where the city's ceaseless crowd moves on the live-long day' (thirteen syllables); 'Withdrawn I join a group of children watching' (eleven); 'I pause aside with them' (six).[4] In contrast, line 11, 'Myself effusing and fluid, a phantom curiously floating, now here absorb'd and arrested', is an almost perfectly balanced triad.[5] The poem's structure, as Helen Vendler observes, constitutes a kind of musical 'reprise', in which the second group of eight lines repeats, with variation, the motifs of the first.[6] And the poet's musical apprehension of the scene he describes, and of its effect on him, is the vehicle of a numinous meaning, like Wordsworth's 'sense sublime / Of something far more deeply interfused'—undefined but not empty.[7] 'The scene and all its belongings, how they seize and affect me': we are not directly told *how* they affect him, yet the statement manages not to seem evasive. It is characteristic of Whitman that this emotion should be found not in Nature but in the city, though the poem's urban setting is not a simple matter.

My first, and still active, response to the poem is an emotional one— the feeling that it is a beautiful and moving poem, that it fulfils Wordsworth's criterion for the purpose and value of poetry, namely to give pleasure, and that this pleasure is an affair of the senses as well as the intellect—of intellect and senses combined.[8] And I would like to persuade readers who are not 'seized and affected' by the poem as I am

4. Revisions in punctuation from the poem's first printing in 1871 sharpen this sense of Whitman's craft: 'Where the city's ceaseless crowd moves on, the livelong day, / Withdrawn, I join a group of children watching—I pause aside with them'. In the manuscript the first line originally read 'Where the city's ceaseless crowd moves up and down', more apt for the vertical axis of Manhattan, but rhythmically awkward. See Fredson Bowers (ed.), *Whitman's Manuscripts: Leaves of Grass (1860)* (Chicago, IL and London: University of Chicago Press, 1955), pp. 254–5. The manuscript of 'Sparkles from the Wheel', though it dates from a decade later than the poems of the 1860 *Leaves*, is included in this volume because it is one of a handful of post-1860 MSS in the Valentine-Barrett collection that forms the basis of Bowers' edition. The Valentine-Barrett MSS are now in the Library of the University of Virginia (Bowers, p. ix).
5. Three phrases of seven, eight, and seven syllables; the pronunciation of 'curiously' makes the middle phrase of almost equal length to the others.
6. Helen Vendler, *Poets Thinking: Pope, Whitman, Dickinson, Yeats* (Cambridge, MA and London: Harvard University Press, 2004), p. 37.
7. William Wordsworth, 'Lines Written a Few Miles Above Tintern Abbey', ll. 96–7, in *Lyrical Ballads*, ed. Michael Mason (Harlow: Longman, 1992), p. 212. The poem was first published in 1798.
8. For the relevant quotation from the Preface to *Lyrical Ballads*, see Chapter 1, n. 3.

to partake of my feeling, which I distinguish from politely agreeing to differ about it. This emotion persists even though I now know more than I did about its contexts and allusions, its analogies and reson-ances—now that I have a scholarly grasp of it, which so often seems like taking a work of art into protective custody.

The contexts are many. The poem belongs to Whitman's poetry about the city, and about himself as observer of urban sights and sounds. These city poems are, in turn, part of a literary tradition which is both ancient and modern, in which the urban crowd is the subject of cele-bration, or satire, or both, and in which the figure of the walker, or *flâneur*, the urban spectator, whether alienated from, or at one with, the city's performances, is equally present. Urban street trades have a long history of representation in literature, music, and painting, as I have already shown in other chapters of this book, and, within that vast general category, the knife-grinder has been the subject of particular kinds of attention.

'This is the city and I am one of the citizens, / Whatever interests the rest interests me.'[9] From the beginning, Whitman was a self-appointed urban laureate, buoyed by the modern city's energy, enjoying its immensity, its restlessness, its cacophony. Already, in the first edition of *Leaves of Grass* in 1855, the soundscape of New York is made up of both human and non-human voices: 'The blab of the pave... the tires of carts and sluff of bootsoles and talk of the promenaders', 'the clank of the shod horses on the granite floor', 'The hurrahs for popular favorites... the fury of roused mobs', 'The impassive stones that receive and return so many echoes': 'I mind them', the poet tells us, 'I mind them or the resonance of them... I come again and again'.[10] The city is a place of limitless opportunity, based on the continuous shock of new encounters: Manhattan is the 'City of orgies, walks and joys', lit up by the 'frequent and swift flash of eyes offering me love'.[11] It is also a crucible of democracy, 'Where the citizen is always the head and ideal'.[12] Whitman was not such a fool as to think that the modern city was without hier-archies of wealth or class. But he believed that the city as a whole was too strong for any group or person to define and possess—except, of course, himself. Despite its pastoral-sounding title, *Leaves of Grass*

9. 'Song of Myself', ll. 1075–6 [sect. 42] (p. 235).
10. From ll. 146–59 of the untitled first poem in the 1855 edition of *Leaves of Grass* (pp. 33–4).
11. 'City of Orgies', ll. 1, 8 (p. 8).
12. 'Song of the Broad-Axe', l. 124 [sect. 5] (p. 335).

belongs to New York, not simply because Whitman lived and worked there in the crucial years during which the poem was gestating, but because it enabled him to forge his poetic credentials—his claim to sovereignty over America. He is 'Walt Whitman, a kosmos, of Manhattan the son' (though he was actually born on Long Island): both name and title, so to speak, are authorized by his affiliation.[13] In 'City of Ships' he addresses the 'Proud and passionate city—mettlesome, mad, extravagant city!':

> Behold me—incarnate me as I have incarnated you!
> I have rejected nothing you offer'd me—whom you adopted I have
>   adopted,
> Good or bad I never question you—I love all—I do not condemn any
>   thing,
> I chant and celebrate all that is yours—[14]

The contrast with Wordsworth has become a critical commonplace, and not one I wish to challenge. What the Lake District meant to Wordsworth, New York meant to Whitman. He was not the first writer to take issue with Wordsworth on this account—Charles Lamb put the case a decade before Whitman was born, in a funny and fiery letter to Wordsworth declining to join the Nature-worshipping choir, giving a Whitmanian catalogue of the sights and sounds of Fleet Street and Covent Garden, and declaring that he 'often shed tears in the motley Strand from fullness of joy at so much Life'.[15] Whitman, too, writing of New York and Brooklyn in 1871, felt the 'splendor, picturesqueness, and oceanic amplitude and rush of these great cities', which 'completely [satisfied his] senses of power, fulness, motion, &c., and [gave him], through such senses and appetites, and through [his] esthetic conscience, a continued exaltation and absolute fulfilment'.[16]

And yet there is something odd about 'Sparkles from the Wheel'—something that doesn't fit the general idea of Whitman as a city poet. As

---

13. 'Song of Myself', sect. 24, l. 1 (p. 210). In the first edition of *Leaves of Grass* (1855) the line read: 'Walt Whitman, an American, one of the roughs, a kosmos' (p. 50).
14. 'City of Ships', ll. 9, 12–15 (p. 430).
15. Charles Lamb, letter to Wordsworth of 30 January 1801, in *The Letters of Charles and Mary Anne Lamb*, ed. Edwin W. Marrs, Jr, vol. 1 (Ithaca, NY and London: Cornell University Press, 1975), p. 267.
16. Walt Whitman, *Democratic Vistas* (1871), p. 938. The caveat that follows—'But sternly discarding, shutting our eyes to the glow and grandeur of the general superficial effect [...] we ask, Are there, indeed, *men* here worthy the name?' (p. 939)—is of great interest, but is not relevant to my argument here.

Dana Brand points out (with hostile intent), Whitman characteristically presents the city in sweeping, panoramic views, and his New York is 'strikingly impressionistic': 'Sense impressions are rarely unique, particular, or extensively described. They are experienced in clusters, subsumed under general categories'.[17] He cites passages from 'Song of Myself', and poems such as 'A Broadway Pageant' and 'Crossing Brooklyn Ferry', to argue that 'The panoramic and impressionistic nature of Whitman's apprehension of the city does not lend itself to concrete and particularized representation'.[18] In a letter written from New York in October 1868, Whitman does his best to supply Brand with ammunition.

You know it is a never ending amusement and study and recreation for me to ride a couple of hours of a pleasant afternoon on a Broadway stage in this way. You see everything as you pass, a sort of living, endless panorama—shops and splendid buildings and great windows: and on the broad sidewalks crowds of women richly dressed continually passing altogether different, superior in style and looks from any to be seen anywhere else—in fact a perfect stream of people—men too dressed in high style, and plenty of foreigners—and then in the streets the thick crowd of carriages, stages, carts, hotel and private coaches, and in fact all sorts of vehicles and many first class teams, mile after mile, and the splendor of such a great street and so many tall, ornamental, noble buildings many of them of white marble, and the gayety and motion on every side: you will not wonder how much attraction all this is on a fine day, to a great loafer like me, who enjoys so much seeing the busy world move by him, and exhibiting itself for his amusement, while he takes it easy and just looks on and observes.[19]

Brand has no time for the poet as *flâneur*, a figure whose 'flaunted laziness' he sees as a form of false consciousness, and he attributes 'The failure of Whitman's urban poetry' to a more general cause, 'The inability of nineteenth-century spectators to look at crowds with a questioning rather than an imperial gaze'. This judgement seems to me to be itself lazy and self-satisfied; but Brand is right to characterize Whitman's approach to the city as favouring perspectives from which, as he puts it in his prose piece 'My Passion for Ferries', he 'could get a full sweep, absorbing shows, accompaniments, surroundings'.[20] Not surprisingly,

---

17. Dana Brand, *The Spectator and the City in Nineteenth-Century American Literature* (Cambridge: Cambridge University Press, 1991), p. 158.

18. Ibid., p. 159.

19. Letter of 9 October 1868, in *Calamus: A Series of Letters Written During the Years 1868–1880 by Walt Whitman to a Young Friend (Peter Doyle)*, ed. Richard Maurice Bucke (Boston, MA: Laurens Maynard, 1897), p. 42.

20. 'My Passion for Ferries', *Specimen Days and Collect* (1882), p. 701.

then, 'Sparkles from the Wheel' does not feature in Brand's analysis. Its perspective is local and accidental, not at all panoramic; Whitman is on foot, not riding in an omnibus or sailing on a ferry; he may still be a *flâneur*, but he is not 'just looking on and observing'. The poem records an encounter rather than an impression, and this encounter is defined by the city street, where events are contingent and inconsequential. The knife-grinder, the children, and the poet will all move on. There are very few poems in *Leaves of Grass* at all like it.[21] It most resembles— to return to this comparison from another angle—those poems or passages from poems in which Wordsworth records an encounter with a figure, solitary or singled out from the crowd—the old man travelling and the shepherd carrying the last of his flock in *Lyrical Ballads*, the Leech-Gatherer in 'Resolution and Independence', the Highland girl in 'The Solitary Reaper', and, in the city, the prostitute's child, the workman with his sickly child on his knee, and the blind beggar, in book 7 of *The Prelude*.[22] Wordsworth invests these encounters with symbolic meanings, but he is also more forthright than Whitman in

21. I would cite the opening lines of section 13 of 'Song of Myself', 'The negro holds firmly the reins of his four horses' (p. 198); from *Calamus*, 'I Saw in Louisiana a Live-Oak Growing' (p. 279); from *Drum-Taps*, four vignettes: 'Cavalry Crossing a Ford', 'Bivouac on a Mountain Side', 'An Army Corps on the March', and especially 'By the Bivouac's Fitful Flame' (pp. 435–6); from *Autumn Rivulets* (besides 'Sparkles from the Wheel'), 'The City Dead-House' (pp. 494–5) and 'Italian Music in Dakota' (p. 523). I am not sure of some of these, and several, clearly, are nothing to do with the city. For such urban encounters we have to look to Whitman's prose, above all to *Specimen Days*, which Brand misleadingly implies takes the same view of the city as the poems. This is true of some sections, but not of many others. Besides specific historical anecdotes, such as Whitman's memory of seeing John Jacob Astor being 'lifted and tuck'd in a gorgeous sleigh' ('Broadway Sights', p. 702), or of hearing the news of the attack on Fort Sumter ('Opening of the Secession War', p. 706), or of seeing President Lincoln receiving visitors at his inauguration levee, 'looking very disconsolate, and as if he would give anything to be somewhere else' ('The Inauguration', p. 758), there are numerous accounts in which Whitman is far from being a privileged spectator, where his movements are haphazard, and his point of view veers from 'documentary' detachment to immersive subjectivity: 'Back to Washington' (pp. 713–14), 'An Army Hospital Ward' (pp. 718–19), 'The Wounded from Chancellorsville' (pp. 720–1), etc.

22. William Wordsworth, *The Poems*, 2 vols., ed. John O. Hayden (Harmondsworth: Penguin Books, 1977): 'Animal Tranquillity and Decay' (originally titled 'Old Man Travelling'), i 242; 'The Last of the Flock', i 295; 'Resolution and Independence', i 551; 'The Solitary Reaper', i 659. *The Prelude: A Parallel Text*, ed. J. C. Maxwell (Harmondsworth: Penguin Books, 1972): the prostitute's child, vii 333–411, pp. 271, 273; the workman, vii 594–618, pp. 285, 287; the blind beggar, vii 635–49, pp. 287, 289. I cite the text of the first edition (1850), the one Whitman would have known; the 1805 text was not published in his lifetime. In 1805 the workman with the sickly child is in viii 42–59, p. 344.

framing them as moral or philosophical *exempla*: the workman with his child, for example, is introduced as an example of 'those individual sights / Of courage, or integrity, or truth, / Or tenderness' which are 'more touching' in the city because of the surrounding 'foolishness and madness in parade'.

Only one of Wordsworth's extended urban encounters is with a street trader or performer; I discussed this poem, 'Power of Music', in my first chapter, but it is worth returning to here because it helps us understand what makes Whitman's treatment distinctive.[23] The parallels between the two poems are clear enough: the musician, like the knife-grinder, holds his audience's attention by something magical and enchanting in his performance; although he is playing in Oxford Street, in one of the busiest streets of London, those whom he enter-tains, all of them poor and some destitute, are 'deaf' to the noise of traffic, indifferent to the prosperous citizens rushing by in their 'coaches and chariots', whom the poet himself addresses with scorn: 'they care not for you, / Nor what ye are flying, nor what ye pursue!' Whitman would sympathize with all this, but not with the poet-spectator's attitude and response to what he sees and hears. Wordsworth does not place himself in the scene, does not implicate himself in what he witnesses; yet he identifies with the musician and rejoices in the exercise of his power. Whitman's description of the knife-grinder, by contrast, is sober, respectful, serious—and purely external. He does not speculate on what the old man is feeling. On the other hand, Whitman's class-consciousness is less in evidence than Wordsworth's. It is not not there, if I may use that awkward formula; clearly the figure who wanders the city streets is at leisure, while the knife-grinder is at work; he can't quite escape his own self-description as 'a great loafer [. . .] who enjoys so much seeing the busy world move by him, and exhibiting itself for his amusement'. There are no labouring poor among the spectators, but the 'group of children' are street children, unaccompanied by parents or nursemaids, and the poet does not come from their neighbourhood.[24]

23. 'Power of Music', *The Poems* i 691–3.
24. Compare 'the bonfire of shavings in the open lot of the city...the crowd of children watching', from the second (untitled) poem of the 1855 *Leaves of Grass* (l. 149, p. 97); in 1856 this poem was given the title 'Poem of the Daily Work of the Workmen and Workwomen of These States' and in 1860–1 it was no. 3 of 'Chants Democratic'; the line is present in both of these texts, but was cut as part of the major revision of the poem in the 1867 *Leaves*, where it has the title 'To Workingmen'; it eventually became 'A Song for Occupations'.

Nevertheless, the effect is much more oblique than in Wordsworth, and Whitman's initial action—'I *join a group* of children watching, I pause aside *with them*'—places him in the scene, at least to begin with, in a way that is not part of Wordsworth's design.

I will return to this group of children; they are part of the iconography of the scene which has a history of its own. I want first to say a little more about the knife-grinder himself. Whitman's knife-grinder combines two kinds of figure, and is represented in two different modes. One is a workman, practising a street trade which was still, in the mid-nineteenth century, a familiar sight in both urban and rural communities. He is realistically depicted, in phrases that delineate first the action he performs, and then the type of man he is. The fact that he is sharpening a 'great knife' may imply that he is not working for a private household, but a local business such as a butcher's. He is a skilled craftsman: he works 'carefully', and his hand is 'light but firm'. In the second stanza we learn that he is an old man, whose countenance and dress tell us that he is poor, and who wears the badge of his trade, the 'broad shoulder-band of leather', as though he were defined by the labour over which he is bent. But this is not the case. The first stanza ends by emphasizing not the knife-grinder's skill in sharpening the blade, or the sound it makes, but the gratuitous beauty his craftsmanship produces: 'Forth issue then in copious golden jets, / Sparkles from the wheel'.

These 'sparkles' are something more than 'sparks'; they combine light and fire. There is also a pun on the knife-grinder's lightness of touch: in the first stanza he 'presses with light but firm hand', in the second, the knife itself is a 'light-press'd blade', as though the 'sparkles' had been produced by verbal play (as indeed they have). In 'So Long!', the poem that has formally concluded *Leaves of Grass* since the third edition of 1860–1, the poet speaks of himself as a wanderer through life, his art made out of casual, unplanned encounters:

At random glancing, each as I notice absorbing,
Swiftly on, but a little while alighting,
Curious envelop'd messages delivering,
Sparkles hot, seed ethereal down in the dirt dropping,
Myself unknowing, my commission obeying, to question it never daring,
To ages and ages yet the growth of the seed leaving[25]

---

25. 'So Long!', ll. 37–42 (p. 610). The poem was extensively revised through successive editions, but this passage remained virtually unaltered, with only a couple of minor

In 'Sparkles from the Wheel', the figure of the poet is split in two: he is the wandering observer, 'a phantom curiously floating, now here absorb'd and arrested', and also the craftsman whose 'light-press'd blade / Diffusing, dropping, sideways-darting' produces the 'sparkles' that resemble the 'Sparkles hot, seed ethereal down in the dirt dropping', and deliver his 'Curious envelop'd messages'.

In thinking about the double identity of the knife-grinder, I don't want to lose sight of the workman, as though Whitman's realistic sketch of him existed only as a front or disguise for the poet's true purpose, which hollows him out and makes him a figure in a self-serving design. (That is a risk that Whitman's poetic method courts: he is so openly bent on appropriating the identities of others that it becomes hard, sometimes, to accept his contention that the process is reciprocal.) But it is also the case that Whitman was not the first to represent the knife-grinder in a work of art, and that his poem takes its place in a contest, or conversation, whose other voices include painters and printmakers as well as writers.

It is a rule of thumb in studying nineteenth-century American literature that, for almost any subject you care to name, James Russell Lowell will turn out to have written either a poem or an essay on it. The knife-grinder duly appears in a poem called 'Under the Willows', published in 1869, in which Lowell indulges in rural meditations that don't measure up either to Horace in the classical past or Robert Frost in the New England future.[26] After welcoming the 'dusty Tramp', whom he characterizes as 'lavish Summer's bedesman', work-shy and immoral, but enviably free and self-possessed, a kind of Robin Hood

---

changes in punctuation and spelling. The association of 'sparkles' and 'seed' was influenced, I think, by the ending of Shelley's 'Ode to the West Wind': 'Drive my dead thoughts over the universe / Like withered leaves to quicken a new birth! / And, by the incantation of this verse, / Scatter, as from an unextinguished hearth, / Ashes and sparks, my words among mankind!' (ll. 63–7, in *Poetical Works*, ed. T. Hutchinson, 2nd ed., corr. G. M. Matthews [Oxford: Oxford University Press, 1970], p. 579). 'Sparkle' and its cognates are not common in Whitman, either as noun or verb; mostly the noun refers to effects of light, as in 'the sparkles of starshine on the icy and pallid earth' in 'The Sleepers' (l. 65, p. 545), or 'the far-away sparkle of the minarets of Mecca' in 'Salut au Monde!' (l. 185, p. 295). The same is true of the verb, which only once, in 'Camps of Green', refers to fire: 'the fires lit up begin to sparkle' (l. 5, p. 606).

26. James Russell Lowell, 'Under the Willows', in *Under the Willows and Other Poems* (Boston, MA: Ticknor and Fields, 1869). Robert Frost's 'The Grindstone' (first publ. in the magazine *Farm and Fireside* in 1921, then in *New Hampshire*, 1923) begins by emphasizing not movement but stasis: 'Having a wheel and four legs of its own / Has never availed the cumbersome grindstone / To get it anywhere that I can see.'

who has a 'secret league with wild wood-wandering things'—after this figure appears at his door, he is followed by his no less Romantic opposite:

> Here
> The Scissors-grinder, pausing, doffs his hat,
> And lets the kind breeze, with its delicate fan,
> Winnow the heat from out his dank gray hair,—
> A grimy Ulysses, a much-wandered man,
> Whose feet are known to all the populous ways,
> And many men and manners he hath seen,
> Not without fruit of solitary thought.
> He, as the habit is of lonely men,—
> Unused to try the temper of their mind
> In fence with others,—positive and shy,
> Yet knows to put an edge upon his speech,
> Pithily Saxon in unwilling talk.
> Him I entrap with my long-suffering knife,
> And, while its poor blade hums away in sparks,
> Sharpen my wit upon his gritty mind,
> In motion set obsequious to his wheel,
> And in its quality not much unlike.[27]

The Pedlar in Wordsworth's *Excursion* is one model for this figure: 'From his native hills / He wandered far; much did he see of men, / Their manners, their enjoyments, and pursuits, / Their passions and their feelings'; in a note to these lines, Wordsworth cites a passage from Robert Heron's *Observations Made in a Journey through the Western Counties of Scotland* (1793), which says of such itinerant merchants: 'As in their peregrinations they have opportunity of contemplating the manners of various men and various cities, they become eminently skilled in the knowledge of the world. *As they wander, each alone, through thinly-inhabited districts, they form habits of reflection and of sublime contemplation*'.[28] But another, more recent figure is also on Lowell's mind: the 'grimy Ulysses' alludes to Tennyson's poem, whose hero proclaims, 'Much have I seen and known; cities of men / And manners, climates, councils, governments'.[29] Lowell's allusion is tinged with bathos, as though the knife-grinder's claim to epic status were both

27. 'Under the Willow', ll. 205–26 (the 'dusty Tramp'); ll. 226–43 (the 'Scissors-man').
28. William Wordsworth, *The Excursion* (1814) i 340–3 (*The Poems* ii 50; the quotation from Heron is on p. 954; Wordsworth's italics).
29. Alfred Tennyson, 'Ulysses' (1842), ll. 13–14, in *The Poems of Tennyson*, ed. C. Ricks, 2nd ed., 3 vols. (Harlow: Longman, 1987), i 616.

valid and absurd, a quality gifted to him, pro tem, by the poet's superior learning. When Wordsworth calls the street musician 'an Orpheus', he means it, or rather the poem finds a way to break out of its self-conscious stance; Lowell is caught in the mock-epic trap he has set himself. He doesn't ignore the hardship of the knife-grinder's life, but in the end this hardship turns to the poet's account. What is 'grimy' and 'gritty' about the knife-grinder's trade enters into his speech and his mentality, as Lowell represents them, and these qualities give his conversation with his social superior its savour and profit.

Whitman would never have the knife-grinder 'doff his cap', a phrase that conveys more than that he simply takes it off, even if he were interested in having a conversation with him. But he isn't. The 'sparkles from the wheel' are more eloquent than anything the man himself could utter, however 'Pithily Saxon'. Nor does Whitman give the knife-grinder any pseudo-Wordsworthian aura of homespun wisdom. In any case, the iconography of the scene has a different focus. It is to do with looking, not speaking. And here Whitman joins, consciously or not, a long history of visual representation of the knife-grinder and his 'audience'.

This history isn't uniform, but complex and sometimes contradictory. Part of it sees the knife-grinder as one of many craftsmen whose social and economic activities are worth documenting and classifying; but this 'documentary' impulse is in itself not neutral. In a sixteenth-century German handbook of trades and crafts, the grinder boasts in verse of his skill and usefulness in the arts of both peace and war: he sharpens 'Messerkling mittl, groß und klein' [cutlery of all sizes] but also 'Helleparten, Dolch, Schwert und Degen' [halberd, dagger, sword, and rapier].[30] In an eighteenth-century engraving of a 'Gagne petit Auvergnat' (itinerant knife-grinder from the Auvergne region), the knife-grinder belongs to a series of artistic 'studies taken among the lower orders' who perform the *cris de Paris* (Figure 7.1).[31] As this example suggests, the knife-grinder would feature as a matter of course in any compilation of the 'Cries' of London or Paris; in a

---

30. *Der Schleifer* [The Grinder] in *Das Ständebuch* [The Book of Trades], Frankfurt, 1568. Woodcuts by Jost Amman (1539–91); accompanying poem by Hans Sachs (1494–1576), the original 'Meistersinger von Nürnberg'.
31. Caylus (Figure 7.1) was an aristocrat, antiquarian, and connoisseur of art and low life.

Figure 7.1. *Gagne petit Auvergnat,* engraving by Anne Claude Philippe de Tubières, comte de Caylus (1692–1765) after Edmé Bouchardon (1698–1762), in *Études prises dans le bas peuple, ou Les Cris de Paris* (Paris, 1737–46)

series of prints issued in London in 1795, the 'cry' is given in both English and French (Figure 7.2).[32] The knife-grinder appears, not surprisingly, in Dutch genre painting, for example in Jacob Duck's *Street Scene with Knife Grinder and Elegant Couple* from 1655 (Figure 7.3), where the wheel is at rest, pointed at and discussed by the onlookers; but Adriaen van Ostade, around 1682, offers a very different image, in which the workman, with his set features, is seen bent to his relentless task, the cobbler to his right already leaning out of his basement workshop to offer him another tool to grind (Figure 7.4).

Knife-grinding, however socially necessary it might be, was hard labour—we speak of the daily grind, or keeping our noses to the grindstone—and it was associated with poverty and loneliness. That did not always imply empathy. In 1797 the Tory statesman and wit George Canning published a satirical poem, 'The Friend of Humanity, and the Knife-grinder', in the *Anti-Jacobin* magazine. The 'Friend of Humanity', a caricature of philanthropic radicalism, addresses a 'Needy Knife-grinder' in the belief that his ragged dress and forlorn appearance tell a tale of exploitation by the rich and powerful. But the knife-grinder denies that he has any such 'story' to tell; his tale is rather one of good old-fashioned working-class dissipation, of a drunken brawl and being arrested and put in the stocks for vagrancy. He concludes by saying that he never 'meddles with politics' and asks the 'Friend of Humanity' to give him sixpence for a pot of beer. Indignant at his lack of political consciousness, the 'Friend of Humanity', in the poem's final stage direction, '*Kicks the Knife-grinder, overturns his Wheel, and exit in a transport of republican enthusiasm and universal philanthropy.*' The 'needy knife-grinder' became a kind of cultural cliché, surviving late into the nineteenth century.[33] But the original political message is the important

32. The English 'cry' is 'Knives, Scissars [sic] and Razors to Grind'; the French 'Couteaux, Ciseaux, Rasoirs à [sic] Repasser'—virtually identical to the *cri* that Proust heard over a century later.

33. He features in James Clarence Mangan's 'Khidder' (see Chapter 1, p. 21), where a specific allusion to Canning's poem is likely, though not declared, as it is in chapter 3 of Matthew Arnold's *Culture and Anarchy*: 'Perhaps Canning's "Needy Knife-grinder" (who is dead, and therefore cannot be pained at my taking him for an illustration) may serve to give us the notion of defect in the essential quality of a working-class' (*Culture and Anarchy: An Essay in Political and Social Criticism* [1869], p. 96). Walter Besant, in the lecture that so provoked Henry James, expects his audience to recognize it as the ground of a simile: 'We have all along been training ourselves how to tell the story, and here is this new school which steps in like the needy knife-grinder, to explain that there is no story left at all to tell' (*The Art of Fiction: A Lecture Delivered at the Royal Institution, April 25th, 1884*), p. 28.

Figure 7.2. Giovanni Vendramini (1769–1839), *Knife Grinder*, after painting by Francis Wheatley (1747–1801), in *Cries of London* (1795)

Figure 7.3. Jacob Duck (*c.* 1600–67), *A Street Scene with Knife Grinder and Elegant Couple* (*c.* 1655)

one: you can see its force in James Gilray's contemporaneous print, which reproduces the poem and identifies the 'Friend of Humanity' with the Whig politician George Tierney, MP for Southwark, where the scene is located; the slogan 'Tiernay [sic] & Liberty' is graffitied on the wall of the building to the left, and the print is dedicated with ironic 'respect' to 'the Independent Electors of the Borough of Southwark', who had put Tierney into Parliament the year before. The knife-grinder is standing outside a pub advertising 'Best Brown Stout' on the signpost and 'Brandy Rum & Gin' over the door, and his face is a caricature of working-class ignorance and dissipation. Yet his sturdy refusal to 'meddle with politics', his candid avowal of his physical appetites, are meant also as a rebuke to the high-flown rhetoric of the 'Friend of Humanity'. The grinding labour of the poor is not the responsibility of the ruling class; it is not the 'Squire', the 'Parson', or the 'Attorney' who have forced this man from his home and onto the streets; the knife-grinder refuses to play along with the narrative of social injustice that he is offered (Figure 7.5).

Canning chose the knife-grinder as the interlocutor of the 'Friend of Humanity' precisely because his was one of the lowest and least

Figure 7.4. Adriaen van Ostade (1610–85), *Knife Grinder* (*c.*1682)

reputable of street trades. Gilray's image reinforces the stereotype: it implies that no more absurd example of the 'dignity of labour' could be found. On the other hand, the image of the knife-grinder could be reappropriated, as it is in Henry James's novel *The Princess Casamassima* (1886). When the Princess tells Mr Vetch that she has heard '[he] had been a great democrat in old days, but that now [he] had ceased to care for the people', he sharply objects to her use of the term: 'Why are some human beings the people, and the people only, and others not? I am of the people myself, I have worked all my days like a knife-grinder,

Figure 7.5. James Gilray, *The Friend of Humanity and The Knife-Grinder* (1797)

and I have really never changed.'[34] Yet even here the suggestion is of a kind of labour that has, in itself, no inherent dignity or nobility. Unlike the blacksmith, who has some status in art and mythology, the knife-grinder is of low caste; there is no knife-grinder god, and one of the most famous representations of the craft in classical sculpture depicts a barbarian whetting his knife for an especially grim purpose. This is *L'Arrotino*, probably a first-century Roman copy of a Hellenistic original, now in the Uffizi Gallery in Florence (Figure 7.6a): it would originally have formed part of a group of figures, one of which would be a hanging satyr: the knife-grinder is also referred to as 'lo Scita', the Scythian, for he is the Scythian slave whom Apollo appoints to flay the satyr Marsyas alive, after defeating him in a musical contest (Figure 7.6b). It is tempting to speculate that Whitman had seen one of the many reproductions of this statue, which was widely copied, imitated, engraved, and photographed, and especially tempting to think that he knew of its associations with one of the most haunting myths about poetic power, but the evidence is lacking.[35] What can be affirmed is that, although *L'Arrotino* was admired for its exceptional quality, it was also known as an image of hard, if not degraded labour. 'I must pause a moment before the "Arrotino," or slave whetting his knife, which is so masterly that it arrests one with an imperious hand', wrote the author of an article on Florence in the New York magazine *The Galaxy*, a journal to which Whitman was a contributor, and which appeared in October 1872, almost exactly contemporaneous with 'Sparkles from the Wheel': 'Here is the well-known, knotty figure, the coarse plebeian form, the vulgar face, the hard hand of the labouring man, the slave chained to his inexorable work'.[36] Paintings that exalt or dignify the figure are

---

34. Henry James, *The Princess Casamassima* (1886), ch. 37.

35. I have come across a photograph dated 1900 by an American firm, Underwood & Underwood (active 1881–1940s): '*L'Arrotino, the "Scythian sharpening his knife to flay Marsyas"—Uffizi Gallery, Florence, Italy*' (Los Angeles, CA: J. Paul Getty Museum). There were almost certainly earlier examples.

36. The author is identified only by the initials 'M.E.W.S.' 'Florence', *Galaxy* 14.4 (October 1872), p. 531. The verbal parallels with Whitman's poem—'I must *pause* a moment... it *arrests* one'—are intriguing, but influence one way or the other cannot be demonstrated. The repetition of the word *slave* has a particular resonance in this American context; in 1876 the sculptor Thomas Ball, as Kirk Savage persuasively argues, used the *Arrotino* as a model for the attitude of the kneeling slave in the Emancipation Memorial, now in Lincoln Park in Washington DC (Kirk Savage, *Standing Soldiers, Kneeling Slaves: Race, War, and Monument in Nineteenth-Century America* [Princeton, NJ: Princeton University Press, 1999], p. 79).

Figure 7.6a. *L'Arrotino o lo Scita* [The Knife-Grinder, or the Scythian]. First century BCE, Roman copy of Hellenistic original

Figure 7.6b. *Marsyas*. First century BCE, Roman copy of Hellenistic original

few and far between, and those by Édouard Manet and Kazimir Malevich are the only ones I have come across where the *sparks* from the knife-grinder's wheel, what Malevich calls its 'scintillation', are a primary object of attention (Plates 5 and 6).

Manet's oil-sketch is the most beautiful of all images of the knife-grinder that I know, and the only one that offers a visual equivalent to Whitman's poem—except that the knife-grinder is on his own. As we have already seen, images of the knife-grinder often place him in a group, which may comprise customers, spectators, and passers-by. Children regularly feature in such groups, to the point where we might say that the knife-grinder as street entertainer is a recognizable town or village 'type'.[37] You can see this association between the knife-grinder and the child in emblematic form on the façade of Buchanan House in St James's Square, London, for which the sculptor Newbury Abbot Trent

37. The French blog site https://remouleurs.wordpress.com (maintained by 'Philogène Gagne-petit') has dozens of illustrations of knife-grinders and children (on chocolate wrappers, advertising for cafés, etc.). In some the children themselves are playing at knife-grinding on miniature wheels.

was commissioned, in 1933–4, to carve a series of bas-reliefs illustrating the 'Cries of London'. The knife-grinder is in eighteenth-century costume, as in the other bas-reliefs (a costermonger, a lavender-seller, an organ grinder, and a town crier) but the child is not—he is wearing dungarees and clutching a sandwich. All the other children in Trent's designs are in period dress, so it seems that this anachronism was deliberate, and that it says something like 'children in all ages have been fascinated by this spectacle' (Figure 7.7). This sense of delight is vividly evoked in a French postcard of a street scene in Marseille, dating from the early 1900s, part of a series illustrating provincial 'types' (Figure 7.8). The image is accompanied by a poem by Elzéard Rougier (1857–1926), a local poet, dramatist, and folklorist:[38]

Dans la rue, on s'égaie à voir	In the street, it cheers us to see
Le Remouleur lorsqu'il aiguise,	The Knife-grinder when he sharpens,
Et fait de la roue, à sa guise,	And makes from the wheel, as he pleases,
Mille étincelles d'or pleuvoir!	A thousand sparks of gold rain down!

Rougier has noticed that you need only add a wheel, an 'o', to the *rue* (the street) to make it into the knife-grinder's *roue* (wheel); *s'égaie* (to be cheered, to rejoice) is close to *aiguise*, to sharpen, which rhymes in turn with *à sa guise*, as though the knife-grinder were making the sparks fly at his will or pleasure. Image and text bring us close to Whitman—close enough to suggest that the street scene in 'Sparkles from the Wheel', with its setting and cast of characters, would have been familiar to readers, not just because they would have seen knife-grinders in their own neighbourhoods, but because this sight was associated with pleasure, with the ability of the knife-grinder to conjure, it seemed at will, those showers of golden sparks.

Helen Vendler, whose observation on the musical structure of 'Sparkles from the Wheel' I cited earlier, sees the poem as divided between reportage and reflection.[39] An initial, objective account of what the poet sees and does is followed by reflection and self-consciousness, in which empathy plays a part, but also artistic design. The shift is marked at line 9, the midpoint of the poem: 'The scene and all its belongings, how they seize and affect me', which functions like the *volta* in a Petrarchan sonnet. I agree that the poem moves through two phases, but the break

---

38. The postcard wrongly spells his first name 'Elzèar'.
39. Vendler, pp. 40–2 (see above, n. 6).

Figure 7.7. Newbury Abbot Trent (1885–1953), *Knife-Grinder and Child*, from a series of five bas-reliefs illustrating the 'Cries of London' (1933–4); Buchanan House, 3 St James's Square, London SW1

Dans la rue, on s'égaie à voir
Le Remouleur lorsqu'il aiguise,
Et fait de la roue, à sa guise,
Mille étincelles d'or pleuvoir !
          Elzéar Rougier.

980   Type Marseillais - L'Amoulaire (Le Remouleur)

Figure 7.8. *Type Marseillais—L'Amoulaire (Le Remouleur).* Postcard, early 1900s

between them is not as absolute as Vendler suggests; in her emphasis on the thoughtfulness of the poem, the way Whitman first depicts the urban scene and then reflects on it, she cannot help privileging the second stage, where both feeling and self-consciousness seem so much more present and appealing. But to my mind the first part of the poem is as imbued with thought as the second.

'Where the city's ceaseless crowd moves on the livelong day': most readers, hearing this as the first line of a poem by Whitman, would expect it to be followed by a rhetorical gesture of rejoicing or solidarity. This is the Whitman of 'Song of Myself', 'Hurrying with the modern crowd as eager and fickle as any', identifying with the 'living crowd' of 'Crossing Brooklyn Ferry', 'merging' with it in 'A Broadway Pageant', celebrating, at the end of 'Give Me the Splendid Silent Sun', 'Manhattan crowds, with their turbulent musical chorus! / Manhattan faces and eyes forever for me'.[40] So the word that begins the second line of the poem,

40. 'Song of Myself', l. 787 [sect. 33] (p. 223); 'Crossing Brooklyn Ferry', l. 23 (p. 309); 'When Broadway is entirely given up to foot-passengers and foot-standers, when the mass is densest, / When the façades of the houses are alive with people, when eyes gaze riveted tens of thousands at a time, / When the guests from the islands advance, when the pageant moves forward visible, / When the summons is made, when the answer that waited thousands of years answers, / I too arising, answering, descend to the pavements, merge with the crowd, and gaze with them' ('A Broadway Pageant', ll. 16–20, p. 384); 'Give Me the Splendid Silent Sun', ll. 39–40 (p. 447).

'Withdrawn', comes as a shock. It is a deliberate negation, but it doesn't signal a Romantic withdrawal from the urban crowd to Nature and solitude; instead, Whitman 'join[s] a group' which has already separated itself from the city's 'ceaseless' rush.[41] 'Crowds of men and women attired in the usual costumes, how curious you are to me!', says the poet in 'Crossing Brooklyn Ferry' (l. 3), but here 'a group of children watching' attracts his curiosity, and he joins them before even knowing what it is they are watching, or at least before telling us. What he knows or intuits is that children are not implicated in the modern city's economic drive. And the figure of the knife-grinder, when he appears, reinforces this detachment. In *Democratic Vistas*, Whitman evoked New York's 'hurrying, feverish, electric crowds of men, their complicated business genius, (not least among the geniuses,) and all this mighty, many-threaded wealth and industry concentrated here'.[42] Neither the children nor the knife-grinder are caught up in the city's 'many-threaded' web. They are too young, and he is too old—old both in himself, and in his being a pre-industrial worker, self-employed and independent, even though this places him on the margins of urban life.

In joining the group of children, in experiencing, along with them, the magic of the knife-grinder's performance, the poet lays himself open to the charge of sentimentality, in which the characters in the story are co-opted into a narrative from which political economy and other threatening adult themes have been evacuated. I prefer to think of the poem as a 'version of pastoral', to use William Empson's term—that is, I think Whitman knew what he was doing, that the scene is not at all naïve—that it is, in fact, polemical.[43] We must remember that the poem dates from the same period as *Democratic Vistas*, the essay in which Whitman, as part of his defence of democracy, required his readers to acknowledge the brutal materialism and corruption of the actual conditions of American life. Those phrases I just quoted about the 'hurrying, feverish, electric crowds' and New York's 'mighty, many-threaded wealth and industry' are the prelude to a ferocious attack on the hollowness and death-in-life that lie behind the 'general superficial effect', so that within a few sentences America's cities are

---

41. Whitman does occasionally make such gestures of Romantic withdrawal, as in the opening section of 'Starting from Paumanok': 'withdrawn to muse and meditate in some deep recess, / Far from the clank of crowds' (ll. 7–8, p. 176).
42. *Democratic Vistas* (p. 939).
43. William Empson, *Some Versions of Pastoral* (London: Chatto & Windus, 1935).

described as 'crowded with petty grotesques, malformations, phantoms, playing meaningless antics'.

Is Whitman himself one of these 'phantoms'? In the poem he describes himself as 'a phantom curiously floating', and while I don't think he means this in the wholly negative sense it bears in *Democratic Vistas*, I do think we shouldn't simply take the word, or the line in which it is embedded, at face value. 'Myself effusing and fluid, a phantom curiously floating, now here absorb'd and arrested': the *self* here may have the libidinous freedom and anonymity of the *flâneur*, concentrated for a brief moment in time and space ('*now here* absorb'd and arrested'), but the imagery of dispersal and flow—*effusing, fluid, floating*—contrasts with the precision of the knife-grinder's actions, the concrete, specific details of his appearance, and this contrast gives the word *arrested* at the end of the line a stronger accent, as though Whitman's identity had indeed been brought to book. But then the poem knows this; the *self* may claim to be fluid, but the *poem* is poised, shapely, definite. *Diffusing* answers *effusing*; the knife-grinder's action is that of a controlled explosion: 'the light-press'd blade, / Diffusing, dropping, sideways-darting, in tiny showers of gold, / Sparkles from the wheel'.

These 'sparkles' are the main components of what I think of as the 'street song' of the knife-grinder's wheel, but the 'scene' Whitman records is not silent. It includes three notations of sound: 'The attentive, quiet children', 'the loud, proud, restive base of the streets', and 'The low hoarse purr of the whirling stone'. These three elements are balanced against each other with deliberate art. The children's behaviour tells us that they, like the poet, are 'absorb'd and arrested', that their normal noisy, scattered motion has been suspended by the knife-grinder's spell. Around them, as in Wordsworth's 'Power of Music', the noise of the city continues: it is unlike the children in being *loud* and *restive*, and it is full of its own importance: the internal rhyme *loud, proud* is a boast, and not an empty one. 'Proud' is a word Whitman associates with New York as a whole, 'this proud, friendly, turbulent city', as he calls it;[44] unlike Wordsworth, he does not want to isolate the knife-grinder's 'song' from the urban soundscape. The noise of the streets is the 'base' (punning on both the musical and material meanings of the word) for the melody, 'the low hoarse purr of the whirling stone', a sound pattern which circles on itself: 'low purr...whirling...stone'. But if Whitman

44. 'First O Songs for a Prelude', l. 55 (p. 418).

differs from Wordsworth in seeing the city's soundscape as a kind of harmony, he is as unrealistic as Wordsworth in the way he describes the actual sound of the knife-grinder at work. This was, by all accounts, one of the most grating of all street traders' noises; it is not included by accident among the street noises in Hogarth's *The Enrag'd Musician*, and there are numerous testimonies in nineteenth-century literature to its intolerable high-pitched sound, including accounts of people treating the knife-grinder like the proprietor of a barrel-organ and paying him to go away, despite the fact that his services were needed by their neighbours. For Whitman to bring the sound of the grinding wheel into harmony with the 'loud, proud, restive base of the streets' required as much poetic licence as Wordsworth had used to imply that the violinist's music was not just audible above the roar of traffic in Oxford Street, but triumphant over it.

The knife-grinder, too, triumphs over the threat that the city poses— the threat that this 'unminded point, set in a vast surrounding' will be lost in a chaotic, undifferentiated mass. 'Unminded' is charged with negative energy, as though the city's obliviousness might also be a form of oblivion; but remember Whitman's claim, in 'Song of Myself', when he lists the sounds of the street and says, *I mind them or the resonance of them*.[45] To *mind* in this double or triple sense is to notice, to pay attention, to look after. Perhaps, however, it is not quite right to say that the *knife-grinder* triumphs over the threat of dissolution in the city. Perhaps this victory belongs to the poet. In fact, the poem implies that the knife-grinder's 'song' is not audible to its singer; that its Orphean quality is created by the action of the poet who pauses to observe him.

Does Whitman see himself in the figure of the knife-grinder, and identify his art with the old man's craft? Yes, but the craft of the poem suggests something else, something that goes beyond this analogy. Whitman's detachment, his being a spectator, is a necessary complement of the old man's concentration on his work. His presence makes the poem possible—it is grammatically signified by the use of the present tense—and, in turn, the poem's circling reflexive pattern converts narrative into form, suspends time, so that what is *seen* becomes a *scene*, to be apprehended not once but each time the poem is read—each time it *takes place*. The poet who composes

---

45. The term 'unminded' also reflects on the condition of the children, whom nobody is 'minding'.

'Sparkles from the Wheel' is a greater craftsman than the craftsman who produces them. To me this makes the poem a supreme example of the art of appropriation which has formed the core of this book, but I don't want to end by suggesting that Whitman's mastery of his art erases or even occludes that of the knife-grinder. On the contrary, Whitman—like Wordsworth, or Joyce, or Woolf, or Proust—can afford to be as generous as he is unscrupulous. Only the great artists pay such tribute to the treasure they plunder.

Index of Persons

Pl. denotes the plates and *f* denotes the figures

Index of Songs, Arias, Tunes, Rhymes and Street-cries